Political Decision Making and Non-Decisions

Political Decision Making and Non-Decisions

The Case of Israel and the Occupied Territories

Ronald Ranta

Lecturer in Politics, Human Rights and International Relations at Kingston University, UK, and Honorary Research Associate at University College London, UK

palgrave
macmillan

First published 2015 by
PALGRAVE MACMILLAN

Palgrave Macmillan in the UK is an imprint of Macmillan Publishers Limited, registered in England, company number 785998, of Houndmills, Basingstoke, Hampshire RG21 6XS.

Palgrave Macmillan in the US is a division of St Martin's Press LLC, 175 Fifth Avenue, New York, NY 10010.

Palgrave Macmillan is the global academic imprint of the above companies and has companies and representatives throughout the world.

Palgrave® and Macmillan® are registered trademarks in the United States, the United Kingdom, Europe and other countries.

ISBN 978–1–137–44798–2

This book is printed on paper suitable for recycling and made from fully managed and sustained forest sources. Logging, pulping and manufacturing processes are expected to conform to the environmental regulations of the country of origin.

A catalogue record for this book is available from the British Library.

Library of Congress Cataloging-in-Publication Data
Ranta, Ronald.
Political decision making and non-decisions : the case of Israel and the occupied territories / Ronald Ranta.
pages cm
Summary: "This book examines Israel's relationship and political decision-making process towards the Occupied Territories from the aftermath of the Six Day War to the Labour Party's electoral defeat in 1977. The period represents the first decade of Israel's occupation of the Occupied Territories and the last decade in which the Labour Party was Israel's most dominant political force. Arguing that the successive Israeli governments headed by the Labour Party lacked a strategic policy towards the Occupied Territories to address the country's objectives and needs, this book demonstrates the detrimental effect this had on Israel, on the Middle East in general, and on the Palestinian people in particular. In addressing key aspects of decision making pathologies, this book raises issues which remain important features of Israeli politics today and an analysis relevant for political decision making worldwide"—Provided by publisher.
ISBN 978–1–137–44798–2 (hardback)
1. Israel—Politics and government—1967–1993—Decision making.
2. Mifleget ha-'avodah ha-Yisre'elit.   3. Israel-Arab War, 1967—Occupied territories.   4. Palestinian Arabs.   I. Title.
JQ1830.A56.D457 2015
956.9405'4—dc23   2015001245

Typeset by MPS Limited, Chennai, India.

Contents

Acknowledgements		vi
Abbreviations		vii
Maps		viii
	Introduction	1
1	Early Days	16
2	The 'Wall-to-Wall' Coalition	48
3	'I don't know, I am looking for someone who does!'	65
4	The Best Man in the Government	84
5	Golda's Kitchenette	101
6	The Grand Debate	121
7	Hand Picked	139
8	Submission to Gush Emunim	156
	Conclusion	173
	Epilogue	182
Notes		189
Bibliography		216
Index		224

Acknowledgements

This book is a product of several years of research and writing, all of which would not have been possible without the support and encouragement I received along the way. I would like to thank the many archivists who helped me: Helena and Michal for the many days and hours of assistance at the Israeli State Archives; Murray, Aharon, and in particular Rivka, who was always very kind to me, at Yad Tabenkin Archive; and Michael at the Labour Party archives at Beit Berl.

I am also extremely grateful to several family members, friends and colleagues who kindly gave their time to assist me with the writing and research for this book. In particular I would like to thank Elen Shute for her advice, constructive criticism and editing work; my brother Adrian for designing the maps; and my partner Kathryn Tomlinson for her patience during the process, going through the manuscript several times, helping me with editing and proofreading, providing valuable comments and for constantly being my biggest critic.

Lastly, I would like to thank my parents for always being there for me and supporting me throughout the project; they were the best research assistants I could have asked for. My only regret is that I could not finish the book fast enough; my father did not get an opportunity to see the final result. I hope he would have been proud.

Abbreviations

AMAN	military intelligence
IDF	Israeli Defence Force
ILA	Israel Land Authority
KFDC	Knesset Foreign Affairs and Defence Committee
MAC	Ma'ale Adumim Committee
MCC	Mapam Central Committee
MCHT	Ministerial Committee for the Held Territories
MK	Member of the Knesset
MSC	Ministerial Settlement Committee
NRP	National Religious Party
NSC	National Security Council
OT	Occupied Territories
PA	Palestinian Authority
PFLP	Popular Front for the Liberation of Palestine
PLO	Palestine Liberation Organisation
UN	United Nations

Maps

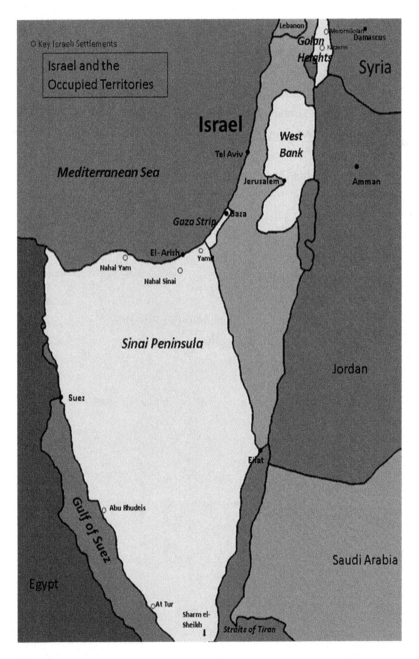

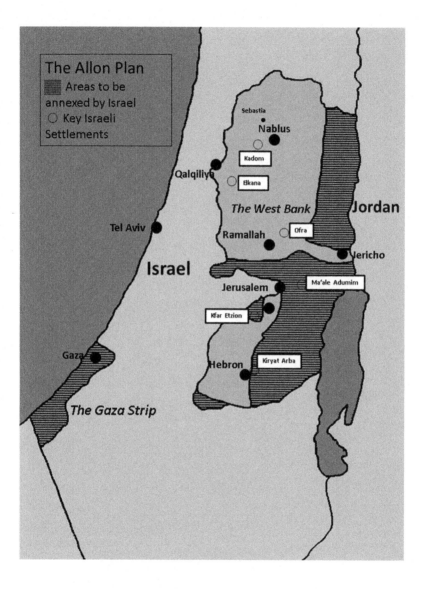

The Allon Plan

Areas to be annexed by Israel
○ Key Israeli Settlements

Introduction

The study of foreign policy in general and Israeli foreign policy in particular is mostly about how and why decisions are made in the context of international, though sometimes also domestic, events. In this regard, this book is not a traditional study of foreign policy. Although it deals with the process and structure of foreign policy decision-making, the book is not about a particular event or decision – at least not in the classical way of understanding the term. It is instead about the lack of a decision, or to put it in different terms, it is about Israel's decision not to decide on the future of the Occupied Territories (OT).

The 1967 Six Day War, also known as the June War, fundamentally changed the dynamics of the Arab-Israeli conflict; in its aftermath the Middle East faced a new reality. Israel emerged from the war in possession of territories three and a half times its own size and in control of a population of over one million, the overwhelming majority of them Palestinian. The occupation of Arab lands and people posed numerous problems for Israel, particularly with regard to security and the economy. The Israeli government needed to take into account the complexity of these problems and define its approach towards them, not only in a manner that addressed the challenges but also in a way that corresponded to its national objectives. The problem of defining such an approach was further complicated by the need to reach a consensus within the confines of the recently established national unity government – a 'wall-to-wall' coalition government bringing together, for the first time in Israeli history, all of the main political parties, from the right to the left and everything in between. The government's first objective was to reach a decision regarding Israel's future borders, that is, which of the territories it wanted to retain and those from which it was willing to withdraw as part of a negotiated settlement. Additionally, and until the Israeli government engaged in negotiations over the future of the territories with its neighbours, it needed to decide on a mechanism of administering the OT.[1]

On 19 June 1967, the cabinet headed by Prime Minister Levi Eshkol reached a unanimous decision regarding some of the OT. Ministers agreed to annex East Jerusalem and the Gaza Strip – after its population was 'resettled' elsewhere – and to withdraw from the Sinai Peninsula and the Golan Heights in exchange for peace agreements. While reaching a decision on most of the territories, ministers were unable to decide over the future of the West Bank. The failure to reach a decision on the future of the West Bank is generally known as 'the decision not to decide'.[2] Despite its apparent decision to withdraw from most of the OT, in response to international and domestic factors, and in the absence of direct negotiations between Israel and its neighbours, the 19 June decisions – as they came to be known – were consigned to the history books. It became clear that Israeli policy-makers were, on the one hand, eager to hold on to some of the territories, while, on the other hand, unable to agree on a clear vision for the future of the territories. Consequently, they settled for a muddled, disjointed and ad hoc approach that neither defined Israel's desired future relationship with the OT and its population nor addressed its national objectives.

In this book I examine the period from the aftermath of the Six Day War to the Labour Party's electoral defeat in 1977. The period represents the first decade of Israel's occupation of the OT and the last decade in which the Labour Party was Israel's dominant political force. I contend that during this period, successive Israeli governments, headed by the Labour Party, did not grasp the opportunity to define Israel's long-term relationship with the OT in a way that addressed the country's objectives and needs. With the exception of East Jerusalem, at no point during this period did Israel have a strategic policy regarding the territories. I say this with regard to the territories as a whole and with regard to specific territories in particular.

What do I mean by stating that Israel did not have a strategic policy towards the OT? I use the term 'strategic policy' to mean an overarching framework that encompasses and links together all aspects of how a government intends to deal with a particular problem or issue, as opposed to ad hoc or operational/tactical policies. The policy decision-making process can be divided into four main stages: identifying and assessing the problem; formulating a response that deals with the problem; formally or informally agreeing and or approving the response;

and implementing the agreed upon response. In this context, a strategic policy means an overarching framework – decisions, laws and regulations, statements of intent, guidance to the military, and diplomatic and political manoeuvres among other things, encompassing and linking together economic, diplomatic, social, political and military aspects – that was assessed, agreed upon and implemented by the government with the intent of pursuing a particular vision for Israel's long-term relationship with the OT and the population living under Israel's occupation.

There is no doubt that during the period examined the Israeli government identified the OT, or rather what to do with the territories and the population under its control, as one of the most important and pressing national problems. The problem was discussed and debated at cabinet, ministerial and sub-ministerial levels; several specialised and ad hoc committees were established to examine the problem and advise the government on the range and feasibility of available options. It was widely discussed in other forums as well, such as meetings with foreign dignitaries, in the United Nations (UN), in Israel's bilateral meetings with US officials, in the international and domestic media and in the army. In short, the pressing need to define Israel's long-term relationship with the OT and the population under occupation was evident and out in the open. Yet at no point during the period did any of the governments examined formulate, approve or implement a policy with the aim of achieving a particular long-term solution to the OT – a policy that defined Israel's preferred approach and provided answers to the pressing issues and challenges arising from the occupation of Arab lands and people. Indeed, I would argue that to this day such a policy has not been formulated or agreed upon. Instead, the government settled on a fragmented and disjointed approach characterised by ad hoc decisions based mostly on short-sighted operational needs, political calculations, risk aversion and non-decisions. I would like to be clear, however, that this is in no way denying the detrimental effect these actions – the creation of 'facts on the ground', the appropriation of land, the establishment of settlements, the integration of the economies of the territories with Israel's own, and the creation of military and civil institutions of occupation – have had on the occupied population, the overwhelming majority of whom were and are Palestinian. The question that should be asked is: to what end were these actions taken? I argue that these actions did not amount to any clear and coherent policy that addressed the multiple challenges faced by the state, but were instead a product of Israel's fragmented political party system and decision-making process, the rise of religious nationalism and the lack of any meaningful international pressure.

An interesting question to ask is to what extent the history and ideology of Zionism, in particular its attitude towards the 'Arab question' and the land of Palestine (*Eretz Israel*), are important for understanding Israel's actions towards the OT. There are indeed parallels between Israel's supposed lack of a clear policy towards the OT and the 'constructive ambiguity' approach adopted by early Zionist leaders, in particular Israel's first Prime Minister David Ben-Gurion. Ben-Gurion, in order to alleviate Arab and Palestinian fears and to not risk jeopardising relations with the major international powers, chose to remain vague on important issues, such as Israel's desired borders in the pre- and post-state period, while pursuing very clear policy goals. A case in point was his attitude towards Israel's nuclear programme. On the one hand, Israel under Ben-Gurion pursued a very clear strategic policy of acquiring nuclear capabilities while, on the other hand, it either denied pursuing such weapons or remained vague as to its true intentions and capabilities.[3] Looking at the OT, and extrapolating from this line of argument, one could argue that Israel purposely chose not to define its approach towards the territories, stating that it had not taken a firm decision on the matter. Nonetheless, and while implicitly rejecting a formal and public policy, Israel then proceeded to create 'facts on the ground' based on the rejection of Palestinian rights and a desire to hold on to as much territory as possible and expand the state's narrow borders. As I will demonstrate, this is a simplistic explanation of Israel's foreign and security policies that does not take into account the complicated nature of Israel's political system and the impact of international as well as domestic factors on Israel's decision-making process. Additionally, and most importantly, the main difference between the Zionist and Ben-Gurion's 'constructive ambiguity' approach and Israel's territorial policy was that the former was based on clear policy calculations, parameters and objectives, while the latter lacked an overall strategy and endgame.

Nevertheless, there is no denying that, in order to comprehend the actions and perspectives adopted by Israeli decision-makers, it is pertinent to delve into some aspects of Zionist ideology and history. In this respect, some of the actions pursued by specific decision-makers do correspond to particular images of Zionism. A clear example of this has been the refusal of a majority of decision-makers to even consider the establishment of a Palestinian state, the right of Palestinians to self-determination, or to recognise the Palestinians as a people. However, too often the examination and judgement of Israeli policies and actions is interpreted through the prism of Zionism. In this regard, while this book will, where appropriate, discuss decision-makers' psychology and images, as well as elaborate on the history and ideology of Zionism, it will, nonetheless, demonstrate that the majority of actions undertaken during this period had more to do with the political and diplomatic dynamics and structures than with Zionist ideology.

Lack of clear policy – 'the decision not to decide'

While there has been a great deal of literature devoted to Israel's relationship to the OT, the question of whether Israel had a strategic policy towards the OT has not been dealt with directly. Nonetheless, it is possible to discern three broad perspectives adopted in the literature regarding Israel's overall policy towards the OT. First, that Israel was willing to or had formulated and approved a policy based on a land-for-peace approach but could not implement it because of the lack of credible partners. Moshe Sasson, Eshkol's special representative to talks with the Palestinians, attributes the absence of meaningful negotiations, in the period leading to the Yom Kippur War, to the lack of credible partners: 'there was no one to talk to'.[4] It is claimed that Israel agreed on a land-for-peace concept, but the lack of Arab reciprocity and popular backing meant the state 'had a map and could not say so'.[5] The idea that Israel either adopted or was willing to adopt a land-for-peace policy, but could not implement it because of the lack of credible partners is simply not based on the historic reality. Israel adopted no such policy, even though, as I will demonstrate, it had several plans to choose from and credible peace partners with whom to negotiate.

The second broad perspective is that Israel had, at least with regard to its settlement activity, a clear long-term policy, which it formulated, approved and implemented. In other words, Israel might not have had a strategic-territorial policy (for whatever reason), but it did have a clear settlement policy based on the Allon Plan. This view, which has been put forward by, among others, Yehiel Admoni and Tzvi Tzur, who were directly involved in Israel's settlement policy-making,[6] will be shown to be factually incorrect. As I will demonstrate, using among others Admoni's own research on the subject, Israel did not have a clear long-term settlement policy based on the Allon Plan. In fact, the Israeli government was unable to formulate either a strategic or a coherent operational policy regarding settlements. Government decisions were in many cases ad hoc responses to settlement activities that were instigated by extra-parliamentary groups. Throughout the period examined governments appeared unable to decide over the appropriate settlement strategy to adopt, changing and rearranging their settlements strategies and maps constantly.[7] This is not to argue that the Israeli governments did not formulate, approve and implement operational or ad hoc settlement policies, many of which were roughly based on the Allon Plan. While the governments did establish and provide support for settlements, they did not put forward or approve a long-term policy with regard to them. They instead decided not to decide and deferred such a decision for a later date.

This leads us to the third perspective: Israel did not have a strategic policy towards the territories; instead, it decided not to decide. Though this perspective is widely shared, there has not been any systematic attempt to prove whether it is factually correct and address the reasons behind the non-decision. Additionally, there is little in the literature on what is meant by Israel's non-decision. This book, while demonstrating that Israel did not have a strategic policy towards the OT, illuminates and expands upon the subject of non-decisions.

The concept of non-decisions was developed and advanced by Bacharach and Baratz and was initially used to refer to the use of power, influence, authority and force by elites to dictate the areas in which decisions can be made in order to dominate the decision-making process.[8] There are two slightly different ways of understanding non-decisions, both of which could be applicable to Israel's case. First, that 'non-decisions' are indeed decisions; they are a deliberate strategic ploy to increase 'margins for manoeuvre',[9] for example, Abraham Lincoln's famous dictum 'my policy is to have no policy' and Ben-Gurion's approach of constructive ambiguity. Political scientist Reuven Pedatzur argues that the 'non-decision' allowed for policy flexibility and political manoeuvres. He agrees that the government did not have a clear policy, but contends that the lack of clear policy enabled the government to continue with its desired settlement activities.[10] According to historian Avi Shlaim this is evident in the Galili Document, which demonstrates that Israel's territorial policy, though not explicit, was basically that of creeping annexation.[11]

On the other hand, 'non-decisions' could also be seen as a result of an inability to reach a decision, normally associated with 'paralysis of the decision-making process'. This is a phenomenon closely associated with multiparty coalition governments.[12] From this perspective, Israel did not have a clear policy and, because of domestic and international factors, was unable to formulate one, even though it strived to do so, most notably during Eshkol's term and the Labour Party's 1972 'Grand Debate'. Examining Israel's economic policy towards the territories, economist Brian Van Arkadie argues that Israel's lack of an economic policy was not deliberate: while the government manipulated the economic interaction with the OT to its advantage, it did not 'conceive or attempt to implement any systematic, large-scale plan to alter the economic structure of the West Bank and the Gaza Strip' and there was no 'Israeli master-plan'.[13] The Israeli Defence Force (IDF) coordinator of activities in the OT Brigadier-General Shlomo Gazit takes this line of argument further and suggests that government ministers never dealt with the strategic questions regarding the territories. In his view, this non-decision caused the IDF to pursue very limited operational objectives in the OT, as it was not given clear political guidance.[14]

Did decision-makers strategically decide not to decide or were they unable to reach a decision? One way of resolving this question is to determine whether the 'non-decision' served a strategic purpose (constructive ambiguity) or was instead a product of an immobilised decision-making process – an extreme form of the incremental policy model referred to as a 'disjointed incrementalism'.

The incremental policy theory is modelled on the premise that a rational decision-making process is unachievable. In order to overcome this problem, decision-makers resort to the art of 'muddling through', coping and agreeing on policies that 'satisfice'. Choices are based on ideological and power struggles within the government and unwillingness, as a consequence, to adopt bold measures, as these might hurt chances of re-election or coalition unity. Understanding the limits of the political process, the government disavows grand schemes for gradual change based on consensus and risk aversion.[15] An extreme manifestation of this is 'disjointed incrementalism'. In cases of political deadlock decisions are made on an ad hoc basis with no long-term policy planning or formulation. In this case the government, characterised by its avoidance of taking decisions and bold measures, is unable to deal with the overall problem and instead adopts policies that are short-sighted and 'lacking clear-cut ends'.[16] This is associated with paralysis of the policy decision-making process, weak leadership and fragmented multiparty coalitions,[17] all of which, I will demonstrate, characterised Israeli politics during the period examined.

Throughout the period, on no occasion – with the exception of 19 June – did the government, manage to formulate an overall strategy for dealing with the territories. Instead the government substituted overall strategy with micromanagement of and reaction to events, while allowing individuals and groups to push forward their own ideas regarding the territories devoid of any long-term planning. The government's approach towards the territories can thus be characterised as 'disjointed incrementalism'. However, as I will demonstrate, during the period examined, for a variety of reasons, different forms of incrementalism and non-decisions occurred or were utilised. For example, under the leadership of Golda Meir the government agreed, as a matter of policy and because of risk aversion, to tactically postpone any meaningful debate on the issue of the territories. In contradistinction, the Eshkol and Rabin governments, though they strived to, were mostly unable to reach a decision. In fact, Israeli foreign policy under Eshkol has been described as a 'policy of indecision'.[18]

What were the reasons behind Israel's non-decisions? Although this question has not been specifically examined in the literature, reading through historical and political accounts of the period it is possible to identify three broad perspectives based on the politics of the Labour Party, the transitional nature of the Israeli state, and the government's decision-making process.

The Labour Party

Former Israeli minister Yossi Beilin argues that the structure and the mechanism of operation of the Labour Party were the main reasons, among other things, behind Israel's inability to put forward a clear long-term policy. It stems, in his view, from the process of unification the party underwent in the period after the Six Day War; Beilin refers to this as the 'price of unity'.[19]

The history of Israel's Labour Party has been a fractious and fragmented one. The party is best understood as a movement that supported and encompassed diverse groups who occasionally split and/or joined forces. This process of splitting and forming new parties under the banner of the Labour movement has been endemic to Zionist politics both during the British Mandate period and after independence. Therefore, it is no surprise that the unified party did not have clear views and tended to incorporate the divergence of opinions within it. The diverse views expressed within the party's factions regarding the 'Arab question', territorial compromise, socialism, and the nature of the Israeli state have been a feature of the Labour movement from the early 20th century. One could point to three main issues that have been at the heart of the debates between the various parties and factions: the power of the elites to dictate the agenda, suppress issues and dominate the nomination and patronage system; the role socialism should play within the state; and the proper approach with regard to the 'Arab question'. Labour factions correspond, to a certain degree, to earlier splits along these lines.[20]

Two particular events illuminate the issues and problems that shaped the Labour Party: the partition plan and the Lavon affair. In both events, reaching a consensus within the party meant sacrificing party unity and, in both cases, a split in the party precipitated a crucial decision on a controversial issue. The partition plan divided the Labour movement into those who were willing to compromise and accept a two-state solution, and those who were not, although the initial signs of disagreement between the different constituents of the movement arose in the early 1930s. Ben-Gurion, the leading figure of Mapai (the Workers Party of Eretz Israel) – at the time Israel's most dominant party – accepted the idea of a partitioning Palestine into a Jewish state and an Arab-Palestinian state out of necessity and as a diplomatic compromise. His counterpart in Ahdut-Ha'avoda (the Unity of Labour), Yitzhak Tabenkin, was unwilling to accept such a plan.[21] Initially, Ahdut-Ha'avoda was a faction within Mapai known as Siya Bet. The debate between Mapai and Ahdut-Ha'avoda concerned the nature of the party and the state. Ben-Gurion pursued a policy of statism and a movement away from the social policies advocated by Ahdut-Ha'avoda. Statism represented a policy shift that occurred within Mapai as it changed from being a narrowly focused entity into a party associated with the state, and considered to be more representative of the nation.[22] Ahdut-Ha'avoda's opposition to the idea of partition, and to Ben-Gurion's statism, caused the faction to split and form an independent party.

During the second event, the Lavon affair, Mapai's Central Committee was pitted against several of the party elites, including its leader Ben-Gurion. The affair revolved around the discovery of an Israeli terrorist organisation in Egypt that sought to implicate the Nasser regime in anti-British activities. At the centre of the affair was the question of who authorised the terrorist operation in Egypt: was it Defence Minister Pinhas Lavon or Binyamin Gibli, the head of the military intelligence unit (AMAN)? The Labour Party was unable to resolve the issue one way or the other without risking a major split. The affair went through several stages, which ended in a battle between Prime Minister Ben-Gurion and the party's Central Committee. Ben-Gurion's unwillingness to accept the party's findings resulted in his resignation and the formation of an independent party Rafi (Israel's Workers List).[23] The affair, or more precisely one of its key figures, Gibli, is infamously known as 'the banana skin' that caused Ben-Gurion to slip and lose power.[24] The Lavon affair, in particular its last stage, brought about realignment within the Labour movement.[25]

The Labour Party factional strife in the aftermath of the Six Day War shared similarities with both the Lavon affair and the partition debate. The Mapai elites were unwilling to plunge the party into a renewed ideological crisis, as occurred during the debate on the partition plan, nor risk a further split, as happened with Rafi. The importance of maintaining unity, and thus the difficulty in achieving a consensus, has been cited as one of the factors contributing to the decline of the party.[26] Beilin argues that it was the infighting which hampered the ability of the Mapai elites to conduct foreign policy as they did before the war. In a sense, the relationships between elites – especially between Defence Minister Moshe Dayan and the Mapai leadership – eroded the authority of the party and its ability to conduct and maintain its previous decision-making mechanisms. The reasons for this are engraved in inter-party factionalism and the structural characteristics of the Israeli political system as a whole, which allows small parties and factions to exert disproportionate leverage on the decision-making process. These factions proved to be more adept at averting actions than promoting them.[27]

Transitional nature of the state

Over and beyond the Labour Party, during the 1960s and 1970s the Israeli state as a whole went through a transitional phase, which included immense demographic, political and cultural changes. These changes resulted in a shift in the views of the electorate and the political power to the right, which contributed to a deeper fragmentation of Israel's polity and resulted in the governments' inability to conduct policy in the manner they were accustomed to before the war. One could divide Israel's history into two periods – before and after 1967[28] – in the sense that the post-1967 period can be seen as the transition from the founding generation to the 1948 generation.[29] The founding generation had neither served as active fighters in the IDF nor in the resistance movements during the British Mandate period. An examination of the age differences among the leading politicians in Israel illustrates this. Eshkol and the leading politicians of Mapai were mostly in their late sixties and early seventies and had served most of their lives as politicians.[30] The younger generation, in their early forties or fifties, were native Israelis and had served as IDF commanders, or in the resistance movements.[31]

The changes affecting the state were not limited to demographics. The manner of the Israeli victory in the Six Day War had a detrimental effect on the state.[32] The OT were referred to as liberated territories and this 'liberation' of biblical Israel assumed messianic and prophetic proportions. An increase in immigration and investment followed a wave of nationalistic and religious fervour that swept through the state, signalling the revival of a new form of Zionism, that is, Religious Zionism or New Zionism.[33] The occupation brought to the fore a territorial discussion not touched upon since the partition era. This discussion revealed a 'growing dissonance' between the Labour Party's foreign policy and the electorate's perception of the OT,[34] in particular a 'breakdown of the Green Line as a Hegemonic Conception'.[35] The public was overwhelmingly in favour of retaining most if not all of the territories.[36] The shift in the electorate's perception and the inability of the Labour Party to respond meant that interest groups took it upon themselves to influence the state's foreign policy. Israel's settlement policy and approach to the territories cannot be understood fully without taking into account the role of these groups, in particular the role of Gush Emunim.[37] Before the Six Day War the public accepted Mapai's national agenda. However, in the aftermath of the war, and even more so after the Yom Kippur War in 1973, the gulf between the party and the public grew, and the party elites were no longer seen as representative of the state.[38]

This situation was starkly different from the one prevailing before the Six Day War. The government decision in 1965 to slow down an overheating economy led directly to a serious economic recession.[39] Immigration, one of the most important social indicators in Israel, reached unheard-of lows, while the numbers of emigrants were at record highs.[40] As a result of this economic hardship, declining immigration and increased emigration, the state of Israel did not resemble the epitome of the Zionist dreams; the nationalistic parties, and Gahal – the main opposition party headed by Menahem Begin – in particular, were seen as losing their way and the idea of a greater Israel faded as a viable political objective.[41] A famous joke at the time asked for the last person leaving the country to switch off the lights.[42] This all changed on 15 May 1967. Israel stood in the middle of an unfolding crisis following Nasser's decision to move Egyptian troops into the previously demilitarised area of the Sinai Peninsula. The period between 15 May and 5 June is known in Israel as the *Hamtana* (Waiting Period). During this period the leadership of Eshkol was publicly challenged by members of his own party, as well as by members of the coalition, the opposition, the IDF, the press and the public.[43] The 'Waiting Period' can be seen as a period in which the generational split became apparent, with the younger leadership pushing for war, and the older leadership trying to find a diplomatic-political way out.

Before the Six Day War, Eshkol used a number of decision-making committees, which included his closest political allies and senior members of the Mapai Party, to formulate and examine potential policies. The inclusion of Gahal and Rafi within a national unity government and the distrust of Eshkol for the members of his party, who tried to depose him during the *Hamtana* period, diminished the capacity of those committees. The government resorted to an ad hoc decision-making process in which various ministers, in particular Dayan, Deputy Prime Minister Yigal Allon and Eshkol, each appeared to operate of his own accord, either through their ministries or, in Dayan's case, through the IDF. This occurred because of Eshkol's increasingly difficult position in the government, and the inclusion of his political enemies, leading to the system being threatened with paralysis. The government was not formulating policies nor was it fully in charge of an increasingly ad hoc process. Instead, the responsibility was taken on by individuals and interest groups with personal agendas.

The decision-making process

Understanding the reason for Israel's lack of a strategic policy towards the OT also requires delving into the nature and structure of its political system. Israel's political history as a parliamentary democracy has been dominated by coalition governments. This means that, from its inception as a state, and to this day, governments and prime ministers have been constrained in their ability to conduct foreign and security policies by coalition politics. As a result, Israeli policy-making has been held hostage to the political considerations and electoral calculations of its coalition parties. This feature is not specific to Israel; coalition governments in general tend to exhibit flawed policy-making and 'produce very little if any coordinated policy because they are so immobilized or deadlocked by their circumstances' and 'at best do not effectively address national problems and at worst spark political instability'. Coalition governments thus tend to be characterised as unstable, prevaricating on important issues, and possessing an immobilised and or paralysed decision-making process.[44]

Another important element is that, because of the rapid changes and crises that occur in the Middle East, Israeli policy-making is reactive in nature and based on improvisation; this has led to the lack of effective leadership, proper consultation, formulation or assessment of policy options, and the preference for short-term tactical decision-making.[45] Examining the period this book deals with, Lewis Brownstein claims that the Israeli government lacked sufficient 'systematic or rational policy-making procedures' and was dominated by a small group of elites who were resistant to outside expertise and lacked policy research, planning, analysis and evaluation systems.[46] Prominent officials and politicians within the government described the decision-making process during the period as 'non-existent', 'lacking definitions and targets' and 'unprofessional'. Even Israel's Foreign Minister Abba Eban (1966–74) described foreign policy-making as 'amateurish' and being 'based on improvisation'.[47] Important decisions were taken by Israeli leaders 'on a spontaneous basis ... relying on personal intuition'.[48]

Purpose of this book

The purpose of this book is four-fold. First, it provides a detailed historical and political analysis of Israel's relationship with the OT, between the years 1967 and 1977. This analysis includes a detailed account of the specific challenges posed by the occupation of Arab territories and (mainly Palestinian) populations, and the approaches and plans that were proposed in order to address them. Through the provision of a historical narrative, the book charts the evolution of policy-makers' beliefs, consultations, approaches, plans and decisions towards the territories. Additionally, through analysing Israel's policy decision-making, this book contextualises these issues within Israel's political sphere: examining the process but also structure of decision-making; relating these to relations among policy-makers as well as images and beliefs held; and situating policy-making within Israel's domestic and international environments.

Second, this book questions whether successive governments, under the leadership of the Labour Party, had a strategic policy towards the OT that addressed Israel's main concerns and was in accordance with its stated objectives. By examining Israel's decisions regarding the specific problems posed by the occupation, this book demonstrates that successive Israeli governments in that period had no such policy. The research shows that, during the period, none of the governments that form the subject of this book managed to define Israel's position vis-à-vis the OT. The majority of the policies formulated during the period never made it to the cabinet for consideration and approval, and were never approved.

Third, while discussing Israel's lack of a strategic policy, the book sheds light on the subject of non-decisions. Throughout the period examined Israeli governments had several opportunities to decide over the future of the OT; at each of these junctures the governments in question decided not to decide. By examining the Israeli decisions not to decide on the future of the OT, this book addresses a lacuna in the study of policy decision-making in general, and foreign policy decision-making in particular, namely the study of non-decisions. In this respect, the book helps define and explain the meaning and types of non-decisions, and highlights the important part they play in foreign policy decision-making.

Last, this book analyses the reasons behind Israel's lack of a strategic policy and use of non-decisions – a flaw that was displayed by each individual government and by successive governments during a 10-year period. There has not been specific research into the reasons behind the inability of successive Israeli governments, under the leadership of the Labour Party, to put forward a clear and comprehensive policy that would define its relationship with the OT. In this respect this book is an attempt to resolve this long-standing question, by providing an explanation for Israel's lack of policy. Why is it that successive governments decided not to decide?

This last point is worth elaborating on. I am not arguing that Israel should have adopted any particular policy, be it land-for-peace or greater Israel. Rather, I argue that it is essential for any government to be clear, at least internally, about the overall direction in which it plans to lead the state on matters of national importance. Israeli governments examined a number of different policies that could have been adopted with regard to the OT. One of the few policies that was unequivocally dismissed was that of annexation leading to a one-state solution. Yet this is precisely the direction in which the actions taken by these governments were leading the state. It is also important to note that these actions had a detrimental effect on the Middle East in general and on the Palestinian people in particular. In addition, the pathologies and constraining factors discussed in this book are still features of Israeli politics. Israel's political system has become, if anything, even more fragmented and rudderless. Despite the fact that more than forty years have passed, the analysis provided and the arguments advanced are still relevant to Israel's current situation. Israeli governments since 1977 have also been characterised by non-decisions and failures to put forward strategic policies towards the OT.

1
Early Days

The war

In his memoirs, Defence Minister Moshe Dayan criticised the conduct of the government and the army in the period leading up to and during the war. He accused Prime Minister Levi Eshkol of mismanaging the country and of being over-reliant on the US. Dayan claimed that the government under Eshkol did not complement the army's operational plans with coherent strategic objectives. According to Dayan, the war was the least planned and the worst prepared in Israel's history. Reactions to the day-to-day events determined the direction of the war, though he acknowledged that the army was successful at exploiting the chances that came its way.[1]

On 1 June 1967, Dayan took his place as Israel's new defence minister, replacing Eshkol.[2] This followed a week of intense political manoeuvring within both the coalition and the opposition parties. It came about as a result of Eshkol's perceived paralysis in the face of an unfolding crisis – one that started with Egyptian President Gamal 'Abdel Nasser's decision to move troops into the demilitarised Sinai Peninsula and close the Straits of Tiran. After a particularly embarrassing incident, in which Eshkol seemed to stutter and stumble during a live radio broadcast that was meant to reassure the nation, public confidence in him evaporated. Demands for his removal from office were made by members of the opposition, the press, the army and even his own Mapai Party members.[3] Threats to dissolve the ruling coalition were made by several parties, in particular Mapai's coalition partner the National Religious Party (NRP). They demanded the formation of a national unity government that would include Rafi and Gahal, and the removal of Eshkol from the Defence Ministry, which, incidentally, was also one of the preconditions set by both Rafi and Gahal. Dayan was the opposition's preferred candidate.[4]

Former chief-of-staff and the architect of Israel's successful conquest of the Sinai Peninsula during the Suez crisis, Dayan, with his many years of military service during the pre- and post-state period, cut a very different figure from Eshkol. With his famous eye-patch[5] and war hero status, kibbutz born and bred Dayan represented the new resourceful and confident native Jew (*Tzabar*). In contrast, 72-year-old Prime Minister Eshkol represented a different generation. Eshkol immigrated to Palestine in 1914 from Russia, and was a life-long bureaucrat and politician famous for his organisational skills and for establishing Israel's national water company. His supporters considered him a cautious and calculated operator who enjoyed colouring his sentences with Yiddish sayings. His detractors pictured him as hesitant and indecisive; a popular joke told of his secretary asking him whether he wanted coffee or tea, to which he replied 'half and half'.

Contrary to popular perception, the formation of the national unity government and the inclusion of Dayan as defence minister did not hasten the decision to go to war. This decision came as a result of the inability of the US administration, headed by President Lyndon Johnson, to put forward a constructive solution to the diplomatic impasse that had been reached. Despite the army's top brass clamouring for action, and existential fears for the country expressed by the press, Eshkol tried to avoid war. He, as well as most of the ministers, believed that the army would win the war, but feared large casualty numbers and an international backlash if Israel went ahead without America's approval. The final decision came on 3 June 1967, during Meir Amit's (Head of Mossad) mission to Washington, where he received what was understood to be a 'yellow light' for operations against Egypt.[6]

Israel's war plan, in response to the Egyptian troop build-up, was clear from the outset. It called for a pre-emptive air strike to neutralise the Egyptian air force followed by a three-pronged armoured thrust into Sinai, sweeping through the Egyptian stationary defensive set-up, and advancing towards the Suez Canal.[7] The Israeli war planners had their sights set firmly on the Egyptian front; Israeli Defence Force (IDF) units on the borders with Jordan and Syria were ordered to remain in defensive positions. This was done despite warnings from AMAN (the IDF's intelligence unit) that Jordan and Syria might be tempted to 'bite the bullet' and join the war.[8] As a precautionary measure, the Israeli government sent a message to King Hussein not to interfere with the war, promising in return to honour Jordan's territorial integrity.[9]

Having examined the plans, Dayan requested that several changes be made. He wanted the IDF to surround the Gaza Strip but not enter it. Dayan felt that conquering the Gaza Strip would be unwise, referring to the Gaza Strip as a 'nest of wasps' bristling with problems.[10] Dayan also felt that the army needed to take Sharm el-Sheikh and secure the Straits of Tiran, arguing that the war was fought over the right of passage through the straits. Furthermore, fearing a war on several fronts, he warned the army generals not to get Israel entangled in a war over the West Bank or Jerusalem. The first digression from the plan occurred early on the first day of fighting (5 June 1967). Major-General Yeshayahu Gavish, head of Israel's Southern Command, sent an urgent request to Chief-of-Staff Yitzhak Rabin for permission to send troops to occupy the Gaza Strip. Gavish complained that Israeli troops were coming under fire from Egyptian and Palestinian forces in the Strip. Knowing Dayan's predisposition towards Gaza, Chief-of-Staff Yitzhak Rabin decided to approve Gavish's request without consulting him.[11]

Encouraged by misleading early reports from Nasser of Egyptian military success against Israel, Syria and Jordan decided to join the war. King Hussein, normally a very cautious and calculated political operator ordered Jordanian air force and artillery units to attack Israeli targets in and around West Jerusalem, reaching as far as the outskirts of Tel Aviv, while Syrian artillery shelled northern Israel. However, by the time their forces entered the war the Egyptian army was 'on the ropes'; its air force had been eliminated in a series of pre-emptive air strikes, while its ground forces were rolled back by the rapidly advancing Israeli armoured thrust.[12] Dayan's fears of a multiple-front war became a reality. Yet, despite the attacks, he called for restraint and warned against diverting troops to the new fronts before the army was allowed to conclude its operations against Egypt. Additionally, the Israeli government tried to invalidate one of the newly created fronts by sending King Hussein a message, imploring him to cease all hostilities; by his own admission, Hussein refused.[13]

As the situation on the Egyptian front and the scale of Egypt's impending defeat became clearer, the voices calling on the IDF to divert attention to the Jordanian front grew louder. In a cabinet meeting, Employment Minister Yigal Allon and Minister without Portfolio Menahem Begin (leader of the Gahal Party) declared that this was a historic opportunity for Israel; they urged the government to order the immediate conquest of East Jerusalem and the West Bank.[14] Eshkol appeared to side with the duo, but demanded time to consider the diplomatic repercussions of such an act.[15] Several ministers were against the conquest of East Jerusalem, including Foreign Minister Abba Eban, and the NRP Ministers Haim-Moshe Shapira (Interior) and Zerach Warhaftig (Religion). Shapira and Education Minister Zalman Aran suggested that the government consider handing over the city, once it had been occupied, to international jurisdiction.[16] Shapira would later claim he meant for international jurisdiction to be applied only to the holy places. Eshkol commented that even if Israel took over the West Bank and East Jerusalem, it would have to withdraw from these areas in the end.[17]

During the second day of the fighting, the government convened to discuss its options, with ministers voting for the conquest of the Samaria (northern West Bank) mountain range, stretching from Jerusalem to Jenin,[18] and for the army to seize the city of Hebron, as well as to surround the Old City of Jerusalem. A government vote on whether to storm the Old City ended in a draw.[19] During the meeting, Amit inquired whether Israel would seek to annex the West Bank and wanted to know more about the diplomatic state of affairs the government would have to face should the worst come to the worst. According to Amit, the lack of strategic planning was characteristic of the Eshkol government, during and after the war.[20] At the same time, realising the extent to which the situation had deteriorated, King Hussein implored the US and British governments to intervene on his behalf and impose a ceasefire, citing his fear for the survival of his Hashemite kingdom.[21] Eshkol offered Hussein a way out, but demanded that the king agree to immediate peace talks; a generous proposition, but one to which Hussein could not agree.[22] From the king's perspective he was between a rock and a hard place. If he ordered his army to stop fighting, and the Arab side lost the war, he would be blamed for the defeat. If the Arab side won and his army stopped fighting, there is every indication that the victorious armies would have continued towards Jordan to liberate it from his rule.

After agreeing to postpone the conquest of the Old City, the ministers deliberated over the Syrian front. Dayan argued against opening another front; he warned against antagonising Syria's Soviet patrons. According to Dayan, the Syrian army had not advanced into Israel and its artillery attacks on northern Israel were manageable and did not pose an imminent threat. On this issue, Dayan became increasingly isolated. The majority of ministers were in favour of dealing with the Syrians 'once and for all', as were Rabin and Major-General David 'Daddo' El'azar, head of the Northern Command, but all agreed to leave the final decision to Dayan and Eshkol.[23]

One of the main concerns expressed by ministers was of a possible international condemnation – a fear which increased with every new territory conquered, but one which eventually turned out to be totally misplaced. The US administration was starting to accept that some territories would remain in Israel's possession. During the first days of fighting, Walt Rostow (the National Security Advisor) wrote to President Johnson suggesting that the US should act, upon the cessation of violence, to find a permanent solution to the Middle East problem, adding that the US should not allow for a return to the pre-war borders.[24] The US position was further clarified when Walworth Barbour (US ambassador to Israel), while conveying King Hussein's urgent request for a ceasefire to Eshkol, did not seek an Israeli commitment on the West Bank. In Barbour's view it was too late.[25]

In the early hours of the morning, on 7 June, Eshkol was informed that the UN Security Council had agreed to a general ceasefire that would come into effect at 22.00 later that night. Eshkol immediately called Dayan, ordering him to send the army into the Old City of Jerusalem and complete the conquest of the West Bank. At a ministerial-level meeting later that morning, Dayan announced that orders had been given to storm the Old City.[26] Despite a Jordanian acceptance of the UN-brokered ceasefire, fighting in and around the city continued throughout the morning. Israeli officials claimed that as long as the ceasefire was not agreed to by Egypt and Syria, the fighting would go on. Around late afternoon, news that the IDF had managed to seize the Old City of Jerusalem prompted a mad rush of government ministers to the site. Dayan, initially sceptical about the need to conquer the Old City, and wanting to avoid what he called 'all that Vatican', was the first on the scene. In full military attire and accompanied by Head of the Central Command Major-General Uzi Narkiss and Rabin, he was the first minister photographed entering the Old City, stealing the limelight from Eshkol in the process. According to Dayan, Israel had returned to its holiest places 'returned in order never to be separated from them again'.[27] By night time the majority of the West Bank was in Israeli hands. Eshkol commented that 'these were historic days for Israel and for the Jewish people'.[28] He expressed his views regarding the territories several times that day, professing a deep desire to keep the Gaza Strip as part of Israel, referring to it as 'a lily with many thorns', while examining the possibility of relocating its population.[29]

On 8 June, the daily broadsheet *Ha'aretz* asked the government, in its editorial, to complete the task and conquer the Golan Heights. Goaded on by the press, the entire leadership appeared to be in frenzy for further conquests. Allon claimed that he did not understand why occupying the Sinai Peninsula, the Gaza Strip and the West Bank was acceptable, while the Golan Heights were 'off the table'.[30] Allon's opinion was echoed by the IDF's high command and most of the ministers, including Eshkol. However, not all shared this view. Warhaftig and Aran expressed concern about a possible Soviet intervention, in response to an Israeli assault on the Golan Heights. Dayan, admonishing the ministers for their enthusiasm, refused to consider any attack on the Golan Heights.[31]

In the early hours of 9 June, and not for the first time, Dayan changed his mind and ordered the army to attack the Golan Heights. When ministers found out about the order they were exasperated.[32] They supported his decision but not the manner in which it was carried out.[33] However, this would not be the last time (during and after the war) that Dayan exhibited fickle behaviour.[34] By 10 June, with the fighting in the Golan Heights going Israel's way, US Ambassador Barbour strongly advised Israel to agree and adhere to the UN's unconditional call for a ceasefire, if it did not want to jeopardise its gains. Fearing that the UN would force Israel to halt before the conquest of the Golan had been completed, Eshkol urged El'azar to finish the job, promising him that the government would do its best to stall. The UN-proposed ceasefire came into effect on 11 June, but Israeli forces continued to fight until 13 June, at which point the entire area was under Israeli control. The immediate result of these actions was a break-up of relations with the Soviet Union.[35]

The war brought about numerous political, diplomatic, ideological, strategic and geographic changes; Israel now occupied territories three and a half times its size. Politically, the war brought to the fore a territorial question that was thought to have been settled with the acceptance of the UN partition plan. This territorial pre-independence debate threatened to challenge Mapai's long-held view of accepting the temporary 1949 ceasefire lines as borders. Additionally, it put the party at odds with several of its coalition partners, most notably Ahdut-Ha'avoda.[36] The war had also left the country with a national unity government, which incorporated a 'wall-to-wall' coalition of the right, the left and the religious parties. Thus the task of maintaining unity within the coalition was made even more difficult by the controversial and polarising issues on the agenda. Moreover, the inclusion of Gahal, and in particular Menahem Begin, in the government was a watershed moment in Israeli politics. Up until that moment, Begin was characterised in the official state, and Mapai-sponsored media as a right-wing extremist, beyond the pale of mainstream politics and a danger to the state. Back in 1948, Israel's first Prime Minister David Ben-Gurion claimed that he would happily include anyone in his coalition, with the exception of Begin and the communists.[37]

On the diplomatic front, the war had provided decision-makers, for the first time, with the necessary bargaining chips to achieve a long-lasting peaceful resolution to the Arab-Israeli conflict. Eshkol expressed hope that the government would have the sufficient wisdom and intellect to deal with 'this property and I do not only refer to the real estate'.[38] In addition, the war instigated a change in the involvement of the superpowers in the region, in particular the increasing Israeli dependency, diplomatically and militarily, on the US.

Ideologically, the war brought about a Zionist revival, albeit in a new form. The re-emergence of Religious Zionism fused together religious and nationalist elements, which resulted in a change in the way most decision-makers viewed the war and the Arab-Israeli conflict. The war was talked about in biblical and even messianic terms, and not only in religious circles. Eshkol remarked that, for the first time, Jews could pray at the Wailing Wall (East Jerusalem) and the Tomb of the Patriarchs (Hebron).[39]

As far as the military were concerned, the two main threats to Israel's security prior to the war were now a distant memory: Syria was no longer able to pose a risk to Israel's northern towns and water supplies, and the threat posed by Egypt to Israel's right of passage through the Straits of Tiran had been eliminated. The new territories also changed the strategic balance in the region. Israel had acquired strategic depth allowing it to change its long-held pre-emptive strike doctrine. However, beyond the strategic gains and achievements, and with the obligation to govern the population now under occupation, the war also brought changes to the army's traditional role.[40]

The military administration

The occupation of the territories raised urgent issues with which the government had to contend, such as the restoration of public and social services and the resumption of day-to-day life for the occupied population. These entailed setting up an Israeli administrative body to govern the territories. A number of years prior to the war, Meir Shamgar – the army's Chief Military Advocate General – following a study into the army's previous experience of governing the Gaza Strip and the Sinai Peninsula,[41] set up regional administrative commands.

These would handle civilian matters in accordance with international law. Shamgar also set out clear guidelines and procedures regarding behaviour towards the population under occupation. These were later integrated into the army's officer training programme. In addition, regional commanders and their personnel were appointed, with former Major-General Haim Hertzog taking responsibility over the West Bank. The military administration and regional commands were set up in the belief that they would soon be required. But as time went on, and no apparent need for a military administration arose, the resources allocated for it understandably decreased. Therefore, it is no surprise that, despite the original contingency plan, the appointment of officials and the preparatory work done by Shamgar and others, the early conduct of the military administration left much to be desired.[42]

During the 'Waiting Period' Brigadier-General Hertzog attempted to staff his command and organise his men in anticipation for the possible occupation of the West Bank. This proved a difficult thing to do. Neither Dayan nor Narkiss had time for him, as they were preoccupied with ongoing events. On the first day of fighting, Shamgar sent a memo to the army's heads of command, reminding them of the principles of international law regarding military conduct procedures in territories inhabited by civilian populations. On the same day, requests were made by regional commanders for clear guidelines regarding setting up military administrations in the areas occupied. Many of the officers had no prior knowledge of the previous appointments and arrangements. On 7 June, Dayan and Narkiss appointed Brigadier-General Moshe Goran as governor of the Gaza Strip, and placed the West Bank under the jurisdiction of Narkiss. There was no mention of Hertzog or his unit.[43]

Hertzog's first week in command was described as an 'absolute confusion'.[44] His administrative units suffered from lack of manpower and adequate resources. They had insufficient communication lines, which harmed their ability to coordinate their activities. Orders given by Hertzog were not carried out. Combat units were either unaware of the role of the administrative units, or simply disregarded them. Furthermore, in each of the West Bank regions, local commanders – facing chaotic circumstances in the absence of clear instructions – were asked to use their own initiatives. This was not the case in the Gaza Strip, where unused combat units were sent to the Sinai front, leaving behind only logistics and support units, which were assigned to operate under appointed Governor Goran.[45] When asked by Narkiss how he planned to restore the basic services to the Arab population, Hertzog proposed using the existing workforce of the Palestinian public sector. The army wanted to avoid using Israeli professionals, who were already in short supply due to national conscription. Narkiss agreed and gave his blessing to the plan. Dayan would later use it as one of the cornerstones of his 'enlightened occupation' approach.[46]

Before the war broke out, Dayan had nominated Colonel Yehuda Nitzan to coordinate the army's activity with regard to civilian matters. Within the first few days of the fighting Nitzan was able to conclude that the army and the Ministry of Defence were lacking the capacity to govern the territories. The scale of the task meant that additional resources and expertise were required, especially in the West Bank. In the aftermath of the war, Nitzan recommended that responsibilities for civilian affairs in the territories should be shared by all relevant government ministries. This led to a reorganisation of the army's administrative units, and to the establishment of a special committee, to coordinate the government's activities. The committee comprised the government ministries' directors-general, under the director-general of the Treasury. This also marked the end of Hertzog's tenure; on 15 June, his command was annulled and the West Bank was placed under the command of Narkiss.[47]

First proposals

On 6 June, while the outcome of the war had not yet been determined, Eshkol summarised the problems Israel's decision-makers were facing:

> In front of us are the problems of our relationship with Egypt: the status of Sinai and Gaza, the question of free passage through the Gulf of Eilat and the Suez Canal, the status of the West Bank, the status of the Old City of Jerusalem, the question of the demilitarised areas in the north, the issue of control over water, finding a solution to the refugee problem and the problems with the Arab population in the Occupied Territories (OT).[48]

The need to formulate comprehensive long-term policies with regard to the newly occupied territories inspired many within the army and the government to put forward their ideas. During those early days, two interesting and thought-provoking proposals were put forward. These plans were designed to deal principally with the West Bank and its Palestinian population. The first of these proposals was submitted to the chief-of-staff and the Ministry of Defence on 9 June. It was the brainchild of the AMAN research department, headed by Brigadier-General

Shlomo Gazit, the would-be coordinator of IDF activities in the OT. Senior officers in AMAN felt that Israel had to dictate the proceedings in the early diplomatic activity. This would act to nullify any Arab proposal that might come up, while showing the world that Israel was sincere in its desire to resolve the conflict. The AMAN proposal called for the abrogation of the 1949 ceasefire agreements and for minor border modifications as part of new agreements which would be based on peace negotiations. With regard to the West Bank and the Gaza Strip, AMAN recommended the establishment of an independent, though demilitarised, Palestinian state. Furthermore, they argued that the Old City of Jerusalem should become an open city, modelled on the Vatican. The plan was never officially discussed and no comments were made by the Ministry of Defence and the General Staff.[49]

Another thought-provoking proposal was handed to the Ministry of Defence and General Staff on 14 June, with Eshkol reportedly receiving a copy as well.[50] Its authors had been members of Israel's intelligence community. They held talks during and immediately after the war with Palestinian notables in the West Bank. This was done with the approval and support of both the head of AMAN, Major-General Aharon Yariv, and Narkiss. The authors identified the Palestinian issue as the most crucial element in the Arab-Israeli conflict. In their view, Israel had an opportunity to resolve this conflict once and for all by adopting what would become known as a Palestinian approach. From their discussions with Palestinian notables, the authors sensed that there was a desire to reach a separate peace agreement with Israel, a move which would effectively bypass King Hussein and Jordan. In their remarks the authors called on the Israeli leadership to seize this unique and historic opportunity. They urged the government to work without delay towards the establishment of an independent, though demilitarised, Palestinian state in the West Bank and the Gaza Strip. Israel, they advised, should annex East Jerusalem and the Latrun Pass. In order to allow for an honourable accord, they proposed transferring some Arab lands in Israel to the newly created state and assigning a special status to the Christian and Muslim holy sites in Jerusalem.[51]

For the proposed solution to succeed, a step-by-step plan was drafted, with several goals being mentioned as points of reference. These included resolving the issue of the Palestinian refugees (re-settlement, repatriation, international support, monetary compensation), convening a gathering of all Palestinian leaders in the West Bank and producing a declaration of intent, ensuring the economic viability of the Palestinian state, free passage between the West Bank and Gaza as well as free port services in Israel.[52] The authors warned that a non-resolution of the issue would 'sow the seed of future violence',[53] but even this did not bring the proposal to the fore, and it was subsequently dropped. Examining the solutions that are currently discussed, the similarities with the above-mentioned proposals are simply remarkable.

During those first days, many additional proposals were submitted, although these did not deal with the long-term future of the OT. Of all the proposals, only one made a significant contribution to Israel's initial policy-formulation process. Brigadier-General Aryeh Shalev and Foreign Ministry representative Hanan Bar-On worked alongside Dayan during the war. They suggested that the Golan Heights and the Sinai Peninsula should be returned to Syria and Egypt respectively in exchange for peace treaties. Furthermore, they proposed that the West Bank should either form the basis of a Palestinian autonomous region or be returned to Jordan, in exchange for peace. In both scenarios, the authors suggested some border modifications in the Jerusalem area, the Latrun Pass and around the city of Qalqilya.[54] The Shalev–Bar-On plan appealed to Dayan and he adopted some of its recommendations, in particular the parts referring to Sinai and the Golan.[55]

In a meeting with his staff on 12 June, Dayan expressed his views on the future of the territories. He believed Israel did not need an additional 1.2 million Arabs. He made it clear that there were only two viable options with regard to the West Bank, that is, the establishment of an autonomous Palestinian entity with Israel in charge of its security and foreign affairs, or withdrawing from the West Bank and handing over the responsibility for the area to Jordan. On the subject of the Sinai Peninsula and the Golan Heights, Dayan felt that Israel should not rush to offer anything, but instead wait and see what Egypt and Syria offered. He was willing to consider an Israeli withdrawal in return for peace treaties and the demilitarisation of these areas, with some minor border adjustments. In addition, he decided to establish a special exploratory committee, headed by Hertzog, which would examine the main issues and report back to him.[56]

Eshkol and Dayan

Dayan's apparent desire to dictate Israel's territorial policy concerned Eshkol. When Eshkol heard of Dayan's exploratory committee he immediately dismissed it, fearing that Dayan was trying to establish his own fiefdom in the territories.[57] In response, he ordered Dayan to refrain from acting independently, and to leave the territorial policy-making to the government.[58] In order to effectively bypass Dayan and the Defence Ministry, Eshkol established a new committee under his control that would advise him on the territorial problems. The ministerial committee for the territories was headed by Finance Minister Pinhas Sapir, who wanted no part in it; the committee convened once on 15 June and was disbanded on 18 June.[59]

Eshkol wanted to find a forum in which he could nullify Dayan's contribution, while continuing to operate as he did before the war. In the pre-war period, policy formulation regarding security and foreign affairs was dominated by a special informal committee headed by Eshkol, which included Golda Meir (former foreign minister and Secretary-General of Mapai), Sapir, Ya'akov-Shimshon Shapira (the Justice Minister) and, on occasions, Foreign Minister Eban. In addition, Eshkol made use of several other forums, depending on the issue. These included the Ma'arach (the Alignment: a political block comprising the Mapai and Ahdut-Ha'avoda) Political Committee (comprising senior Mapai and Ahdut-Ha'avoda members), the Ministerial Defence Committee, and the 'Sarinu' (*our* ministers; i.e. Ma'arach ministers) forum, headed by him, and comprising ministers close to him.[60] The challenge facing Eshkol was to find a useful mechanism for dictating policies and reaching desired consensus, while preserving the national unity government. Eshkol was unable to find an appropriate forum. He therefore attempted to utilise several different ones, depending on the issue, in an attempt to preserve his control over the decision-making process, especially now that his influence had been reduced, he was no longer defence minister and his political allies had failed to stand by him during the 'Waiting Period'.[61]

The two ministerial meetings on 11 and 13 June illustrated Eshkol's method of operation. The first meeting dealt primarily with the question of Jerusalem and was attended by all ministers. It was an attempt to reach a unanimous decision on a matter that enjoyed broad consensus. Eshkol, favouring the unification of Jerusalem, felt the ministers should differentiate between Jerusalem and other territories when voting over the city's future.[62] Eshkol stated that Jerusalem had been 'liberated and united', arguing that the government 'should do what it needs to do quickly', that is, formally unify the city.[63] The ministers did not need convincing and all agreed on the need to unite the city, with the exception of Education Minister Aran, who raised several concerns regarding the possible repercussions the act would have on future Israeli-Arab relations and the political damage that could be caused by the need to do an abrupt U-turn in the face of potential international pressure.[64]

Haim Shapira convinced the rest of the ministers that the government should unify the city quietly, and without much fanfare. He proposed to extend the municipal borders of West Jerusalem, so as to include East Jerusalem, without having to vote on unification or annexation. Police Minister Eliyahu Sasson added that this was how things were done in 1949.[65] The proposal was accepted unanimously and a special committee was established to look into the future boundaries of the Jerusalem municipality.[66]

In contrast, the meeting on 13 June was an attempt by Eshkol to marginalise Dayan, and clarify to him that Israel's future foreign and security policies would remain in the hands of the prime minister. The meeting on 13 June dealt with the need to define Israel's long-term policies and was attended only by Eshkol, Eban, Dayan, Allon, Minister without Portfolio Yisrael Galili and former Chief-of-Staff and Special Advisor to Eshkol Yigal Yadin.[67] The meeting established the basis for the conduct of the military administration and led to the establishment of the Directors-General Committee to oversee the activities of the government ministries in the territories. It was the first time that Israel's long-term or strategic territorial policy was deliberated, with ministers hinting that they would be willing to offer Egypt and Syria peace treaties on the basis of Israeli withdrawal to international borders. This meeting was an example of the prevailing political mood; most ministers believed that the bulk of the territories would be returned as a result of international pressure. In an interview given on the 11 June, Eshkol echoed those very sentiments, conceding that Israel would probably have to withdraw from the Golan Heights in order to appease US and international pressure.[68] Eshkol had previously informed the US ambassador to the UN, Arthur Goldberg, that Israel would return all the territories it conquered in return for peace.[69]

Jerusalem

The attempt to limit Dayan's contribution to the decision-making process had succeeded only in part. With the military administration coming under the Defence Ministry's jurisdiction, Dayan had an alternative avenue to circumvent Eshkol and the government and influence policy. Dayan believed that neither Eshkol nor Sapir had sufficient understanding of 'the Arab mentality' and were therefore incapable of governing the territories.[70] Furthermore, when it came to the core issues, the indecisiveness exhibited by ministers prompted Dayan to 'relieve' them of their day-to-day duties in the territories. As a result, his relations with Eshkol and the Mapai old guard deteriorated, even though most ministers appeared to be content with, or at least did not challenge, his running of the territories.[71] Dayan's actions with regard to Jerusalem are a case in point.

On 10 June, and before the government managed to discuss the *small* matter of Jerusalem, events on the ground already shaped a new reality. In the courtyard of the Wailing Wall stood the Moors neighbourhood with its decrepit houses – a product of Jordanian rule. On 8 June, and accompanied by the mayor of Jerusalem Theodor 'Teddy' Kollek, David Ben-Gurion arrived at the site and was horrified. He became furious when he realised that public toilets were situated directly in front of the Wailing Wall, and demanded that Kollek do something about it. The same day, during a meeting between Dayan and the proposed military governor of East Jerusalem Brigadier-General Shlomo Lahat, Dayan asked Lahat to find 'a way' for hundreds of thousands of Jews to visit the wall through the narrow alleys and the small courtyard.[72] In coordination with civilian engineers, and supported by Kollek, the army started demolishing the Moors neighbourhood, expelling dozens of local families in the process. When, on 11 June, Eshkol called Narkiss to enquire about the demolition rumours, Narkiss claimed he did not know anything about it. Dayan and Kollek urged the contractors to finish the job quickly before the government succumbed to international pressure and had to cease the work.[73] It is alleged that when Kollek asked Justice Minister Shapira about the legality of the demolitions, the latter replied, 'Do it fast, and god will help.'[74]

The government needed to decide on the fate of the Temple Mount with regard to the control over the site, and whether to allow Jews to pray there. While ministers argued, Dayan decided to bar Jews from praying at the Temple Mount, returning it to the control of the *waqf*.[75] Furthermore, against the wishes of the army, Dayan decided to remove all the barriers between the two parts of the city, using army engineers for the job. He also relinquished the need for permits, against the advice of Narkiss, and decided to allow Muslims to pray at the Temple Mount, with immediate effect.[76] This set a precedent for state officials, the army or private individuals to act 'not in line with government policy, but in order to set it'.[77]

The Ministerial Defence Committee

On 14 and 15 June the Ministerial Defence Committee held discussions about the territories and produced the first official recommendations to the government. These bore a resemblance to the suggestions made in the Shalev–Bar-On plan. On the matter of the Sinai Peninsula and the Golan Heights, the committee advised the government to agree on an Israeli withdrawal if several conditions were met. These included the abrogation of the 1949 ceasefire lines and the signing of peace treaties. The committee also insisted that Israel demand the right of passage through the Tiran Straits; the demilitarisation of the Sinai Peninsula and the Golan Heights; a guarantee for the continuation of the flow of water from the Jordan tributaries; as well as the removal of the Arab economic embargo. The committee suggested that, as long as there was no peace, Israel would continue to hold these territories.[78]

The committee was unable to reach a decision on the future of the West Bank, though it did look at several proposals regarding its governance, among them making it an autonomous region, and the formation of cantons with military rule.[79] The committee suggested that the West Bank remain under Israeli control until a long-lasting constructive solution was found. The committee went on to suggest that Israel negotiate with Jordan in an attempt to promote good relations and achieve economic integration between the two states, while declaring the Jordan River as Israel's eastern border. It also recommended that East Jerusalem should be annexed, with special arrangements to be made for the Christian and Muslim holy sites. The committee deliberated over the Gaza Strip, but could not reach a decision. Dayan disagreed with the committee over several issues and submitted his own proposals to the government. He suggested that Israel annex the Gaza Strip, and that any long-term solution for the West Bank should be based on a Palestinian approach. He envisioned a semi-autonomous Palestinian entity, with Israel in charge of its foreign and security policies.[80]

The 19 June decisions

On 18 and 19 June, the cabinet convened to discuss its position with regard to the OT. These meetings were held in response to a US request that Israel reveal its position prior to discussions in the UN on 19 June;[81] Allon stated that 'What has been decided here is not meant for the assembly [the UN General Assembly], but for talks with the Americans.'[82] Eshkol remarked that Israel was forced to tell the US what it had planned. He advised the ministers not to shy away from setting clear policies, explaining that Israel could not operate in a vacuum and would need to consider the views of the international community.[83] These meetings were the government's first attempt at defining Israel's territorial policy; it would be the first and last time the government clearly laid out its position on the matter. Despite dissenting views, ministers, taking their cue from the recommendations of the Defence Committee, were able to reach a consensus on the Golan Heights, the Gaza Strip, the Sinai Peninsula and East Jerusalem.

Ministers decided to annex East Jerusalem and the Gaza Strip, although Eshkol remarked that while they were willing to die over Jerusalem, the thought of incorporating an additional 400,000 Arabs left a bad taste in the mouth.[84] With regard to Egypt, the government agreed to withdraw to the international border in return for a peace treaty, excluding the Gaza Strip. Furthermore, they decided to look into the idea of relocating the Gaza Strip's population before annexing it. Begin questioned how the government would transfer hundreds of thousands of Arabs from Gaza, and suggested that it might be possible to do so, but only if they were transferred to northern Sinai.[85] It is important to note that, at that time, the Gaza Strip was regarded by even the dovish Mapam ministers as essential to Israel's national security.[86] It was further decided that the peace treaty with Egypt would be conditional on Israel's right to pass through the Tiran Straits and the Suez Canal, and on the demilitarisation of the Sinai Peninsula.[87]

With regard to Syria, ministers proposed a peace treaty based on an Israeli withdrawal to the international border and in accordance with Israel's security needs.[88] The government made its withdrawal conditional on the demilitarisation of the Golan and an agreement not to sever Israel's water supplies from the Jordan River's tributaries. Until such an agreement was signed, ministers agreed to continue holding and administering the territory.[89] Several ministers remarked that Israel would probably end up holding most of the territories for a long time, believing there would be no willingness from the Arab side to negotiate.[90] Despite this, Eshkol remarked that he did not believe the world would allow Israel to retain possession of the Golan Heights.[91] The decisions regarding the Sinai Peninsula, the Golan Heights, East Jerusalem and the Gaza Strip are known as 'the decisions of 19 June'. These decisions were kept secret from the IDF and the Knesset. Chief-of-Staff Rabin only learned of these decisions from the US administration when he became Israel's ambassador to Washington.[92]

The apparent consensus did not apply to the West Bank, despite the fact that the area stood at the centre of the discussions. A motion, proposed by the Health Minister Yisrael Barzilai, to decide on the issue of the West Bank was rejected.[93] The discussion revolved around whether to adopt a Palestinian or Jordanian-based approach, with six ministers (Dayan, Barzilai, Sapir, Aran, Ya'akov-Shimshon Shapira and Haim Shapira) supporting a Jordanian approach. The rest adopted some form of a Palestinian approach, while only Begin differed, advocating an outright annexation. Begin argued that Israel 'did not sacrifice its sons in order to create an additional Arab state', or, indeed, to return the area to Jordan. Furthermore, Begin feared that the establishment of Arab cantons, in an age of decolonisation, would be a mistake. Begin questioned how 'seasoned and intellectual politicians' could even raise the idea of cantons, which he described as an 'Arab ghetto'. Therefore, Begin proposed that Israel declare its sovereignty over the West Bank.[94]

Justice Minister Shapira, in agreement with Begin, asked how Israel, in an age of decolonisation could control the lives of Palestinians. He did not think anyone would accept it, suggesting Israel either annex the West Bank and deal with the demographic repercussions, or negotiate with King Hussein over it. He warned that the world would accuse Israel of being the bearer of colonisation and imperialism, effectively trying to create an Israeli colony in the West Bank. Shapira claimed that any decision made by Israel, other than withdrawal, would be regarded as annexation by international standards. Shapira, however, acknowledged that some territorial modifications were essential (e.g. East Jerusalem).[95]

Sapir warned the government that, by annexing the West Bank, Israel would find it difficult to maintain a Jewish majority.[96] Aran added another note of caution, warning that, by annexing the West Bank, 'Israel might manage to snatch defeat from the claws of victory'. He suggested that Israel instead negotiate with Jordan, stating 'a great deed did God do by giving us this thing called Hussein, on whom we can drop this burden [the West Bank]'.[97]

Dayan also advocated a Jordanian approach, but a slightly different version of it. Dayan proposed joint Israeli-Jordanian control over the West Bank. Jordan's role would be restricted to administrative matters, while Israel would control the territory militarily. He suggested declaring the Jordan River as Israel's security border, beyond which no Arab army will be allowed to advance.[98]

The idea of negotiating with Hussein was rejected by the Ahdut-Ha'avoda ministers Allon, Galili and Transport Minister Moshe Carmel, who viewed the problem mainly from a strategic-military perspective. For them, the best way to achieve long-term security was to retain either part, or the whole, of the West Bank. In this respect their ideas were closest to Begin's. However, while accepting the demographic considerations, they were unwilling to grant citizenship to the population in the territories Israel chose to retain. Galili declared that he was willing to accept the social and political problems that could arise from Israel maintaining its control over the West Bank. Acknowledging Shapira's 'colonial' warning, Galili proposed solving the demographic problem through some form of a Palestinian-administered autonomy.[99]

Allon, echoing Galili, proposed a solution based on Israel's national security needs, stating that 'peace agreements are the weakest form of guarantees regarding future peace and security'.[100] Allon acknowledged the demographic problems associated with controlling the West Bank. He admitted that, if he was forced to choose between adding the Palestinian population to Israel and withdrawing from the West Bank, he would choose the latter. He therefore proposed establishing an independent Palestinian state in the West Bank that would be surrounded by Israel.[101] Allon argued against a return to the pre-war situation, proposing instead to unilaterally annex several strategically important areas. In those areas, Allon proposed creating facts on the ground that would emphasise Israel's refusal to return to the pre-war border.[102] He went on to argue that Israel would not be able to retain areas in which it did not settle; Allon suggested settling in the Jordan valley, the Jerusalem area and the Hebron mountain ranges.[103] Allon's comments prompted Eshkol to remark that every minister was deciding for himself what is good for Israel, 'We are playing chess with ourselves.'[104]

Trade Minister Zeev Sherf argued that there was no need to decide, as there was no real chance of reaching peace at the moment. He, therefore, proposed to leave the matter of the West Bank and to re-examine it in a few weeks' time, once Israel was able to assess the 'international mood'.[105] Sherf's proposal was accepted and the debate regarding the West Bank was postponed.[106] In other words, ministers decided not to decide. However, the government did not take a strategic decision to prevaricate in order to increase its 'margins for manoeuvre' or in order to leave open its diplomatic options; it was genuinely unable to reach a decision. The differences among ministers were so great that they were unable to reach a consensus, or even a majority view, on the matter. The failure to produce a policy for the West Bank is referred to as 'the decision not to decide'.[107]

Johnson's five principles

On 19 June, President Johnson laid out the US administration's position regarding the situation in the Middle East. In his speech Johnson proposed 'five great principles of peace in the region'. First, 'that every nation in the area has a fundamental right to live and to have this right respected by its neighbours'. Second, 'There will be no peace for any party in the Middle East unless this [refugee] problem is attacked with new energy by all.' Third, 'the right of innocent maritime passage must be preserved for all nations'. Fourth, 'limits on the wasteful and destructive arms race'. Fifth, 'respect for political independence and territorial integrity of all the states of the area'. Johnson argued that only direct negotiations between Israel and its neighbours could lead to a peaceful resolution. According to Johnson 'an immediate return to the situation as it was on June 4' was 'not a prescription for peace but for renewed hostilities'.[108] Johnson steered clear of describing the final borders, preferring instead the term 'territorial integrity'. In addition, Johnson did not mention the Palestinians, other than stressing the importance of resolving the refugee problem. Arguably, the US did not view the Palestinians as a nation and did not foresee a viable long-term solution based on a Palestinian approach for either the West Bank or the Gaza Strip.

From the perspective of the Israeli government, Johnson's argument ('no return to the pre-war situation') was a de facto American acceptance of Israel's right to hold on to parts of the territories. Israeli decision-makers did not expect Johnson to argue along those lines. It is conceivable that the Israeli government would have modified its 19 June decisions had it known Johnson's position in advance. The government would have argued for an Israeli withdrawal to 'recognised and secure borders' (Dayan's suggestion) as opposed to withdrawing to the international border.

Encouraged by the US position, Foreign Minister Eban presented Dean Rusk (the US Secretary of State) with Israel's position, as stated in its 19 June decisions. Eban claimed to have been surprised when he first learned of these 'moderate' decisions, which signalled Israel's desire for peace.[109] Eban commented later that the US administration viewed these decisions as being far-reaching.[110] Rusk was overall pleased with Israel's position, but the 'non-decision' regarding the West Bank, and the unresolved status of East Jerusalem, troubled him (Israel did not inform him of its decision to annex the city). Rusk cautioned against unifying the city, advising Eban to seek accommodation with Hussein instead.[111] The US conveyed Israel's willingness to negotiate on the basis of its 19 June decisions to Syria and Egypt. Both states did not reciprocate, which helped to justify the feeling in Israel that these were not partners for negotiations. This reinforced the view (expressed by Dayan, Allon, Galili, Sherf and Begin) that Israel should be allowed to hold on to the territories indefinitely, or until suitable peace partners emerged.[112]

In recent years there has been some controversy over Israel's willingness to negotiate at the time. According to Shlaim, Eban did not actually ask Rusk to convey Israel's intentions to Egypt or Syria, and so no offers were made to those states.[113] Bavly argues that, because of its own interests in the region, the US decided not to convey Israel's position to Egypt and Syria, informing Israel that both states refused to reciprocate.[114] If true, this would place the responsibility for the failure of Israel's initiative on the American administration. Nevertheless, it is clear that Eban informed the US of Israel's 19 June decisions. Regardless of what happened next, there is no doubt that the lack of reciprocation, whether it was due to Egyptian and Syrian intransigence or US machinations, played into the hands of Israeli hardliners. The lack of a diplomatic breakthrough provided ammunition for those ministers, that is, Allon, Galili and Dayan, who argued in favour of retaining areas Israel deemed essential for its national security.[115]

Israel's 19 June decisions were not intended solely for the American administration; they were also motivated by the desire to clarify Israel's position, prior to a debate on the matter at the UN. In the UN, the Soviet delegation, supported by Egypt and Syria, demanded that Israel withdraw unconditionally to the pre-war borders. The USSR and several Arab delegations believed that, when 'push came to shove', the US would support a resolution condemning Israel and calling for its unilateral withdrawal. This assumption was based on the Suez Crisis precedent, where the Eisenhower administration pressured Israel to withdraw from areas it occupied after the crisis.[116] However, the US refused to accept the Soviets' demand, claiming that an Israeli withdrawal to the pre-war lines would only serve as a precursor to the resumption of hostilities.[117] Among the permanent members of the Security Council, the American position was supported by France and Britain. The British, through Foreign Secretary George Brown, called for an Israeli withdrawal in conjunction with peace negotiations.

In contrast to the Americans, Brown discussed the intricate details of the problem, arguing that the UN should not recognise an Israeli move to unify Jerusalem. The move, according to Brown, would 'isolate them not only from world opinion, but will also lose them the support which they have'. This remark, as well as a similar statement regarding the inadmissibility of acquiring territories by means of war, were seen in Israel as an attempt by Britain to appease the Arab side and further increased the pressure on the government to speed up its plans to annex East Jerusalem.[118]

Jerusalem again

The British comments on Jerusalem were used by Eshkol to open a cabinet debate on the subject of unifying the city.[119] Israel had previously decided to annex the city, as part of its 19 June decisions. Only the municipal boundaries of the proposed unified city were left undecided. For advice on the issue of municipal boundaries, the government established a special ministerial-level committee. The committee's proposed map tripled the size of Jerusalem, and added many Arab villages and open spaces (e.g. surrounding hills) which were never part of Jordanian Jerusalem.[120] The committee claimed to have increased the municipal boundaries in order to provide 'room' for future growth. The main considerations expressed by the committee were of political and military nature, as opposed to urban planning. Areas were linked to or cut from Jerusalem according to their perceived strategic importance. The main idea behind the proposed map was to surround the unified city with populated 'strategic ridges',[121] with these urban changes being presented as reversible (which arguably they were anything but).[122]

Between 20 and 27 June the government deliberated over the map presented to it by the committee. Despite Eban's insistence that a vote to change the status of the city prior to the conclusion of UN discussions would harm the Israeli cause, ministers proceeded to vote on the committee's recommendations. The map was approved unanimously.[123] Following the recommendations of the justice minister, the government decided to annex the city by 'adjusting' the judicial system. A new section was added to a 1948 regulatory law, stating that the judicial and administrative law of the state would apply to any part of the land of Israel the government saw fit.[124] The government – wanting to avoid publicity – proposed to extend the municipal boundaries of West Jerusalem to include East Jerusalem, as opposed to formally unifying or annexing the city, hoping a clever use of semantics would 'do the trick'.

The following day, the Knesset was convened for a special session. With the exception of the Communist Party and the Arab Members of the Knesset (MKs), the Knesset voted unanimously in favour of the new law. The vote was followed by a government decree, stating that the new lands (the extended boundaries of Jerusalem) were part of Israel, and therefore Israel's law and sovereignty applied in them. In order to disguise the real purpose of the new law, the extended municipal boundaries were only ever mentioned as coordinates (i.e. point 1678613520 north towards point 1673613678).[125]

The decision to annex East Jerusalem was taken without a serious discussion on the long-term implications of such an act. Despite Eshkol's initial remarks and the remarks made by the special ministerial-level committee, the decision was taken in full knowledge that it was not reversible. The decision was spurred on by overwhelming public support and was made possible by a rare consensus among the major political parties. Israeli leaders, fearing an international backlash, decided to act before international pressure forced Israel to withdraw.[126] The decision clearly paid dividends, as the UN Security Council waited until May 1968 to officially condemn Israel's decision; much of the delay was due to American diplomatic obstructions. The American administration said it 'strongly deplored' Israel's unilateral action, but did not put any pressure on Israel to reverse its decision.[127]

At the UN, after struggling to find a compromise, on 20 July, the US and the USSR reached an agreement on a joint draft resolution. Presented by Arthur Goldberg (US ambassador to the UN) and Andrei Gromyko (Soviet Foreign Secretary), the Goldberg–Gromyko draft resolution called on all states to withdraw immediately from all territories acquired during the war. The withdrawal would be accompanied by a statement calling on all states to recognise each other's right to live in peace and security, ensuring the rights of maritime passage, finding a just solution for the refugee problem and allowing for UN peace-keeping deployment in the region.[128]

To the Israeli government the Goldberg–Gromyko draft resolution was unacceptable. Eban complained vociferously to Goldberg, objecting on the grounds that the sides were not required to negotiate a settlement. Israel did not believe the UN was an honest broker and refused to allow UN peace-keepers to be stationed in the territories. In addition, Israel refused to accept a return to the pre-war borders, distancing itself from its 19 June decisions. In order to alleviate Israeli fears, Johnson promised Israel that a withdrawal would not precede the other conditions mentioned and would occur only at the final stage. To Israel's surprise the Arab delegations refused to accept the compromise.[129] This refusal played into the hands of those in Israel, who refused to see the Arabs as peace partners.

The debates in the UN, coupled with requests made by several hawkish ministers, as well as the general public opinion, all strengthened the desire in Israel to keep the territories indefinitely. The claim 'there is no one to talk to' became prevalent as the perceived Arab refusal to compromise helped foster a climate of denial and eroded the perception, among policy-makers, of the OT as diplomatic bargaining chips.

The failure of the expected international demand for an Israeli withdrawal to materialise proved that the world would not, or could not, force Israel to withdraw. Moreover, the US acceptance of the 'no return to pre-war boundaries' concept allowed Israel to distance itself from the 19 June decisions and keep at least parts of the territories without suffering any repercussions. In the cacophony of the hectic diplomatic activity, Israel's refusal to accept the Goldberg–Gromyko compromise faded to a distant echo. In fact, ministers in Israel doubted whether an additional American diplomatic initiative was either desirable or necessary. They believed the 'existing stalemate ... is exercising a positive influence' on the Arab sides.[130]

In the midst of the UN diplomatic activity, Director-General of the Prime Minister's Office Ya'akov Hertzog met with King Hussein. The talks, which were held in London, were part of a secret channel of communication that had existed between the two states for years (Hertzog had previously met the king several times). Due to its inability to formulate a policy towards the West Bank, and the general unease felt by several ministers towards Hussein, the government hoped to learn more by listening to the king's position first, and therefore instructed Hertzog not to propose anything. The king arrived in London from Washington, where he was advised by the Americans to pursue peace with Israel, informing him that they would not impose a diplomatic settlement on Israel. The king explained to Hertzog that the Arab world was at a crossroads, but agreed that achieving peace was the preferred destination. Hussein did not put forward any proposals; instead he asked for time. The king was hoping that he would be able to convene an Arab summit, one in which the moderate sides would set the tone for peace negotiations with Israel, before he would proceed to present his views.[131]

The West Bank

In its 19 June decisions the government avoided defining its preferred approach towards the West Bank. In order to at least overcome the challenges presented by occupying the West Bank and examine which approach – Palestinian or Jordanian – held more promise, the government established several committees to explore the matter and report back with their findings. During July 1967, these committees presented their papers to the government. The first report came from the Foreign Ministry and was presented on 13 July. The report outlined and analysed seven possible solutions, as far as the Foreign Ministry was concerned.

1. *Annexation* – the report advised against annexation. The option was listed as unrealistic because of the demographic problem.
2. *Withdrawal or returning the West Bank to Hussein* – the report suggested that this option was unrealistic. It would not solve Israel's security problems.
3. *Returning part of the West Bank to Hussein provided it was demilitarised and provided he accepts Israel's annexation of Jerusalem and the Gaza Strip* – the report concluded that this would be a favourable solution from an Israeli perspective, but Hussein would probably consider it unacceptable.
4. *Leaving the problem without a clear solution* – this option would allow Israel greater flexibility but would pose many social and political problems. It would also raise the suspicion that Israel was annexing the territory and the demographic problems would remain unresolved.
5. *The establishment of a Palestinian state in the West Bank* – the report added that the establishment of a Palestinian state would create a breakthrough in Israeli-Arab relations. However, for this solution to be feasible Israel would need to annex the Gaza Strip and transfer its population to the West Bank.
6. *A Palestinian state linked to Jordan* – this option was listed as a possibility only as long as Jordan accepted an Israeli army presence in the West Bank, the annexation of Jerusalem, and the relocation of the Gaza Strip population to the West Bank. The report did not clarify whether the Palestinians or Hussein would agree to this solution.
7. *An Israeli/Palestinian confederation* – this option would solve Israel's security problems but would pose the same political and social problems as annexation.

The committee concluded that the creation of a demilitarised Palestinian state would be the most favourable course of action, as long as this did not include East Jerusalem and the Gaza Strip, after its population was resettled in the West Bank. The report suggested that the establishment of a Palestinian state would create a breakthrough in Israeli-Arab relations and solve many of Israel's security and demographic problems. Nonetheless, the paper fell short of recommending this option, outlining some of the problems of establishing a Palestinian state: it would be viewed as an Israeli creation and 'shunned by the Arab world'; it would mean the end of a Jordanian-based solution; the newly created Palestinian state would be separated from the Palestinian diaspora 'which might lead to irredentism'. [132]

A second committee (referred to in the literature as the Committee of the Four) established by the Prime Minister's Office delivered its recommendations to Eshkol the following week on 20 July. In contrast to the Foreign Ministry's report, this committee concluded that Israel should negotiate with King Hussein. The authors argued for an intensive diplomatic effort to reach a peace settlement with Hussein. The report suggested that Israel did not have time on its side as it risked losing a historic opportunity. The committee claimed a Palestinian entity was undesirable for Israel. After conducting discussions with Palestinian notables, they concluded that only a minority of them were willing to 'go it alone' (without the support of the Arab world) and establish an independent Palestinian state. The report suggested that Israel conduct an intensive diplomatic effort to reach a peace settlement with Hussein conditional on: an Israeli annexation of the Gaza Strip; the resettlement of the Gaza population in the West and East Banks; demilitarisation of the West Bank; minor border modifications; and the establishment of a joint Israeli/Jordanian control over the West Bank. The authors concluded that until such a settlement was achieved, the West Bank should be administered as a separate entity and be placed under the jurisdiction of a separate government department headed by a minister, and that most of the junior administrative positions should be manned by Arabs.[133]

On 21 July, an ad hoc committee (composed of the authors of the previous two papers) titled the Committee of the West Bank met to discuss the Foreign Ministry's seven scenarios. This committee reached a similar conclusion (to that of the Committee of the Four) regarding the viability and feasibility of a Palestinian-based approach. The committee recommended pursuing only a Jordanian-based approach. Nonetheless, the committee suggested four options should this solution prove unsuccessful:

1. Complete integration of the West Bank with Israel.
2. Turning the West Bank into an autonomous province with administrative self-rule.
3. Turning the West Bank into a canton with minimal representation.
4. To wait and not to decide on the future political status of the West Bank.[134]

In what would appear to be an additional blow to the Palestinian approach, the Heads of Services Committee (a committee composed of the heads of the Foreign Ministry, AMAN and the Mossad) submitted a report to the prime minister on 27 July suggesting that Israel should negotiate with Jordan. The committee argued that only two immediate viable solutions existed: direct negotiations with King Hussein, and, in the absence of such talks, strengthening Israel's political and economic control over the West Bank. Nonetheless, the committee did not completely rule out the chances of a future solution based on a Palestinian element:

> There does not appear to be a place for the establishment of a Palestinian independent unit ... at this stage, as it is preferable for Israel to keep all of the options available and to re-examine them in relation to future developments ... The chances of cooperation among the population are dependent upon creating the sense that the chances that Hussein will return to the West Bank are low.[135]

The report relied on a brief prepared by the Committee of the Four detailing its perception of Palestinian attitudes in the West Bank. The brief claimed that most Palestinians preferred an Israeli-Jordanian solution:

> Only some [underline in the original text] are willing today to immediately reach a bilateral solution with Israel. Only some recommend trying to discuss first of all with all Arab states without exception. The overall majority demands that Israel first exhaust all of the options of reaching a peace agreement with Jordan. Some are willing to participate personally in this Israeli effort.[136]

It appears that, after the recommendations of these committees, the Palestinian approach was side lined for several months while Israel explored the possibility of negotiating with Jordan.

The Allon Plan

On 26 July, Employment Minister Allon presented the government with his plan to resolve the political impasse that had been reached with regard to the West Bank. As befitted a former military man, the plan, later known as the Allon Plan, was based on a mainly military-security orientation. Allon had had an illustrious military career from 1936, as part of Israel's paramilitary forces in the Mandate period, to 1950, when he was overlooked for the position of chief-of-staff. During his military career he was considered a brilliant strategist who was unafraid to speak his own mind and meddle in politics. Allon had famously argued with Ben-Gurion in 1948 over the West Bank. Allon called Ben-Gurion's decision to accept a ceasefire and not order the conquest of the West Bank and East Jerusalem a historic mistake; he also disagreed with Ben-Gurion's decision to withdraw from the Gaza Strip in 1957, after the Suez crisis.

The Allon Plan was the first attempt by a minister to propose a strategic territorial policy. In the introduction to his plan, Allon explained the importance of establishing clear policies with regard to the territories. He advised the government to act quickly, before the US and the USSR managed to find a compromise resolution on Israel's behalf. Allon's original plan did not deal with the Sinai Peninsula and the Golan Heights; he explained that these would be dealt with separately. The main features of the Allon Plan are summarised below.

1. The establishment of the Jordan River as Israel's eastern border.
2. In order to guarantee Israel's security, the following territories would be annexed.
   - A 10–15 km-wide strip along the Jordan valley from Beit-She'an valley to the north part of the Dead Sea.
   - A several-km-wide strip from the northern-most part of the Dead Sea to northern Jerusalem.
   - The Hebron Mountain or at least the area from the Judean Desert to the Negev.
   - Minor modifications in the Hebron Mountain and the Latrun regions.
3. In the annexed areas Israel would establish settlements and permanent military bases.
4. In East Jerusalem, new Jewish neighbourhoods would be built in addition to the repopulation of the Old City's Jewish quarters.
5. In the areas not annexed by Israel, negotiations would start with local notables for the establishment of an autonomous Palestinian region, which would be linked to Israel by security and economic pacts.
6. Israel would work with the international community to resolve the refugee problem and would allow their resettlement in the West Bank and/or Sinai.
7. The Gaza Strip would be annexed by Israel once its population has been resettled.
8. An administrative office would be established to deal with the territories and the resettlement of refugees.[137]

Allon divided the West Bank into separate areas based on their perceived military-strategic value, and called for the annexation of those
areas deemed essential for national security; the rest of the West Bank
was assigned for the establishment of a Palestinian autonomy. The
Allon Plan was based on the notion that Israel had no interest in controlling the Palestinian population and was about securing 'greater
Israel's demographic integrity rather than its geographic integrity'.[138]
Furthermore, the plan, with its emphasis on agricultural settlements
and their added value in terms of security, rather than urban centres,
represented a return to the Zionist way of thinking prevalent during the
Mandate period.

The Allon Plan, however, was not well received and, when ministers
met to discuss its merits, they dismissed it as unsuitable. The plan was
dismissed by the right (Gahal), the centre (Mapai) and the left (Mapam).
According to Allon, ministers, influenced by Eshkol, refused to take a
stand on the territorial issue before the Arab world expressed its willingness to negotiate. In short, the government preferred to maintain
its 'non-decision'. The plan did not fare any better when presented to
Ahdut-Ha'avoda members. The party base were in favour of the Greater
Israel ideal and party leader Yitzhak Tabenkin warned against the establishment of a Palestinian autonomous region, accusing Allon of giving
away the West Bank.[139]

Other plans

Despite the reluctance shown by the government towards accepting it,
the Allon Plan did not disappear from the political scene. Moreover,
the plan slowly took on a life of its own and was discussed at great
length during a special meeting of the Ma'arach Political Committee
on 18 August. This committee was composed of the Mapai and Ahdut-
Ha'avoda ministers and the purpose of the meeting was to discuss
Israel's territorial policy. The committee was presented with three alternative plans: the Allon Plan, a settlement plan by Ra'anan Weitz (head
of the World Zionist Organisation's Settlement Department),[140] and an
additional plan created by Dayan.[141]

The Weitz Plan bore a stark resemblance to the Allon Plan. When
asked to comment on it, Allon endorsed it as a 'settlement interpretation' of his plan. Weitz proposed the establishment of 30–50 settlements in the West Bank, established mostly in unpopulated areas along
the Jordan valley. This would allow for the creation of a Palestinian
entity in the areas not settled by Israel, including the Gaza Strip.

However, according to Weitz, Israel would still maintain its military control over the territories.[142] Weitz and Allon professed not to have known about each other's plans, but this would appear highly unlikely. On 27 July, the date the Allon Plan was submitted to the government, Allon outlined in his diary a settlement plan almost identical to the one Weitz submitted: the page in Allon's diary is titled R. Weitz, and is dated 27/06/67.[143] Furthermore, Allon's close collaboration with Weitz on the Eliqa settlement would suggest that they had some knowledge of each other's ideas and aims. Whether they were working together to influence territorial policy is unclear.[144]

Knowing Dayan's historic rivalry with Allon, which stretched back to their time in the paramilitary and then Israel's military forces, it was probably not a surprise that he decided to present the committee with a different approach to the West Bank. The Dayan plan, known later as the Functional Solution, was first presented to the Ministerial Defence Committee on 14 August and was further elaborated upon on 3 September, at a Rafi Party meeting.[145] Dayan, like Allon, also approached the issue of the West Bank from a strategic-military perspective; the West Bank provided Israel, for the first time, with strategic depth. This convinced Dayan that there was no need for static defence along the Jordan River (implied in the Allon Plan), proposing instead a plan based on 'mobile defence'. According to Dayan, this would be achieved by creating five permanent army bases on the mountain ridges of the West Bank. In order to support Israel's position in the West Bank, and alongside the army bases, Dayan proposed the establishment of large urban settlements. These, in addition to the army bases, would break the territorial integrity of the West Bank and ensure Israel's control. Dayan dismissed Allon's settlement philosophy, arguing that agricultural settlements had little security value. Additionally, Dayan envisioned that the administrative responsibilities of the West Bank would be shared between Israel and Jordan and the population would continue to hold Jordanian citizenship.[146] Allon acknowledged that Dayan's plan provided better security for Israel, but at a great demographic cost;[147] under the Allon Plan Israel would not hold the main Palestinian population centres and would not govern their lives. Allon, as well as many others, argued that the idea of a Functional Solution would eventually lead either to annexation or to an Israeli rule that denied Palestinian political rights.

The committee did not actually agree on either of these plans, but its members responded favourably to Weitz's. There was a broad consensus that the Dayan plan did not provide an answer to Israel's demographic problem. Eshkol commented that the Dayan plan would add more Arabs to Israel's population, while the government was trying to avoid exactly that. Nevertheless, the committee was receptive to the security elements in the Dayan plan and recommended it to the government. Two days later, the government voted for the creation of military bases across the mountain ridges, evidently acknowledging the importance of the military elements in the plan.[148]

An additional plan was made public by Mapam on 18 August. Mapam was the only party to present a concrete peace plan, which resembled the government's 19 June decisions but added that the West Bank should be returned to Jordan with some minor border modifications, and that Israel should strive to solve the refugee problem.[149]

It was apparent that the main disagreements among coalition members were about the West Bank. While the Israeli government's position with regard to the West Bank remained unclear, four schools of thought emerged. It is interesting to note that all four are still present in Israeli politics today. The first school of thought (Mapam) called for a withdrawal from the West Bank with some minor border modifications (based on negotiations with Jordan). The second, expressed by Dayan, envisioned a joint Israeli/Palestinian or Israeli/Jordanian administrative rule. The third, as outlined in the Allon Plan, proposed to annex parts of the West Bank for security reasons and, in the territories not annexed, either to create a Palestinian entity or to return them to Jordan. Lastly, Begin called for the annexation of the West Bank, with some form of transitional period in which its residents' civil rights would be assessed, after which they might be able to acquire citizenship.

Dayan

While the government and its various committees debated over Israel's policy approach without reaching any clear decisions, the Defence Ministry and the IDF dealt with the reality of the occupation. Dayan, while briefing the Knesset's Foreign Affairs and Defence Committee (KFDC), explained that the Defence Ministry and the IDF administered the territories according to government policies. He was, however, unable to elaborate on these policies, and on whether or not the government had formulated any.[150] The main reason Dayan did not detail the economic or political policies was that there were none. The lack of policies created a culture of 'wait and see' which put a strain on the Ministry of Defence and the IDF, and led to the retention of administrative powers by the ministry.[151] This fitted well with Dayan's general perception of his fellow ministers who, he believed, lacked long-term vision, and, unlike him, did not understand 'the Arab mentality'. Dayan's own views on Arabs and the Arab world were based partly on his extensive military background (Dayan also fought in the pre-state paramilitary group Haganah) and partly on his own upbringing in Mandatory Palestine where he frequently met with Arabs. Dayan 'liked their way of life and respected them as hard workers'; he had no doubt that peace with them was possible, but also acknowledged that a 'deep national and religious chasm' separated them.[152]

Dayan believed Israel would have to keep the territories for an extended period of time as no solution was forthcoming. This left Israel with a reality of having to manage the territories and their population without creating a 'pressure cooker'. Israel had to do so while improving the living standards of the local population and without allowing the territories to become an economic burden on Israel's economy. For Dayan, the way to manage the territories was through Arab self-rule (*Minhal 'Atzmi*) and economic integration with Israel. Dayan did not accept the proposition that the West Bank and the Gaza Strip should remain separate economic entities in order to preserve their status as bargaining chips.[153]

As for the IDF and the military administration's conduct in the OT, Dayan established his guidelines, which were based on three principles: non-intervention, open borders and non-visibility.[154] Dayan felt it was essential that Israeli officials had minimum contact with the local population and ordered the IDF to remain as far as possible from large population centres in order to allow day-to-day life to proceed uninterrupted (the 'Invisible Occupation'). Dayan made it clear to Palestinian notables that all matters concerning the military administration or the conduct of the army would be dealt with exclusively by the Ministry of Defence. Dayan did not expect the population to love Israel or accept its rule, but asked that they refrain from anti-Israel activities and cooperate with the administration.[155] He remarked that if he had to choose to be occupied, he would have preferred being occupied by Israel over any other nation.[156]

Arguably, the defining policy of the military administration was the Open Bridges policy. Dayan claimed in his memoirs that this policy was his brainchild; in reality it had very little to do with him. During the early weeks of the occupation, IDF officers uncovered attempts by West Bank traders to smuggle their produce across the Jordan River. After the matter was brought to his attention and because of lack of resources to stop the trend, Narkiss, head of Central Command, decided to turn a blind eye. Dayan, however, was quick to spot the inherent advantages when informed of the incidents a few weeks later. Dayan was allegedly against the Open Bridges at first, but eventually changed his mind after spotting an opportunity – an ability for which Dayan was renowned.[157] The export of excess agricultural produce to Jordan increased Palestinian living standards while protecting the Israeli market from cheap imports. The Open Bridges policy came into effect on 21 August and, from Dayan's perspective, served as a 'pressure release valve' for the Palestinians and ensured that the West Bank would not become an economic burden. Dayan may not have conceived the policy, but he understood its advantages and therefore authorised it, long before the government was aware of it.[158]

In short, Dayan's vision was self-contradictory. On the one hand, Dayan pushed for economic integration and the establishment of army bases and Jewish settlements in the West Bank. On the other hand, he genuinely wanted to improve the living standards of the Palestinian population; to provide them with the opportunity to resume normal lives without Israeli intervention; to allow them to exercise self-rule; and even maintain their ties with the Arab world. You could argue that he tried to create a 'Benevolent Occupation'.[159]

2
The 'Wall-to-Wall' Coalition

Merom Golan

On 23 June, Hakibbutz Hameuhad (the United Kibbutz) convened to discuss the post-war situation. Originally a non-political grassroots organisation, it considered itself a vehicle for the realisation of Zionism; it had contributed to the creation of numerous kibbutzim in the state's pre- and post-independence era. The organisation also served as an electoral base for Ahdut-Ha'avoda, through which it expressed its political aspirations. The meeting was dominated by Yitzhak Tabenkin, the 80-year-old leader and one of the founding fathers of Hakibbutz Hameuhad and Ahdut-Ha'avoda. For Tabenkin, the Six Day War represented an opportunity to fulfil the Zionist dream and an opportunity to correct Mapai's historic mistake of accepting the UN partition plan. Tabenkin was behind Ahdut-Ha'avoda's split from Mapai in 1948 as a result of the latter's acceptance of the partition plan. Tabenkin called for the annexation of all the territories and the immediate establishment of settlements. According to Tabenkin, settlements represented the natural way for the development and strengthening of all spheres of Jewish life.[1] Tabenkin's words resonated with Hakibbutz Hameuhad members. The resolution they put forward called upon the government to: abrogate the 1949 ceasefire agreements; unify Jerusalem; continue to hold the territories; make no differentiation between the territories held; establish settlements; and refuse to conduct peace negotiations on the basis of the pre-war borders.[2]

Several of the members took these words literally. During the meeting they discussed the possibility of establishing a settlement on the Golan Heights. It is unclear whether they informed Tabenkin, but it is probably safe to assume that he would have supported their decision. After organising themselves, they announced their intentions to harvest the fields and tend to the cattle abandoned by the Syrians in the Golan. On 14 July, the group established Eliqa (later to be known as Merom Golan) – the first settlement in the territories. The establishment of Eliqa created a precedent in that the government had allowed a semi-private initiative, backed by high-ranking officials, to create 'facts on the ground' and influence policy. In its 19 June decisions the government had decided to withdraw from the Golan Heights in return for peace. During the discussions leading to this decision, the only areas mentioned in relation to settlements were Hebron, East Jerusalem and the Jordan valley. The Golan Heights were not part of the government's initial settlement plans.[3]

The fact that the group managed to circumvent the government and create a 'fact on the ground' was due in a large part to the support they received from the Upper Galilee Regional Council, the IDF, Allon and Ra'anan Weitz (head of the Settlement Department). On 9 July, a few days before they settled in the Golan Heights, the group met with the Upper Galilee Regional Council (an area adjacent to the Golan), which agreed to allocate funds and assist the group with their agricultural undertakings. Although there was no mention at that point of complicity, it is hard to imagine that the council members were oblivious to the implications their actions would have. After the war, the IDF declared the Golan Heights a closed military zone, accessible only with permits.[4] Through Dan Lerner (commander of the IDF's forces in the Golan and a member of Hakibbutz Hameuhad), the Eliqa group enlisted the support of the head of Israel's Northern Command El'azar. El'azar provided the group with permits, food supplies and tractors, and later on also authorised IDF soldiers guard the settlement.[5] On 30 July the army moved the settlers to a disused Syrian army base and authorised their stay. The order was signed by the military-appointed governor of the Golan Heights.[6] The most important contributions to the group's effort came from Allon and Weitz, who were privy to the group's plans; Allon would later claim that it was he who organised the group. It is clear that Allon was actively trying to implement his own plan, with or without the government's formal approval, and operated on the basis that Israel would never withdraw from the Golan Heights.[7] On 3 July, a few days after the Eliqa group found a suitable area to settle, Allon submitted a proposal to the government for the establishment of two or three agricultural work camps in the Golan Heights.[8] Allon did not mention the Eliqa group. He knew the government would rule out any request to settle the Golan and decided to circumvent any obstacles that might have arisen from treating these camps as settlements, by proposing the establishment of agricultural work camps.[9] In addition, Allon provided the group with funds, which were diverted from the Employment Ministry, which he headed, without the knowledge of the government.[10]

Weitz understood from the outset that the principal motive behind the establishment of agricultural work camps was to settle the Golan.[11] Nevertheless, Weitz agreed to provide substantial funds to the group, through the Upper Galilee Regional Council, for the purpose of establishing Eliqa. It is important to note that the Settlement Department had conducted surveys in the Golan and looked into establishing settlements before meeting with the Eliqa group. Arguably, it was acting of its own accord, even though it would not normally act independently.[12] During the war, Weitz discussed with Eshkol the need to conduct surveys in the territories in order to determine land ownership, water supplies and evaluate development plans. Eshkol thought this was unnecessary, as Israel would be forced to give the territories back, but gave him his authorisation nevertheless.[13] Therefore, it is plausible that the Settlement Department provided funds to the settlers with the tacit authorisation of government officials.

Committees

On 27 August, six weeks after the Eliqa group established the first settlement, the cabinet convened to discuss its policy regarding the Golan Heights. On the agenda was the creation of agricultural work camps. Eshkol made it clear these camps were necessary for the purpose of working the land: 'It's clear that you neither destroy orchards nor start permanent settlements … but if orchards exist, you have to maintain them.'[14] Ministers decided to approve the agricultural work camps as well as set up an ad hoc committee for defining the size and locations of these camps. Agriculture Minister Haim Gvati claimed 'the government's decision is sufficient … and in consultation with the Agriculture Ministry [Gvati], the Defence Ministry [Dayan], and the Employment Ministry [Allon], we [the ad hoc committee] will decide how to do it'.[15] At the same meeting, the government also authorised the establishment of an additional agricultural camp in El-Arish (Sinai).[16]

It was probably not a surprise that, with Allon and Dayan at its helm, the new ad hoc committee deviated from the task given to it by the government. Its first briefing paper was titled 'Discussion on Outposts in the Held Territories'. The committee decided to establish two Nahal[17] outposts in the Golan Heights, and agreed to provide official

authorisation for the existing outpost of Eliqa. Furthermore, it authorised the creation of additional outposts in the Golan and Sinai. In its
briefing, the committee stated that the government had empowered it
to decide on settlement matters.[18]

On 1 September, the leaders of the Arab League, with the exception of
Algeria and Syria, gathered in Khartoum to discuss the situation in the
Middle East. The leaders agreed to coordinate their activities to ensure
that Israel withdrew to the pre-war boundaries. The summit's concluding resolution called for 'no peace with Israel, no recognition of Israel,
and no negotiations with Israel' (known as 'the three no's'). There has
been a lot of controversy as to what the resolution 'really' meant. Some
argue that the resolution was a genuine attempt at a two-state solution
through third-party mediations.[19] In Israel, the resolution's three no's
were interpreted as an Arab rejection of Israel and its peace initiative.[20]
For the government, the Khartoum resolutions served as a reality check.
After the Six Day War there were expectations that the Arab states
would stand in line for peace negotiations and would accept Israeli
conditions.[21] The Khartoum resolution helped sway the debate within
the government in favour of those who saw no credible negotiation
partners. Galili remarked that it was unfair to expect Israel to assume a
passive grip on the territories while the Arab world refused to negotiate
with it.[22]

On the heels of the Khartoum Summit, the cabinet convened to discuss the subject of settlements. At the meeting the ad hoc committee
provided a brief on the decisions it had reached, with Dayan reminding the ministers that the committee was actually authorised to make
decisions about settlements. Eshkol, who earlier criticised Dayan's independent activities in the territories, did not object to the committee's
'new range of activities'. Tourism Minister Moshe Kol (Independent
Liberal Party) was the only one to state the obvious, remarking that the
government had not authorised the committee to look into the matter of settlements. The meeting ended without a decision. By failing to
reach a decision, the government all but decided to leave the matter in
the hands of Gvati, Allon and Dayan – showing, not for the first time,
an unwillingness to deal with the complexity of the territorial issue.
In leaving the future of Eliqa undecided, the government effectively
authorised it. There were direct implications to this non-decision: by
not reprimanding the ad hoc committee, the government provided it
with the authority to formulate and implement territorial policies on
its behalf. By failing to decide, the government allowed for a decision
of great significance, that is, the establishment of settlements in the

Occupied Territories (OT), to be taken by an ad hoc committee, without ever discussing the long-term implications. In fact, by leaving the matter in the hands of the committee, the Eshkol government effectively retracted its 19 June decisions without articulating an alternative vision.

The ensuing policy vacuum was exploited by Allon and Dayan, through the ad hoc committee, in order to implement their territorial plans. On 10 September, Allon presented the government with a proposal to allow the ad hoc committee to establish settlements in Gush Etzion and the Jordan valley. According to the proposal, which coincidentally was along the line of the Allon Plan, Israel would annex both areas. Allon argued that the government had already authorised the committee to establish agricultural work camps in the Golan Heights, and it should therefore provide it with the same authority with regard to the Gush Etzion and Jordan valley areas.[23] Eshkol supported the idea of settling Gush Etzion. He informed ministers that a large group of people were willing to settle there if the government approved it.[24] Eshkol did not mention that he had been contacted by the adult children of former Gush Etzion inhabitants, who wanted to resettle there.[25] Gvati objected to the idea of resettling Gush Etzion, stating that the government had not yet decided on the future of the West Bank and that a decision to settle Gush Etzion would entail appropriating land. Gvati believed it would be prudent to decide the future of the West Bank prior to establishing settlements there.[26] While the issue of settling Gush Etzion clearly troubled him, Gvati did not object to settling the Golan Heights. Justice Minister Shapira explained that Gush Etzion had a different status to the other areas, as the land was legally owned by Jews before the 'War of Independence'. Additionally, Gush Etzion was one of the sites suggested by Dayan as suitable for the construction of a military base. One of the problems of deciding over Gush Etzion was that ministers were confused about the legality of establishing outposts, settlements and military bases in the territories. This was apparent in the language they used when referring to the territories, which were described as 'Freed Territories' (*Meshuhrarim*), 'Held Territories', 'Occupied Territories' and as 'Territories held by the IDF'.

In order to clarify the uncertainty over the legal status of the OT, the government requested the advice of Theodor Meron (the Foreign Office Attorney General: later a judge at the International Criminal Court). In his opinion, Meron argued, there was in fact a legal precedent for settling in the Gush Etzion area. The area had previously been owned and occupied by Jews, and Israel could claim the settlers were simply returning to their homes. With regard to the Golan Heights, Meron informed the government that, in legal terms, the area was an occupied territory and therefore, according to the Geneva Convention (which Israel had signed), Israel was categorically prohibited from establishing civilian settlement there. Israel's claim for legal ambiguity regarding its control over the West Bank and the Gaza Strip was not totally unjustified, keeping in line with the previous rule by Egypt and Jordan. However, Meron added that the international community would not accept an Israeli counter-claim. According to international law, states are prohibited from annexing occupied territories or settling their populations in them. Meron explained that international law applied to civilian settlements, but not to military outposts. Therefore, the establishment of temporary army bases on what had previously been public lands would be legally permissible. Meron accepted the government's claim for establishing Nahal outposts in the territories in order to carry out agricultural work.[27] Meron's legal advice opened the way for the establishment of temporary Nahal outposts.

On 22 September, Eshkol met the children of former Gush Etzion residents. Eshkol explained that no firm decision had been taken regarding the future of the West Bank, but promised to look into their request and give them an answer within a few days.[28] Allegedly, the Gush Etzion group told Eshkol they were ready to establish an outpost in the area with or without the government's consent, to which Eshkol replied with 'Go on!'[29] It is interesting to note that the settlers, who included several of the would-be founders of Gush Emunim, were politically supported by the Land of Israel Movement (known in Hebrew as the Movement for Greater Israel). This movement was founded by disillusioned members of the Labour Party and included members of every political orientation committed to the idea of establishing 'the land of Israel as a unified national entity' in the territories 'now in the hands of the Jewish people', that is, Israel and the OT.[30]

Two days later, Eshkol received a settlement plan for Gush Etzion from the Settlement Department, which had worked on it in the knowledge that the area would be resettled.[31] Eshkol informed the government that he had approved the settlement in Gush Etzion, which would be established in accordance with Dayan's plan, that is, the same plan the government and the Ministerial Defence Committee had previously rejected. For the majority of the ministers this was the first time they had heard of this decision. Health Minister Barzilai (Mapam) complained that they (the ministers) only agreed to vote on the issue of agricultural work camps and Nahal outposts, but not on civilian settlements.[32]

Ministers, the majority of whom were purposely or voluntarily excluded from the territorial decision-making process, became upset with the conduct of the government. They complained that it was not a question of whether Gush Etzion was to be a civilian or military outpost, but whether the decision-making process had been taken out of the hands of the government. Ministers were frustrated at not being informed about settlement activities, and complained that the work done by the ad hoc committee was not sufficiently transparent. Eshkol explained that they did not need to know everything and that no formal decision had been made, even though it was apparent that some decisions had been already taken.[33] According to Allon, Eshkol agreed that the ad hoc committee, and later the Ministerial Settlement Committee (MSC), would establish settlements where they saw fit, as long as it was done within the parameters of the Allon Plan,[34] because 'the government [probably meaning most ministers] was of minor importance'.[35] Allon himself admitted that the government only acted as a rubber stamp, fulfilling its role by agreeing with the motions put before it.[36] This would suggest that the government's non-decision on settlements was in fact a political tactic used by Eshkol to have the matter dealt with in a more favourable setting.

The activities of the ad hoc committee represented a clear change in the dynamics of the government's decision-making process. Several prominent ministers, among them Eshkol, were able to participate in the decision-making process, while most were excluded. Thus the government was undermined by private enterprises (the Eliqa and Gush Etzion groups), individual ministerial activity (Allon and Dayan), the work of ad hoc committees (dominated by Eshkol, Allon, Dayan and Gvati) and the Settlement Department (operating with or without the consent of ministers). This created a situation in which – while the government did not have a strategic policy of its own – Allon and Dayan were implementing decisions according to their own interpretation and long-term plans. It did not help that Eshkol was unable to control the activities of his increasingly independent ministers.[37] Nonetheless, it is evident that Eshkol supported the efforts of Allon and Dayan. However, because of the unlikelihood of reaching a decision regarding the Allon Plan, or for that matter any long-term plan, within the confines of the national unity government, Eshkol approved the ad hoc committee's incremental approach. Eshkol, for reasons of political convenience, avoided putting forward clear long-term territorial policies. In other words, any attempt by Eshkol to force a clear decision on the matter of the OT would have been politically complicated and maybe even against his own interests. This last point needs to be emphasised. The lack of a strategic territorial policy suited Eshkol and his main coalition partners.

The 30 October decision

Following the breakdown of the 19 June consensus and the ensuing territorial policy vacuum, the government debate was no longer on whether to establish outposts, but rather on where and of what nature. This exposed the problematic nature of decision-making within the national unity government, with a vote on whether to allow civilian settlements to be established in the Golan Heights ending in a stalemate.[38] This was particularly apparent during the debate over Gush Etzion: ministers appeared confused and unsure as to whether Gush Etzion would be a Nahal settlement or a civilian one. The confusion arose over the fact that most settlers were former soldiers. Eshkol – side-stepping the issue – commented that 'even Nahal soldiers grow old'.[39] Eshkol himself expressed confusion over which settlements were Nahal, which should be Nahal and what should be the standard. In order to avoid further confusion over this matter, Galili suggested paraphrasing all settlement activity as of transitory nature (Nahal).[40]

This was not just an issue of semantics. In response to a *New York Times* article accusing Israel of establishing civilian settlements, the Foreign Ministry asked Israeli embassies to explain that these were transitory Nahal outposts, established in accordance with international law and Israel's security needs.[41] Israel's ambassador to the US, Avraham Herman, urged the government to suppress reports of this nature, as they were having a 'catastrophic' effect on Israel's position in the UN and vis-à-vis the US.[42] In its reply, the Foreign Ministry accepted Herman's stance and asked him to stress that the settlements were transitory and of military and not civilian nature.[43] The government contacted the US administration to clarify that all these settlements were being established according to security requirements and that Israel had not changed its flexible policy regarding the territories. In response, the US administration made clear its discontent with such activities, informing Israel that its illegal settling of occupied land harmed US foreign policies.[44] At the same time, the administration refrained from publicly admonishing Israel or applying pressure on it to stop, a fact that was acknowledged by Israel.[45] Arguably, by sending out mixed messages, the US administration complicated the ongoing debate within Israel regarding the long-term future of the territories. One could make the argument that had the American administration put its foot down, Israel would have trodden very carefully on this issue.

On 30 October the cabinet decided to review its 19 June decisions. Ministers had originally agreed to withdraw from the Sinai Peninsula and the Golan Heights to the international borders in return for peace treaties. The decision was rephrased, and now referred to Israel's willingness to negotiate with Syria and Egypt on the basis of 'secure and recognised borders', while the exact definition of 'secure and recognised borders' was left open. In essence, ministers decided to formally retract the 19 June decisions, though the new decision was not relayed to the Americans.[46] The 30 October decision should not be understood as the adoption of a new long-term territorial policy, but rather as a deliberate attempt to revise Israel's original commitments by making these vaguer and less binding. In essence, the government, in its 30 October decision, chose not to deal with the complex issue of the West Bank and left the decision over the long-term status of the Sinai Peninsula and the Golan Heights for future negotiations.

The evolution of Israel's territorial policy was directly related to the passivity of most ministers. While some ministers took an active role in reshaping the territorial policy (e.g. Eshkol, Galili, Allon and Dayan), others – despite being excluded from the decision-making process – simply supported their actions. One of the explanations for this behaviour was the selective information ministers were being fed. For instance, when referring to their plans, Allon and Dayan focused on the military's needs but, with most ministers not having any military experience, ministers relied on the IDF to explain and brief them on military and security matters. This created a situation in which ministers were dependent on an organisation that only exposed them to a particular view.[47] To complicate matters further, most army generals argued in favour of remaining and maintaining the status quo in the OT.

The army's top brass chose to express their views in a closed meeting with Eshkol and Dayan on 5 December. Chief-of-Staff Rabin broke down into three the choices that Israel had regarding the West Bank, that is, annexation, negotiations with Hussein and the creation of a Palestinian entity bound to Israel. Rabin dismissed the first two options while presenting the third as Israel's only valid choice.[48] As expected from the head of AMAN (the military intelligence unit), Major-General Yariv stressed the need for strategic planning, although he agreed with Rabin that Hussein was not a viable partner and that the Arab states were not ready to negotiate with Israel. He concluded that Israel did not need to find an immediate solution to the territories, as time was on its side.[49] Major-General Gavish asserted that what Israel gained during the war was exactly what it had wanted, that is, strategic depth, and was therefore happy with the status quo.[50] Former Chief-of-Staff Tzvi Tzur stated that Israel needed to find a way of remaining on the current lines while solving the demographic problem that arose as a result. He suggested (in line with Rabin) the creation of a Palestinian entity in the West Bank and the Gaza Strip.[51] This line of thought was supported by Major-General Haim Bar-Lev (who would later replace Rabin as chief-of-staff). Bar-Lev claimed that the status quo was not a bad solution for the time being: 'I am against a Palestinian state, but we must continue to control the West Bank militarily and remain on the Jordan River.'[52]

Hussein

Despite the reluctance of the army's top brass and most ministers to consider him as a reliable partner, talks with King Hussein continued in the midst of a new round of UN discussions on the Middle East. These talks took place in part because of the expressed support given to negotiations with Jordan by the American administration.[53] Israel – represented by Hertzog – held its second post-war meeting with Hussein in London on 19 November. Hertzog inquired whether Hussein would consider holding direct negotiations with Israel. In reply, Hussein explained that direct negotiations could only proceed if they were part of a wider Israeli-Arab settlement. Hussein wanted to know whether Israel would return the West Bank to him. Hertzog claimed to have come to listen rather than to talk. Hertzog proceeded to explain the different views held within the government and the fact that no firm decision had been taken regarding the West Bank. The king explained that he was willing to entertain 'harmonising' Israel's security require-ments with his own vision, while taking into account Israel's historical association with the West Bank.[54] Moreover, Hussein was willing to make an offer to Israel, which he claimed had Nasser's support. This offer included an end to all forms of hostility, recognition of Israel's existence, free passage through the Straits of Tiran and Suez, and a just solution to the refugee problem, coupled with the withdrawal of Israeli forces from all of the occupied territories.[55]

Hertzog, with Hussein's consent, summarised their meeting:

1. The king favours a package deal to end the conflict.
2. He understands Israel's demand for direct negotiations and a peace accord.

3. He understands Israel would not make any moves without direct negotiations and a peace accord.
4. He will work to persuade other Arab states to agree to direct negotiations.
5. He asks Israel to clarify its position with regard to the West Bank.
6. Hussein urges Israel 'not to recognise a Palestinian entity'.[56]

Several weeks later a secret paper outlining Israel's position regarding a separate settlement with Hussein was handed to Eshkol. The paper – written by Eshkol's close advisors, with input from Hertzog and Yariv (head of AMAN) – questioned Hussein's ability to hold separate talks with Israel. The paper proposed was based on the Allon Plan with a Jordanian orientation. It proposed that the areas not annexed by Israel be returned to Jordan on the condition that they remain demilitarised and Israel would be allowed to keep five permanent army bases. In addition, King Hussein would be recognised as the protector of the Islamic holy sites in Jerusalem and Israel would allow free transport of Jordanian goods to and from Israeli ports. Finally, Israel would support plans to resolve the refugee problem and cooperate with Jordan on joint development plans.[57]

The Israeli proposal, as outlined by the paper, consisted of the Allon Plan with the military elements of Dayan's plan, neither of which was agreed to (or voted on) by the government. The same proposal was discussed and analysed by the Foreign Ministry in its 13 July report, where it concluded there was no chance Hussein would accept it. Needless to say, the government never got to vote on or to discuss this proposal.

Resolution 242

The second meeting between Hertzog and Hussein was held in the midst of a new round of UN discussions on the situation in the Middle East. The new international drive to solve the Middle East problems was prompted, in part, by the resumption of hostilities between Israel and Egypt. On 21 October Egyptian forces sank the Israeli battleship *Eilat*, with Israel retaliating by bombing Egyptian oil refineries near the city of Suez.

During the new round of discussions in the UN, the US delegation proposed a draft resolution based on the Goldberg–Gromyko version, which did not sit well with the Israeli government. Eban complained to Goldberg that 'endorsing the withdrawal of Israeli forces from the territories occupied in recent hostilities would jeopardise the prospect of creating a new security system in the area'.[58] The Israeli government claimed that only a resolution that put the emphasis on direct talks without requiring it to withdraw until agreements were reached would suffice. However, Eshkol privately admitted this claim was disingenuous, as Israel had decided against returning to the pre-war borders on all fronts, 'I am afraid of the moment they [the Arab states] will say: with pleasure' (i.e. agree to direct negotiations).[59] Eshkol acknowledged that the US was trying to resolve the situation, but admitted his relief at Egypt's refusal to accept Goldberg's compromise.[60]

On 9 November the Security Council met to discuss the US draft. The Israeli delegation had reasons to fear this meeting, as a report by Israel's Foreign Ministry suggested the US managed to get the support of Jordan and Egypt for its draft.[61] In order to placate Israel, the Americans agreed not to introduce their draft without Israel's approval. Israel's refusal to accept the American draft resulted in the introduction of competing drafts, which contained less favourable terms for Israel.[62] To the US and Israel's relief, the Security Council did not seriously consider the other draft proposals and decided to vote on a British compromise draft instead. This draft resolution, tabled by the British, gained the support of the US, the USSR and the Arab states, with the exception of Syria and Algeria. This resolution was not accepted by Israel, and Eshkol tried to convince the Americans to vote against it.[63] Nevertheless, this draft resolution, which became known as Resolution 242, was adopted unanimously. The resolution, among other things, maintained 'the inadmissibility of acquiring territories by war' and called for 'the withdrawal of Israeli forces from territories occupied in the recent conflict'. The phrasing of the last part was particularly problematic. Egypt and Jordan interpreted it as meaning an Israeli withdrawal from *all* the territories. For Israel it meant an Israeli withdrawal from territories, though not all, the extent to which would be determined through negotiations. The resolution also called upon the Security Council to appoint a special representative to help promote efforts for peace. The Security Council appointed Gunnar Jarring – a veteran Swedish diplomat and former Swedish ambassador to the USSR – as its representative to the region.

The White House

The debates in the Security Council confirmed Israel's growing dependence on the US. Israel was in a problematic situation vis-à-vis the American administration since it could not openly pursue policies which contradicted the American position, as it was dependent on the US for diplomatic support. To compound the problem, Israel was under a French arms embargo,[64] while Egypt and Syria were being rearmed at an increasing pace by the USSR,[65] which forced Israel to seek American military support. Eshkol's visit to Washington at the beginning of

January 1968 – the first official visit by a serving prime minister – provided the opportunity to cement Israeli-American relations. Israeli politicians and generals were unsure as to which plans and ideas should be presented to the US administration and, in particular, whether Israel should inform the US of its retraction from its 19 June decisions. The problem was urgent due to Israel's immediate need for aeroplanes and military equipment – a fact which significantly reduced Israel's diplomatic manoeuvring ability.[66]

In Washington, Eshkol encountered two US approaches towards Israel. On the one hand, Secretary of State Rusk appeared unconvinced by Israel's military needs and was troubled by Israel's inflexible diplomatic stance. Rusk believed Israel should be willing to undertake trust-building measures in the region, and that US supply of military equipment should be conditional upon Israel's actions.[67] Rusk was supported by many in the administration who felt that Israel should agree to withdraw from all the territories – in principle – in exchange for military hardware.[68] Moreover, according to the Chairman of the Joint Chiefs of Staff, Israeli military needs were not as urgent; he predicted continued Israeli air superiority for the next 18 months.[69] On the other hand, Johnson accepted Israel's immediate need for military wares and promised Eshkol to do something about it. Furthermore, he assured Eshkol that he would not take any steps regarding the territories without discussing them with Israel first.[70] Nevertheless, Johnson stressed that the US would work with the Soviet Union to prevent a possible arms race and to promote peace in the region.[71]

At one point during these discussions Rusk and Johnson wanted to know to what extent Israel was willing to negotiate and how much it was willing to give up. Eshkol explained his dilemma. He had a 'wall-to-wall' coalition of the right and left, there were no Arab states with which to negotiate, and Israel was a small country surrounded by enemies. Therefore, Eshkol informed them, Israel had decided – until it had other viable options – 'not to decide'.[72]

Gunnar Jarring

In January 1968 Jarring requested that each state, with the exception of Syria, which refused to negotiate with Israel, publicly accept Resolution 242 and declare their willingness to implement it. While Jordan and Egypt made their stance known, Israel's response fell short of accepting the resolution. Israel stated it would comply but, despite pressure from the US, it would not publicly accept this resolution.[73] One of the main problems was that both Israel and Egypt interpreted the resolution differently. Egyptian officials informed Jarring that their precondition for implementing the resolution was that Israel withdraw from all the territories it occupied, while Israel demanded that peace negotiations proceed before any withdrawal, the exact reverse of Egypt's terms.[74] Furthermore, Jarring's insistence on the acceptance of Resolution 242 as a precondition created a problem for Israel which, in commenting on the document, needed to tread carefully. On the one hand, Israel needed to maintain the integrity of its national unity government while, on the other hand, it had to be seen as being sensitive to the demands made by the American administration.

While the government stated its desire to hold direct negotiations with Egypt in order to achieve peace, it concluded that this was not feasible.[75] According to Dayan 'what is being offered [by the international community] to us [Israel] is withdrawal from the territories without peace',[76] under these conditions, he surmised, peace between Israel and the Arab states was 'something that cannot be attained'.[77] In a joint meeting, the heads of the Foreign Ministry and AMAN's research department reached a similar conclusion.[78] Nasser, according to AMAN, was working diplomatically to bring about an Israeli withdrawal from the OT without having to make any diplomatic concessions towards Israel. Furthermore, it predicted that Nasser would initiate a limited war across the canal if he did not get his way diplomatically.[79]

Israel had several opportunities to negotiate with Nasser; these, however, were never fully explored.[80] The Eshkol government concluded that Nasser was not a reliable peace partner and opted to maintain the status quo, a situation that was possible because the government was under no pressure from the US,[81] even though there were calls within the US administration to put pressure on Israel.[82] In other words, the perceived lack of suitable peace partners provided Eshkol with a diplomatic and political 'fig leaf'. There was no reason for him to make controversial decisions and risk political instability. Additionally, the adoption of a non-committing approach facilitated one of Mapai's most important endeavours during this period, the unification of the Labour movement.

The Labour Party

One of the most important reasons behind Israel's lack of a strategic territorial policy was the formation of the Labour Party. On 21 January 1968, the political parties associated with the Labour movement, with the exception of Mapam, united under the banner of the Labour Party.

This was preceded by protracted negotiations between the three main constituents: Mapai, Rafi and Ahdut-Ha'avoda. The process of unifying the Labour movement started on 13 June 1967 when Rafi's Central Committee decided to adopt a resolution by Rafi's Secretary-General Shimon Peres, and called for re-unification talks with Mapai. These were held against the wishes of party leader Ben-Gurion, who, as a result of Dayan's popularity after the war, became marginalised.[83] Peres had earlier written to Mapai stating Rafi's intention to return 'without any pre-conditions'; this signalled the start of a new period in the history of the Labour movement.[84] During the following months, the unification talks and territorial debate dominated Israel's politics. The Mapai-led government needed to avoid controversial decisions in order to maintain consensus and promote unity. For Eshkol and many in Mapai the unification of the Labour movement was a long-held dream;[85] it presented an opportunity to 'welcome the unruly sons back to the bosom of the founding party'.[86] In addition, it resonated well among Mapai's young guard (*tze'irim*), and many of the local political branches, as they did not share the historical animosity towards Rafi.[87]

According to Mapam leader Ya'akov Hazan, the unification process represented an opportunity for Rafi to replace Eshkol with Dayan and to take over the Labour Party from within.[88] Dayan appeared to be the natural successor to Eshkol, as long as he remained the defence minister. The choice facing Rafi was clear; either wait for an opportunity to capture the leadership through elections in two years' time, or capture the leadership from within the unified party,[89] which made Dayan's position dependent on the success of the unification process: there was a growing fear among Rafi members that the Mapai elites would not allow them to remain in the government for long if they did not agree to the unification process.[90]

Rafi's calls for re-unification proved a divisive issue for Ahdut-Ha'avoda. On the one hand, they opposed the move, fearing an attempt by Rafi to gain control from within. On the other hand, the security-minded hawks in Ahdut-Ha'avoda (among them Tabenkin) thought it was an opportunity to nullify the dovish elements in Mapai, regarding Rafi as a natural ally on national security matters. Rafi's manifesto, as far as the territorial debate was concerned, was closer to Tabenkin's ideology than to Mapai's. Rafi's manifesto called for 'the new nature of Israel to be designed by a policy of building settlements and outposts'.

Ahdut-Ha'avoda considered the unification a political necessity that would help preserve and increase its political strength while keeping in check Rafi's and Dayan's influence.[91] Ahdut-Ha'avoda's main concern was of a merger between Rafi and Mapai which would effectively leave it out and eliminate the possibility of its young leaders, Allon and Galili, assuming power. In other words, the party felt it had no other choice but to agree. Ahdut-Ha'avoda called for the inclusion of Mapam – whom they viewed as a more suitable candidate for unification for political and ideological reasons – an idea supported by Mapai's elites. Mapam was seen as a socialist ally against the 'revisionist economic thought' of Rafi.[92] Mapam, while still part of the coalition, decided not to join the unification talks, preferring its political independence.

The unification process highlighted the demographic changes that were taking place in Israeli society and the transition from the 'founding generation' to the '1948 generation'.[93] Mapai's elites appeared old, weak and out of touch when compared to the young and charismatic technocrats and former IDF generals of Rafi and Ahdut-Ha'avoda. The old generation had immigrated to Israel during the second and third *aliyas*, had Yiddish accents, and had neither served in the IDF nor the pre-state paramilitary organisations. They were mostly in their late sixties and early seventies and had been politicians for most of their lives. The younger generation of leaders, mainly from Rafi and Ahdut-Ha'avoda, assumed that they – and not the older, more hesitant leadership – represented the views of the new generation.[94]

The unified party suffered from the lack of a well-defined national security agenda and a territorial policy, as Mapai's elites were unwilling to plunge the party into a renewed ideological debate. The party became increasingly unable to contain the diverse views within it without risking a split.[95] The perverse nature of the unification proved to be one of the main difficulties. The agreement reached dictated that representation within the party's institutions would be based on electoral strength (Mapai 57 per cent, Rafi and Ahdut-Ha'avoda 21 per cent each), with each faction choosing its own list of candidates, thus turning the new party into a 'façade behind which the three parties continued to compete and coexist … as factions'.[96] The characteristics of the inter-party factionalism allowed the smaller factions to have disproportional leverage on the decision-making process.[97]

In its first convention, the Labour Party failed to formulate a territorial policy due to intra-party divisions. A decision not to decide put forward by Mapai Secretary-General and former foreign minister Golda Meir was accepted:

If I were the prime minister, I would tell my friend [US President] Johnson two things: there is no one to talk to; in my country, among my people there are differences of opinion; as the prime minister I cannot and will not create internal strife for no good reason; so long as there is no one to talk to – there is nothing to talk about.[98]

Meir's proposal was accepted and the party decided to hold on to the territories until viable peace partners emerged and a long-lasting peace agreement was reached. In order to maintain unity, the party unanimously decided not to decide.[99]

3
'I don't know, I am looking for someone who does!'

The settlements

The lack of any meaningful American and international pressure, as well as the complexity of maintaining the national unity government and preserving the unity of the Labour Party, inhibited any meaningful debate on the long-term future of the Occupied Territories (OT). This policy-making vacuum provided Allon with an opportunity to influence Israel's territorial policy. The government, for a lack of alternative, and without scrutinising the activities of its ad hoc committees, was incrementally implementing parts of his plan, and new outposts and settlements were constantly being established.

This incremental approach of 'another settlement' started to resemble the pre-state Zionist policy of 'another dunam'.[1] This was the result of having to deal with the authorisation of individual settlements and outposts instead of focusing on the fundamental implications inherent in the settlement policy.[2] As a result, settlement activity became routine and, by the end of January 1968, there were 24 proposed settlements and outposts, and 12 either established or in the process.[3] Of the proposed settlements, two were in the Jordan valley;[4] one in the vicinity of Jericho (Ma'ale Adumim) that would 'strengthen Israel's grip on Jerusalem'; and a Nahal outpost in Sharm el-Sheikh, citing a ministerial recommendation to maintain a military presence in the area.[5] There were also seven outposts in the Golan Heights, even though Israeli citizens were still prohibited from entering the area without army authorisation.[6]

The need to use the façade of Nahal outposts for the creation of civilian settlements meant that the army was involved in areas with little or no military purpose.[7] According to the Allon Plan, settlements were established in areas Israel deemed essential for its security. The fact that early settlements were largely based on the Nahal concept helped emphasise their pseudo-military strategic purpose.[8] However, early settlement activities rarely related directly to Israel's security needs. This fact was corroborated by the commander of the Nahal, Colonel Moshe Netzer, who confidentially claimed that the settlement policy was not directly related to Israel's security needs,[9] with the exception of settlements along the Jordan valley.[10] Netzer went even further and stated that, in the period immediately after the war, there was no clear settlement policy.[11]

For Allon, the progress made in the establishment of settlements was not sufficient. Allon explained that the fact that the government had not decided over the future of the West Bank should not stop it from creating 'facts on the ground' which would promote Israel's vital national security needs. According to Allon, the matter of establishing these settlements should be left to the Ministerial Settlement Committee (MSC; Allon, Gvati, Dayan and Eshkol).[12] Within weeks of Allon's proposal, the Settlement Department submitted plans for the settlement of the Jordan valley, based on the establishment of up to 16 outposts with 1800 houses.[13] This was preceded by an Allon proposal to construct a road along the Jordan valley, which would serve the settlements; this road would be later named the Allon Road.[14]

Although the government was unofficially implementing parts of his plan, Allon was continuously expanding its scope. This was possible precisely because the parameters of the plan were never agreed upon and no official maps were ever distributed or approved. On 14 April, he proposed to transform all the Nahal outposts in the Golan Heights into civilian ones,[15] which eventually led to an explicit request to annex the Golan Heights.[16] Allon argued that there were already nine established outposts, as well as several more in different stages of development, and that the local Druze community had accepted Israel's presence (Allon had previously submitted a request to have Israeli law applied to them).[17] For Allon, Israel made a de facto decision to remain in the Golan Heights and all that was left was for the process to be formalised. However, the government decided against annexing the Golan. According to Eban, annexing the Golan would not only invite a UN counter-resolution and affect Israel's relations with the US, it would also antagonise Syria and the USSR.[18] However, despite agreeing not to annex the Golan Heights, the government was actively integrating it. This occurred despite the concerns raised by Theodor Meron, who called on the government to halt the social and economic integration of the Golan Heights.[19]

On 21 January 1968, Israel removed all economic and political restrictions regarding the Golan Heights, and this applied to the Druze population and Israeli citizens;[20] this action was taken without a decision over the future status of the Golan Heights.

One of the main problems was that the government was implementing parts of Allon's plan without deciding to formally approve it. In the KFDC, Mapam's leader Hazan admonished the government for failing to decide on the matter. He argued that the government could not intentionally decide not to decide, while it created facts on the ground. Israel, he added, should settle only in areas it intended to keep, and this required making a decision.[21] This point of view was shared by the Health Minister Barzilai, who stated that by not having a clear policy and by establishing settlements, Israel was de facto annexing parts of the territories and narrowing its diplomatic options.[22]

The Gaza Strip

While the government's position regarding the Golan Heights and the Sinai Peninsula had changed, it had remained steadfast in its decision to annex the Gaza Strip.[23] Nonetheless, Eshkol stated that annexing the Gaza Strip with 400,000 'Arabs' left a bad taste in his mouth.[24] In order to address the demographic implications of annexing the Gaza Strip with its population, the government decided to examine the idea of resettling its population, or at least a majority of them, elsewhere.[25]

The idea of annexing the Gaza Strip had broad political support, to the extent that it was even included in Mapam's peace plan.[26] Furthermore, the ministries and committees that advised the government reached similar conclusions. The Foreign Ministry argued that 'any solution regarding the Gaza Strip that may come requires the movement of a large or even major proportion of the refugee population elsewhere'.[27] The Committee of the Four recommended that talks with Jordan were contingent upon annexing the Gaza Strip and resettling its population in the West and East Bank.[28] A similar conclusion was reached by the Heads of Services Committee, which argued that it is Israel's intention and in its interest to move 'Arabs' from the Gaza Strip to the West Bank.[29] An appendix written by the Foreign Ministry, looking at economic implications of diplomatic decisions, pointed out that 'it is not reasonable to assume that it will be possible to empty it [the Gaza Strip] from refugees in a short time. This process will continue for several years.'[30]

Unexpectedly, the idea also received support from Theodor Meron. Asked to examine the subject of resettling Palestinian refugees by Eban,

Meron stated that, in accordance with international law, any resettling of the refugees had to be done with their consent and in a transparent manner. He made it clear that only the voluntary movement of refugees would be seen as legitimate, but that, even in that case, many would see it as an Israeli-directed action. Specifically discussing resettling them in Sinai and the West Bank, Meron claimed that this is more complicated because these areas are claimed by Egypt and Jordan respectively. His recommendations, therefore, were that Israel should encourage the Gaza refugees to settle in areas not under Israeli control, but that their movement should not appear to be a result of Israeli actions.[31]

However, despite enjoying broad consensus, the government was unable to implement its resettlement or transfer policy. It was unable to clarify how, in the age of decolonisation, it would transfer more than 100,000 people without drawing the international community's ire. In addition, the government was unable to find a suitable area to which it could transfer the population. Eshkol's frustration at the lack of progress was very evident. In a meeting to discuss the problem, Eshkol was asked how it would be accomplished, to which he answered 'I don't know, I am looking for someone who does!' In the same meeting he added that he was 'in favour that they all go, even if to the moon'.[32]

The government employed four broad mechanisms to facilitate the transfer of population out of the Gaza Strip: financial incentives, investment in education, employment opportunities and a tough security stance. A Special Task Force was formed, whose aim was to encourage Palestinians to emigrate by providing financial support. The military administration, with the support of various governmental departments, invested in technical schools and further education in the belief that educated and skilled Palestinians would have a better chance to emigrate.[33] The military administration also created infrastructure projects in the West Bank in order to entice the unemployed from the Gaza Strip to move to the West Bank.[34] In addition, the military encouraged emigration by using a harsher security measures than were employed in the West Bank.[35]

A year after the war, the number of people who had left the Strip was estimated at 50,000, with most being young men looking for jobs, and families with relatives in Jordan.[36] Arguably, most of those who left would have done so even without Israel's intervention. The government's failure to implement its policy was due to several factors. First, the question of where to transfer people to was never truly answered. A team assembled by Eshkol advocated the use of the West Bank and were supported by Weitz and several ministers.[37] But some ministers were against this, among them Allon, as it did not fit well with his plan. Attempts to solicit the help of the West Bank mayors to accept Gaza's refugees by promising to invest in local projects and industries failed, with these mayors flatly rejecting the idea.[38] Allon suggested El-Arish (northern Sinai) as an alternative;[39] however, the area was not well suited and it would have proven costly and impractical.[40] The Foreign Ministry also mentioned emigration of educated and skilled workers to immigration states such as Australia, Brazil, Argentina and Canada.[41] Second, the operation was undertaken half-heartedly and without real conviction.[42] The Special Task Force assembled numbered initially five, then ten members, and Eshkol was unwilling to make available the substantial sums of money requested by them. Eshkol sarcastically questioned whether an increase in funding would lead to greater success.[43]

Third, there was no detailed plan on how to implement this policy. Dayan remarked that if the government provided a detailed plan of how this could be done he would have supported it.[44] Fourth, Arab states and the local population were aware of Israel's desire to annex the Gaza Strip and transfer its population, and would not actively support such an effort.[45] Finally, the resumption of hostilities across the Jordan River led to the tightening of Jordanian border controls and subsequently to a reduction in the numbers of Palestinians immigrating to Jordan.

Israel's Gaza Strip policy was not practical. The government had made it clear it would not annex the territory without transferring a substantial part of its population. Its inability to implement this policy was evident from the start.[46] Israel's reluctance to annex a populated Gaza Strip and its inability to depopulate it left the area in a political limbo.[47] Israel did not have a viable policy and at no time did it seriously contemplate the long-term implications of holding the Gaza Strip, an area to which it referred before the war as 'a hornets nest'. In a sense, Israel's actions towards the Gaza Strip were a classic example of how 'muddling through' without a policy would have serious long-term implications.

Hebron

The conquest of the territories and the subsequent occupation revealed a 'growing dissonance' between the Labour Party's official position and the public's perception of the OT.[48] The public were by and large in favour of retaining most of the territories.[49] In addition, the conquest of the West Bank, and in particular East Jerusalem and Hebron, with their religious symbolism, rekindled several ideological debates regarding some of Zionism's main tenets: the state's boundaries, the nature of the

state, the relationship between Zionism and Judaism, the right to settle and the state's demographic composition – questions for which the
government had no clear answers. The government's lack of a strategic
policy left a vacuum in which interest groups with a strong ideological
agenda mostly based on religious Zionism could operate.[50]

Israel had hitherto established settlements (unofficially) according to
the Allon Plan. Allon's broad concept was based on what he perceived
to be Israel's national security needs. The first departure from this
occurred when a group of young religious students, led by Rabbi Moshe
Levinger, asked the military governor of Hebron for permission to hold
the Passover feast in the city. Hebron differed from other areas settled
by Israel in that it was not included in the Allon Plan and was of no
military or security importance. Furthermore, establishing a settlement
within the heavily populated Palestinian city stood in contrast to the
government's professed position of avoiding population centres.

The first to raise the issue of settling in Hebron was none other than
Ben-Gurion. During the war he told Rafi members that Jews must resettle East Jerusalem and Hebron.[51] In the following months, Hebron was
mentioned several times by ministers and Knesset members;[52] some
even petitioned Eshkol on behalf of the Hebron Yeshiva.[53] The Yeshiva
was originally situated in Hebron but was relocated to Jerusalem after
the 1929 massacre.[54] In March 1968, Allon proposed the creation of a
Jewish settlement in Hebron; in his proposal Allon listed several groups,
among them the Levinger one, which were willing and ready to settle
in the city.[55]

It is important to note that Levinger did not act alone as not only did
his actions receive public support, but he was also supported financially
and politically by the Land of Israel Movement.[56] Emboldened by the
success of the Gush Etzion initiative, members of the movement petitioned Eshkol for the resettlement of Hebron.[57] Levinger's group, which
included many of the would-be founders of Gush Emunim, was driven
not only by a belief that their actions would make a direct contribution to Israel's security, but also by a religious zeal. The conquest of
the West Bank was described by some religious scholars as the 'advent
of redemption', that is, the period before the coming of the messiah.[58]
The renewal of the Jewish presence in Hebron was seen by them as a
divine mission; the city was the second holiest after Jerusalem and held
the Tomb of the Patriarchs.[59] Also, they saw their actions as a way of
undoing the events of 1929.

On 12 April 1968, the Levinger group rented several rooms in a Hebron
hotel, allegedly for the sole purpose of conducting the Passover feast.

They had earlier received the army's permission to stay overnight; the permission was granted despite advertisements in the national press calling for the renewal of the Jewish settlement in the city.[60] Levinger claimed the army and the government were aware of his plans. Allon would later attest to have known of the move to resettle Hebron, and that he expressed willingness to help them on the condition that, if the government decided not to establish a settlement in Hebron, they would accept its decision.[61] The following morning, the settlers – true to their cause – refused to leave. Despite the settlers acting illegally and against the government's wishes, the government proved reluctant to order their forcible removal. In several rounds of discussions the ministers were unable to reach a decision regarding the settlers, with Gahal and the National Religious Party (NRP) ministers supporting the settlers. Additionally, and because of the unique place of Hebron in the Jewish psyche, most leading Labour ministers (but not Eban and Sapir, who opposed the resettlement of Hebron), appeared unable to make up their minds; this was particularly true of Eshkol and Dayan.[62] The settlers' refusal to leave the city did not dissuade Allon from showing his support, promising to help them find jobs in the area. This was followed by visits from Gahal and NRP ministers, and a resolution congratulating the endeavour by Hakibbutz Hameuhad. Eshkol claimed ministers were making a mockery of the government, being eager to show their support in spite of the government's position.[63]

Dayan suggested moving the settlers to an army base outside of Hebron until a decision was reached; the government approved. Levinger accepted the move, in the knowledge that the government's 'non-decision' was a de facto authorisation. The government's non-decision was taken despite a plea from Hebron's mayor, Ali al-Ja'bari, not to create a Jewish settlement in the city.[64] Several months later, the government decided to authorise the establishment of a Jewish neighbourhood in Hebron and another (Kiryat Arba) on the strategic hills overlooking the city of Hebron, on lands appropriated by the Israeli Defence Force (IDF) for 'army purposes'. This decision was taken despite concerns raised by a preparatory committee, which was tasked with finding suitable alternative solutions for the Hebron settlement. The committee raised concerns regarding the large number of private lands that would need to be appropriated in the case of Kiryat Arba and the logistical problems, such as the limited availability of suitable housing, associated with the establishment of a Jewish settlement in Hebron.[65] The establishment of the settlement would later be explained by the Israeli government as a response to the problematic nature of settling

Jews in Hebron.[66] The government initially planned for 900 residential units, but later included plans for a commercial and an industrial site.[67]

The case of Kiryat Arba exposed the fact that the government did not have a clear settlement policy, or a definitive settlement map, and did not always act in accordance with the Allon Plan; Kiryat Arba contradicted Allon's principal objective of avoiding the heavily populated areas. The lack of clear settlement policies enabled Allon to incorporate Kiryat Arba into his plan while claiming that it left all diplomatic options open and served Israel's security needs.[68] Kiryat Arba was an example of how a non-decision intended to postpone a controversial debate morphed into a decision that fundamentally changed the nature of Israel's relationship with the West Bank.

Meetings with Palestinians

In the aftermath of the Six Day War, the Israeli government decided not to decide on the long-term future of the West Bank. Nevertheless, the government made it clear that it was against any solution that would leave it in control of the heavily populated areas. Israel's options towards the West Bank were therefore narrowed down to either a Palestinian or a Jordanian-based approach.

The idea of using a Palestinian approach was first raised by AMAN (the military intelligence unit) and was subsequently adopted by Allon and Dayan. At the heart of this approach was the idea of establishing a demilitarised Palestinian entity (either independent or autonomous) in the West Bank (there were some suggestions of including the Gaza Strip), bound by security arrangements to Israel. Eshkol decided to pursue both the Palestinian and Jordanian approaches simultaneously; he nominated Moshe Sasson as his official representative and asked him to examine the possibility of establishing a Palestinian entity in the West Bank while, at the same time, he sent Ya'akov Hertzog and Eban to negotiate with King Hussein. Sasson, an orientalist by training, had earlier served as an Israeli diplomat in Turkey and was the head of the Middle East desk in the Israeli Foreign Ministry. Sasson was to conduct talks with Palestinian notables and liaise with a special steering committee, which included Eshkol, Dayan, Eban, Hertzog and Brigadier-General Shlomo Gazit (coordinator of the army's activities in the OT).[69]

According to Sasson, Israeli-Palestinian engagement proceeded in three stages. Initially, Israel's aim was to establish contact, and dialogue was limited to evaluating the relative strength of Palestinian elements, testing their willingness to support and promote an Arab-Israeli agreement. The second stage involved deepening and strengthening ties and contacts with Palestinians known to be associated with Jordan, in order to have an additional line of communications with King Hussein and 'other diplomatic elements beyond the ceasefire lines'. The third stage involved evaluating the potential for Israeli-Palestinian negotiations. According to Sasson, Israel did not see itself obliged to provide Palestinians with specific plans, but to explore and examine the relations between the sides.[70] Nonetheless, Eshkol authorised Sasson to suggest several different options, including an autonomous region and even a Functional Solution.[71] The offers Sasson could make, it was stipulated, would not include an independent Palestinian state, and there would be no discussion on East Jerusalem; the Gaza Strip; and the Palestinian refugees.[72]

In his first report in January 1968, Sasson informed the steering committee that the Palestinians were waiting to hear what Israel had to offer; Palestinian leaders told Sasson that Israel should set the tone for these talks and declare its intentions before they expressed their opinions. Sasson explained that some prominent Palestinian leaders were advocating direct negotiations with Israel. Nevertheless, they were suspicious of Israel's motives. In particular, many feared Israel was using the talks with them to apply indirect pressure on Jordan.[73]

According to Sasson, Palestinian leaders in the West Bank were deeply divided into independents, nationalists (PLO, the Palestine Liberation Organisation)[74] and pro-Jordanians. Despite the political division, Sasson claimed that there was a general willingness to pursue a separate deal with Israel.[75] However, he made it clear that Palestinians were adamant that any deal would have to include East Jerusalem, the Gaza Strip and a solution to the refugee problem,[76] issues Israel was unwilling to discuss. He also added that almost all Palestinians with whom he held talks demanded that Israel deliver its terms and commit to dealing with them. In the words of 'Aziz Shehadeh – a known supporter of an independent Palestinian state:

> Will you be willing to support us honestly to the end for a Palestinian solution? Will you guarantee us that you will not go behind our backs with Hussein? ... What is the point of acting and endangering ourselves if it transpires that you too do not want a Palestinian state?[77]

From July 1967 to February 1969, Sasson conducted over 120 meetings with Palestinian mayors, former Jordanian ministers, tribal sheikhs, and religious and political leaders of all persuasions, in the West Bank and the Gaza Strip. Most of the talks were exploratory in nature and were used to gauge Palestinian reactions to Israeli policies and international developments, while others were used as a back-channel to King Hussein.

Of the talks held between Israeli and Palestinian leaders, perhaps the most intriguing is one that never took place. At the end of March 1968, Nablus-based notable Waleed al-Shaka'a requested a formal meeting with Dayan. Dayan was seen by many Palestinians as the main Israeli authority concerning the West Bank. Al-Shaka'a wanted to present to Dayan and to the Israeli government ideas, which according to him, came from the PLO and Fatah.[78] According to Sasson, Dayan refused to meet with al-Shaka'a because the latter was a PLO supporter. This decision appeared unreasonable due to the fact the al-Shaka'a had previously met with Eshkol.[79] However, since that meeting it transpired that al-Shaka'a had travelled to Beirut and met with PLO and Fatah leaders.[80] Among those he met were PLO Chairman Yahya Hammouda,[81] and former chairman Ahmad Shuqairi.[82] According to al-Shaka'a, PLO leaders were interested in what Israel had to offer, and Hammouda had expressed his willingness in writing for contact with Israel 'dependent on certain conditions'.[83] The fact that PLO and diaspora leaders were willing to exchange ideas and hold talks with Israel was confirmed by other Palestinian leaders with whom Israel held talks,[84] as well as by Sasson himself. According to Sasson, representatives of several organisations – though in the documents available these are not specified – asked Israel to let them know what it was offering.[85] In other words, Palestinian leaders within the diaspora, and within the PLO, including PLO Chairman Hammouda, were willing to listen to what Israel had to offer. This would indicate that there was much more willingness, especially early on, among Palestinian factions in the West Bank and the diaspora, to consider negotiations with Israel.

In this respect, Dayan's response, as noted by Sasson, is indicative of Israel's attitude towards the PLO and Fatah during the period and afterwards:

He [Dayan] is unwilling to accept Waleed's [Shaka'a] request [for a meeting] ... He [Shaka'a] did not inform us on whose behalf he is talking and it is not clear whom he represents ... The men of Fatah are busy with terrorism. First they should stop their terrorism and say that they want a political solution ... we will not respond to their vague request to meet ... as long as they demand to negotiate while they hold a gun to our temple ... The way to deal with them is to kill them.[86]

It is important to note that the attitude among PLO members towards dealing with Israel changed dramatically towards the end of 1968, when Fatah, headed by Yasser Arafat, gained control over the Palestinian National Council and the PLO Executive Committee.[87, 88] At that stage, Israel was informed that Fatah and the PLO made their disapproval of talks with Israel known to the West Bank leaders; several of whom informed Sasson of the pressure applied on them to desist from their talks with Israel.[89] One can only speculate what would have happened had Israel provided Palestinians with an alternative to the armed struggle in late 1967 or early 1968.

Instead of meeting with al-Shaka'a, Dayan accepted a meeting with Nablus Mayor Hamdi Can'an and 'Aziz Shehadeh. This occurred despite the fact that the duo also represented elements of the Palestinian leadership in exile, including the PLO. Presumably, it would have been difficult for Dayan to refuse a meeting with a Palestinian mayor (Can'an). In the talks, Can'an and Shehadeh complained that Israel was not forthcoming with constructive proposals (Dayan informed them that he was not authorised to negotiate with them), though they professed a willingness among Palestinians to negotiate directly with Israel. Dayan was, however, willing to define the main guidelines that they would be expected to accept, before any meaningful negations could take place:

1. The solution would have to be agreeable to the American administration.
2. There could be no change to the status of Jerusalem (which would stay under Israeli control).
3. There could be no return to the pre-war situation.
4. The solution would be based on the signing of peace agreements.[90]

Can'an and Shehadeh were unhappy with Israel's position on Jerusalem and its unwillingness to discuss the future of the Gaza Strip. Nonetheless, Can'an and Shhada expressed their willingness to reach a separate deal with Israel, even if other Arab states would not. They demanded at least an agreement on joint sovereignty over Jerusalem (agreeing not to divide the city again) and that any border modifications should only be carried out on the basis of reciprocity.[91] Though they were both frustrated with Israel's position, they expressed a willingness to proceed with the talks.[92] This was in contrast to fellow Palestinian leaders, who were informed of the content of the talks and became exasperated by Israel's position.[93]

Dayan informed Eshkol that he thought these talks should continue at a higher level, sensing that there was a possible chance for success. Eshkol, however, was lukewarm towards the idea and decided not to pursue the matter. The solution Eshkol favoured was a Palestinian entity of limited sovereignty.

In May, Sasson informed the committee that most Palestinian notables had publicly expressed their loyalty to King Hussein. They had publicly denounced the idea of a Palestinian state and had described themselves as Jordanian nationals.[94] Sasson claimed that the change of heart came as a result of a Palestinian belief that Israel was about to conclude a deal with Jordan behind their backs, and had used the talks with them to put pressure on Hussein. Sasson expressed his belief that Israel should continue these talks, but only if the government was fully committed to the Palestinian approach.[95]

Limited administrative Palestinian self-rule

By June 1968, the Israeli government decided to change its approach and focus on the establishment of limited administrative regional self-rule. In other words, Israel would remain in control of the West Bank, while providing Palestinians with some measure of self-rule. The idea of establishing Palestinian self-rule was raised by Dayan and by several Palestinian leaders.[96] According to Sasson the *modus vivendi* required by Israel could only be achieved through limited Palestinian self-rule, 'on the condition that it is based on cooperation with and not on separation from Israel'. This *modus vivendi* included: the economic integration of the West Bank and Israel; Israeli overall control; and the exclusion of the Gaza Strip and East Jerusalem from any agreement.[97]

From May to August 1968 Israel discussed with Palestinian leaders the idea of a limited self-rule. Sasson claimed Palestinians looked favourably on the idea, though their view of self-rule was substantially different – it included extended autonomy and East Jerusalem and the Gaza Strip.[98] However, only the establishment of self-rule in the Hebron region, headed by the long-term mayor of the city 'Ali al-Ja'bari – who had been in his position since the 1940s – came close to fruition. In addition to al-Ja'bari, several West Bank mayors requested self-rule, though they all later retracted their requests.[99] In fact, the very limited nature of Israel's offer made it difficult for Palestinian leaders to accept it without appearing to be colluding with Israel.

Sasson presented four alternative options for pursuing Palestinian self-rule:

1. Appointing al-Ja'bari as the governor of the West Bank.
2. Granting self-rule to the regions of Bethlehem, Ramallah and Jericho, as these cities enjoyed a Christian majority and did not want to be governed by al-Ja'bari.
3. Granting self-rule to all of the West Bank regions, starting from Hebron and Bethlehem.
4. Granting self-rule only to Hebron and appointing al-Ja'bari governor of that region.[100]

After some deliberations it was decided to look into the idea of nominating al-Ja'bari as governor of the Hebron region only. The idea of appointing the mayor of Hebron as governor of the West Bank came from al-Ja'bari himself.[101] Al-Ja'bari estimated that several large Palestinian towns and municipalities would support his bid, in particular Hebron, Beit Jala and Jericho.[102] Eshkol hoped that this would act as a precursor for appointing additional regional governors, with Bethlehem earmarked as Israel's second candidate.[103] However, Israeli leaders were fully aware that prominent Palestinian leaders were antagonistic towards the self-rule plan.[104] Al-Ja'bari proceeded to put into writing a formal request to be appointed as governor of the Hebron region. In his letter he asked for the creation of an Arab civil administration with the same responsibilities as the Israeli military administration.[105] The day before the government convened to discuss his appointment, al-Ja'bari professed to have had a change of heart and was now demanding to be appointed governor of the West Bank or not to be appointed at all.[106] Israel refused his demand, thus bringing to an end the idea of regional governors. Nonetheless, Israel continued to hold talks with al-Ja'bari, but nothing more came of them.[107]

In retrospect, the apparent Israeli willingness to appoint al-Ja'bari is misleading. The authority Israel planned to grant al-Ja'bari was limited; he would have needed approval for virtually every move and would have been dependent on Israel for policing and budget.[108] This despite the fact that al-Ja'bari made it clear he did not wish to be a 'puppet'.[109] However, Israel's offer was of limited self-rule, while the overall authority was to remain in its hands. According to Eshkol:

from the outside [al-Ja'bari] will appear as the king of Baghdad ... but from the inside, talking between ourselves, he comes to us for every matter and we sort things with him.[110]

With the culmination of the al-Ja'bari affair, Israeli-Palestinian talks were relegated in favour of talks with Jordan. By August 1968, Sasson, in a report summarising the al-Ja'bari affair, appeared pessimistic about the possibility of achieving a solution based on the Palestinian approach.[111] Israeli-Palestinian talks would not resume in earnest until the early 1990s.

The failure of Israel's Palestinian approach was due to several factors. First, Israel perceived Palestinians as not having a united leadership and being represented by a myriad of groups and individuals with different aims and objectives. Eshkol in particular found Palestinian leaders to be divided among themselves, with some claiming Israel was not making sincere offers, while others urged Israel to talk to Hussein.[112] He nonetheless, supported the continuation of the talks, alongside the talks with Jordan, 'We need to hold the iron in two ovens, even if nothing comes out of either.'[113] Second, Israel's refusal to include the Gaza Strip and Jerusalem in the negotiations would have made it unlikely for any Palestinian leader or group to agree to a separate deal with Israel. Finally, the establishment of a Palestinian entity was not high on the agenda of any state, bar Israel; the idea lacked international support and was fiercely opposed by Jordan.

Jordan

After proposing to pursue both, the failure of the Palestinian approach convinced Eshkol that the Jordanian approach was more feasible. He explained to Allon that he preferred the Jordanian approach because it meant that the million or so Arabs would become the king's citizens and not Israel's, and this was more palatable to the US.[114]

Eshkol informed the Alignment Political Committee (the Ma'arach's Political Committee – MPC)[115] of his decision to concentrate on Jordan and agreed to bring the matter before the committee for a decision. He described how the Americans had asked him to negotiate more vigorously with Jarring and to start making 'concrete offers'.[116] As a result, he had decided to elevate the talks with Hussein to a higher level and to push for a final agreement, which he believed was possible.[117] Nevertheless, Eshkol called for a discussion on what should be offered and on the next course of action in case the talks failed. He did, however, remark that negotiations with Hussein were the only available option for Israel, as he did not see any possibility of advancing negotiations with Egypt as long as Nasser was in power,[118] a sentiment shared by the Foreign Ministry.[119]

Education Minister Aran asked cynically, 'How is tonight different from all other nights?' (referring to one of the questions asked during the Passover feast). Aran did not see why they needed further discussions if nothing meaningful ever came out of them. He challenged the committee to agree on something and to put it to a vote.[120] Eban proposed several points that would serve as Israel's starting position for negotiations; Aran was quick to point out that these points were basically a different version of the Allon Plan. Eban conceded that, but added that the plan had been slightly modified and it now included some input from Dayan.[121] Golda Meir admitted she had little faith in these negotiations altogether, since Israel would not agree to divide Jerusalem while Hussein would not agree to sign a treaty without it and, therefore, there was little chance for peace.[122] Meir added that the Allon Plan was not a suitable solution as it conceded too much, to which Police Minister Sasson replied, 'What are we conceding, 800,000 Arabs?'[123]

Finance Minister Sapir remarked that he did not normally deal with 'these issues' but he understood the need to make decisions, telling ministers that adding more Arabs to Israel was a recipe for a disaster and that Israel should negotiate with Hussein over the West Bank. Additionally, he claimed that Israel did not need military bases in, nor did it need economic integration with the West Bank; both remarks were intended for Dayan.[124] Concluding the meeting, Eshkol expressed his gratitude for the candid discussion and the meeting ended, as most meetings did, without any decisions being taken.[125]

In a follow-up ministerial meeting Eshkol agreed to send Eban to meet with Hussein, but confessed he was still unsure as to whether the Allon Plan should serve as the basis for these talks, claiming that the plan left Hussein with only two-thirds of the West Bank. Eshkol admitted that he had recently seen a map of the Allon Plan in the press and was shocked: because the Allon Plan was never approved, there was no official map. He questioned whether settlements in the Jordan valley provided any security in case of an attack and whether they were necessary at all. Allon replied that most of the land that would eventually be taken according to his plan would be desert and had no real value. In reply, Eshkol made it clear that, in that case, Israel could afford to make some alterations to the plan.[126]

The wrangling among ministers over what to offer Hussein continued for several months. On 20 September, Eshkol briefed the MPC on Eban's forthcoming meeting with Hussein and proposed to offer the Allon Plan.[127] Dayan was quick to speak out against this idea; he claimed that the plan did not represent Israel's territorial policy, it was never adopted by the government, and that Hussein had already rejected it. Dayan's remarks caught Eshkol off guard. Eshkol retorted that Dayan was being fickle: 'You [Dayan] said you were against the Allon Plan and in favour of your own, but that if the Allon Plan was accepted you would accept it too.'[128] Justice Minister Shapira remarked that Israel did not need to decide over the Allon Plan, but merely to use it as a basis for negotiations with Hussein.[129] Eshkol summarised the debate and informed the committee that Eban and Allon would meet with Hussein and offer him the Allon and/or Dayan's Plan.[130]

On 27 September, Allon and Eban met with King Hussein. Allon pulled out a map and presented his plan. Eban explained to Hussein that 'We have no interest in major frontier changes in the western part of the West Bank' and that the changes proposed in the Jordan valley were based solely on Israel's security needs.[131] Hussein rejected the plan categorically.[132] The most he would be willing to accept was some minor border modifications based on reciprocity. With regard to Jerusalem, Hussein offered to discuss a 'new status for the city which would guarantee free access and movement to all', as well as recognise Israel's rights to the Jewish holy places. Hussein refused to accept a plan that took no notice of Jordan's security needs and left the West Bank demilitarised apart from Israeli army bases and settlements.[133]

Several months later, in a briefing to the MPC, Eban said that, although the king found the Allon Plan 'insulting', he was still willing to continue discussions with Israel. Eban raised the possibility of finding a compromise with Hussein, suggesting the inclusion of the Gaza Strip in the deal. Hussein had earlier expressed an interest in accommodating Palestinian refugees only if he was given the Gaza Strip.[134] Eshkol, who had earlier been against any deal that would include Gaza, appeared content with Eban's suggestion. He remarked that if Allon could sell the Gaza Strip for the Jordan valley he would be 'blessed'.[135] According to Allon, Hussein favoured the idea of receiving the Gaza Strip, but not in exchange for parts of the West Bank.[136]

Although they did promote better relations, the talks with Hussein failed to produce any breakthroughs, though there was a sense that these talks could prove fruitful.[137] The negotiations failed because the sides were too far apart to allow for a compromise. Ministers found it hard to accept that Israel would have to compromise and they believed that the Allon Plan was a generous offer. Furthermore, Hussein was viewed with suspicion, not least by Hertzog, who is alleged to have used his influence to hamper the talks.[138]

One of the most remarkable aspects of Israel's negotiations with Jordan was that it had taken the government over a year before it was ready to make an offer to Hussein. This offer was based on the Allon Plan, but at no time was it considered as Israel's official policy, or even its final position on the matter. Arguably, Israel's actions were clouded by vague security considerations and misconceptions. In the end, the government and the Labour Party placed greater importance on preserving the status quo in the West Bank, and maintaining unity and political stability, than on finding a viable long-term solution to the West Bank.

Economic integration

In the period after the war, Israel's economy grew rapidly, resulting in severe labour shortages.[139] The annexation of East Jerusalem and the ending of restrictions on Palestinian movement meant there was nothing stopping Palestinians from finding employment in Israel. The wages were higher and the skills sought by Israeli employers (e.g. construction, agriculture, textile industry, etc.) were readily available in the West Bank. Attempts by the government, and in particular Sapir, to limit the numbers of Palestinian labourers in Israel, had little effect. Israeli firms, unable to attract labour, started to subcontract firms in the West Bank and the Gaza Strip.[140] As a result, the economy of the territories grew rapidly and unemployment decreased substantially in the first years under Israeli occupation. For Dayan this was a positive development, and he sought to further promote Palestinian economic and social well-being by deepening economic integration and encouraging investment. In cooperation with Trade Minister Sherf, he gave Israeli firms incentives to set up enterprises in the territories, which were rapidly becoming a second market for Israeli goods.[141] Dayan's actions were taken despite a clear warning, given to the government by a committee of economic experts, against lifting the restrictions on investment and the free movement of labour in order to protect Israel's economy. The committee stated that the economic justifications for such an act were secondary to the political implications of an economic integration.[142]

On 6 November, Dayan gave a speech in which he openly called for the economic integration of the territories. When asked to clarify his position, Dayan reiterated his call for economic integration and added that this was in accordance with the decisions taken by the relevant government committees.[143] His words sent shockwaves through the political system. The following day Eshkol sent a strongly worded memo to Dayan, demanding to know his intentions. Eshkol appeared baffled by Dayan's suggestion that the government was somehow advocating economic integration.[144] Following Dayan's speech, Sapir gave several interviews in which he spelled out that neither he nor the government agreed with Dayan's ideas, 'I don't believe in this policy; I don't want it. I am against the integration.'[145]

The idea of economic integration was central to Dayan's plan, with the government's lack of a clear policy playing into his hands. The government, despite being against the idea, was not playing an active part in defining its economic policies towards the territories.[146] The government had left the running of the territories to Dayan and chose not to deal with the economic problems of the territories, not least because Sapir was reluctant to get involved.[147] Arguably, the main tenets of Israel's de facto economic policy in the territories (Open Bridges, economic integration and limited internal autonomy) were a by-product of the 'inexorable economic forces on both sides'.[148] Israel's economic needs dictated to a large extent its involvement and the level of integration. But it was Dayan who used the economic inertia and internal political debate to promote and deepen the integration.[149] In fact, Dayan confirmed that, because of the economic reality, it was not possible to stop the process of integration other than by legislation.[150]

The economic policies towards the territories became a battleground between Sapir and Dayan. The government, encouraged by Sapir, decided to try to restrict the flow of labourers. Sapir's fears of producing a nation of manual workers were being realised, as economic needs dictated the opening of Palestinian vocational centres intended to address Israel's labour shortages; Israel was now creating a nation of metalworkers and carpenters.[151] In addition, Sapir decided, against the wishes of Dayan, to place restrictions on the flow of Palestinian goods into Israel in order to protect Israel's economy, and to restrict investment in the territories' infrastructure and public services. Nevertheless, Sapir's restrictions on labour and refusal to invest could not stop the economic tide. While ministers were bickering and disagreeing, Dayan, through the Defence Ministry, continued to promote the employment of Arab labour and increased Israeli investment in the territories.[152]

The fight over economic integration came to a head during the first week of December. The government convened to discuss the Functional Solution, with a rejection by ministers a foregone conclusion. Sapir argued that it would prove impossible in the long run to administer the territories without granting their populations full civic rights. Eban claimed that the plan would lead to annexation, something the government was against. Justice Minister Shapira said that if the government wanted to keep the West Bank, then Dayan's plan was a good idea, but the government did not want to keep the West Bank. He therefore confirmed that the only real option Israel had was the Allon Plan, for the simple reason that it left most of the West Bank either with Hussein or with the Palestinians.[153] The government decided to limit Israel's economic exposure to the territories and to restrict Israeli investments in the territories.[154] However, this had little effect due to the half-hearted nature of the government's actions – Dayan was still left governing OT – the booming Israeli economy and the need of Israeli employers for cheap labour, coupled with unemployment in the OT and the huge wage disparity between Israel and the OT.

4
The Best Man in the Government

Golda Meir

Towards the end of 1968 rumours of Eshkol's deteriorating health circulated in the Israeli media. As a consequence of his ill health, Eshkol was mostly absent from cabinet meetings and the government mostly operated on the basis of internal inertia; Labour Party leaders and ministers waited patiently for his death.[1] Behind the scenes an intense succession battle was brewing. What was at stake was not solely who would be the next party leader, and potentially prime minister, but also the position the party and the new government that would form would take regarding the Occupied Territories (OT). The two leading contenders were Allon and Dayan,[2] each of whom brought with him a particular perspective regarding the OT: the Allon Plan and the Functional Solution. The two candidates also represented the two junior factions in the Labour Party: Ahdut-Ha'avoda (Allon) and Rafi (Dayan). Therefore the succession battle had the potential to undermine the dominant position of Mapai – the largest faction – in the united party.

In an effort to avoid a succession battle, Finance Minister and acting Labour Party Chairman Sapir proposed nominating former Foreign Minister and Party Chairwoman Golda Meir. Meir was famously described as the best man in the government by David Ben-Gurion during her time as the foreign minister. Sapir could have promoted his own candidacy but was apparently not interested in the job; he thought the prime minister's job came with too much responsibility and pressure.[3] Sapir explained the decision to nominate Meir as an attempt to secure Mapai's dominant position within the Labour Party, until a more suitable candidate from Mapai could emerge; it was reported that Meir was sick and it was rumoured that she would not last the year, which made it easier for

Dayan and Allon to accept her nomination.[4] Moreover, it was known that Sapir held a historic animosity towards Dayan relating to Ben-Gurion's favouritism towards Dayan; Sapir also feared that an Allon nomination would precipitate a Dayan and Rafi split from the party.[5]

Meir's nomination was, surprisingly, supported by the Ahdut-Ha'avoda and Rafi factions, which were relieved that Dayan, in the case of the former, and Allon, in the case of the latter, were not nominated. Additionally, Meir's political views were broadly in line with both Rafi's and Ahdut-Ha'avoda's; the latter's leader, Tabenkin, viewed Meir as someone who would stand up to the moderates in the united party and commented that she would save Israel from the threat of giving back the territories.[6]

Meir's nomination was presumed to be temporary: it would turn out to be one of the most defining moments in Israeli history. Meir, a 72-year-old chain-smoking widow with health problems, dominated the political scene, and her stranglehold on the decision-making process ensured that no serious discussion on Israel's territorial policy took place. Meir was in no rush to find a comprehensive solution to the OT; despite her Jewish grandmotherly demeanour she 'repressed dissent and criticism as creating unnecessary conflict, and insisted decisions could be made later'.[7] Meir propagated the myth that time was on Israel's side and that the Arab states would eventually accept Israel's new concept of 'secure' borders; she also famously stated that there were no such people as the Palestinians, that they did not exist. Meir claimed that, in view of the Arab refusal to make peace, the ceasefire lines were Israel's best security guarantee. For Meir, the need to maintain the integrity of the national unity government and the Labour Party superseded the need for a strategic policy. Therefore, she publicly and formally advocated a policy of 'non-decision', arguing that any decision taken would risk alienating parts of the coalition and the Labour Party; on the flip side, Meir's deliberate stance enabled the various elements within the coalition and party to coexist.

The 'War of Attrition'

The defeat in the Six Day War was a defining moment for Egypt and for Nasser. The war, alongside a disastrous military intervention in Yemen, severely weakened Egypt's economy and military, which became even more dependent on the USSR for support. Nasser's aura of invincibility and his popularity inside Egypt and across the Arab world were diminished. In order to regain his lost territories and political clout, Nasser referred to the Six Day War as the *Naksa* (the setback), and started preparing for a new war. From the end of the Six Day War, the situation between Israel and Egypt along the ceasefire lines was very tense and there were sporadic clashes and exchanges of artillery fire. According to Israeli assessments, Nasser was using the UN-sponsored talks as a cover for gaining time and gearing up for war.[8]

On 8 March 1969, after several 'calm' months, Egyptian artillery bombarded Israeli forces along the Suez Canal. The Egyptian attack was part of a new four-stage campaign by Nasser to regain control over the Sinai Peninsula. Nasser planned for an initial period comprising massive artillery bombardment of Israel's positions, followed by limited cross-border raids by commando units. The third and fourth stages comprised canal crossings by multiple forces, culminating in a full-scale attack.[9] Egyptian war-planners believed Israel would face severe difficulties sustaining a long-term war of attrition; they therefore planned for a 'long battle to exhaust the enemy'.[10] The ensuing war – Israel's most protracted – became known as the 'War of Attrition'; it never progressed further than the first two stages and was characterised by artillery bombardments and limited cross-canal excursions.

Against the backdrop of increased volatility along the Suez Canal and the impasse reached in the diplomatic arena, Richard Nixon, who was perceived by many Israeli politicians to be more 'pro-Israel', took office in the White House. Nixon, together with his Secretary of State William Rogers and National Security Advisor Henry Kissinger, introduced a new era of American involvement in the region and relationship with Israel.[11] Assuming office, President Nixon was presented with a National Security Council (NSC) briefing paper outlining America's Middle East options. The NSC proposed pursuing a more active US policy in the region, including cooperating with the USSR. In terms of resolving the Arab-Israeli conflict the NSC presented Nixon with a new policy blueprint:

1. The administration's long-term objective is to reach a binding agreement – not necessarily a peace treaty.
2. Israel should withdraw to the international border with minor adjustments, while special arrangements should be made for the Gaza Strip.
3. Critical areas should be demilitarised.
4. Jerusalem should remain unified but, Jordan should be allowed to assume religious and municipal roles within it.
5. The parties 'must' participate in the negotiations at some point.

6. A final solution must be reached with Israel's consent and participation.
7. Any agreement must include a final and comprehensive solution to the refugee problem.[12]

Following the new blueprint, and in response to increased instability in the region as a result of the 'War of Attrition', Nixon and Rogers met with the leaders of the Arab world; they became convinced that the only way out of the diplomatic deadlock was to bring Nasser to the negotiating table. Although they were sympathetic towards Jordan, they concluded that Hussein would be unable to reach a separate peace agreement with Israel without Nasser's support; an assessment shared by many in Israel. The new American initiative was therefore based on the belief that there could be no solution to the conflict without Nasser's participation and the assistance of the USSR, and that a solution should resemble Israel's 19 June decisions. In a meeting several months later, Joseph Sisco (Assistant Secretary of State for Near-Eastern Affairs) informed Yitzhak Rabin (Israel's former chief-of-staff and newly appointed ambassador to the US) that the US was working towards a settlement based on Israel's 19 June decisions.[13] However, while Rogers accepted Israel's demands that the final borders should be in line with Israel's security requirements, he stated that the final agreement would not be based on the Allon Plan or on major modifications to the 1967 borders.[14] Nevertheless, neither Rogers nor the US administration spelt out how they envisioned the future borders, and they continued to do little to force Israel to define its territorial policy.

Newly appointed Prime Minister Meir clarified Israel's position with regard to the US initiative. Meir, who had a deep affinity with the US – she spent her teenage years in Milwaukee – expressed deep reservations about Nixon's decision to find a solution to the conflict through talks with the USSR.[15] She informed the Americans that she did not agree with their call for an Israeli withdrawal from the OT, allowing for some minor border modifications, and for special arrangements for East Jerusalem and the Gaza Strip. Furthermore, while reiterating the importance of its relationship with the US, Meir added that Israel would have no reservations in rejecting a US–USSR plan if it was not in line with its own policies.[16] Meir's position was backed by the government, which decided not to participate in the American initiative.[17]

The Oral Law

The period following the outbreak of the War of Attrition and leading to the general elections (in October 1969) saw an intense debate within the Labour Party on the future of Israel's territorial policy, though this issue was not an important pre-election issue among the electorate and there was scant public debate on the subject.[18] The government called for the continuation of the flexible and vague understanding reached by the Eshkol administration, based on direct negotiations on the basis of 'secure and recognised borders', while leaving the exact definition of those boundaries open for interpretation. This practice of leaving the main issues vague was not acceptable to all ministers. Several ministers, most notably Dayan and Allon, rejected this approach and called for the adoption of clear policies.

The debate over the territorial policy came to a climax in the run up to voting on the Labour Party's electoral platform. The debate among the main factions – Mapai, Rafi, Ahdut-Ha'avoda and Mapam[19] – made a mockery of the idea of a united party. As head of the Rafi faction, Dayan used his popularity,[20] and the threat of leaving the Labour Party and possibly joining the right-wing Gahal Party, to call for the adoption of clear territorial policies based on his Functional Solution.[21] Dayan's ideas, including economic integration and 'self-rule', alienated the more dovish members of Mapai – the dominant faction with over 50 per cent of the internal party vote – who preferred to maintain a flexible approach. Mapai members feared that his ideas would lead to a demographic problem, possibly annexation, and would prove to be an economic burden, and consequently rejected Dayan's plans.

Dayan, however, found a receptive audience among Ahdut-Ha'avoda members.[22] While Ahdut-Ha'avoda members were weary of Dayan's threats to leave the party, they also viewed him and Rafi as natural allies with 'hawkish' credentials.[23] Although the factions clashed on several issues, most notably over the role of Mapam in the Alignment and the nomination of Allon as deputy prime minister, they shared a common vision with regard to Israel's territorial and security policies which allowed them to collaborate. In fact, the factions chose to present a united front during the electoral platform negotiations. On the issue of the settlements, they presented a joint amendment which called for the expansion and strengthening of existing settlements in the Golan Heights, the West Bank, the Sinai Peninsula and the Jordan valley.[24] In contrast, Mapai called for a more vague initiative to create settlements in response to future needs.[25] Rafi and Ahdut-Ha'avoda were pushing for immediate action while Mapam and Mapai opted for vague definitions that would leave room for political manoeuvring. The collaboration between Rafi and Ahdut-Ha'avoda was more intricate and complex than merely a mutual desire to bring about changes to the party's electoral platform. On the one hand, the factions were rivals within the Labour Party, while, on the other, they were natural allies in opposing Mapam and Mapai's 'dovish' positions.

At the beginning of August 1969 the Labour Party convened to decide its electoral platform, while a political storm was brewing behind the scenes. The convention came after several months of negotiations on the platform by a special steering committee. Dayan, despite being a member of this committee, was unhappy with the phrasing of the electoral platform and chose the occasion to assert his will on the process.[26] In his diary, Allon provides a breakdown of the main points of disagreement between Dayan and Mapai (in particular with Sapir) leading to the convention. Sapir rejected Dayan's idea of economic integration and his proposals for encouraging Arab labour in Israel, Palestinian 'self-rule' and increased investment in the territories. These, he feared, would lead to the slow but gradual annexation of the territories.[27] In fact, Sapir's fears were not without merit: several weeks earlier the Ministerial Committee for the Held Territories (MCHT) decided to regulate the employment of Palestinians in Israel,[28] and the idea of establishing Israeli law in the territories was discussed by the Interior Ministry.[29]

Eban – speaking for the Mapai elite – was adamant that the party should not split over the territorial issue, arguing that the party was big enough to accommodate different points of view. In the negotiation period, Eban tried to persuade Dayan to use the more flexible term 'economic coordination' as opposed to 'economic integration', to describe Israel's economic relations with the territories.[30] Eban added that no firm decision had been taken on the future of the territories and that the current situation should be preserved until a suitable peace partner emerged; in other words, Eban preferred propagating the 'decision not to decide'.[31]

In response, Dayan argued that Israel needed to dictate the diplomatic proceedings, which would ensure that its preferred outcome would be achieved, refuting the premise that creating facts on the ground was detrimental to peace. For Dayan there were only two possible future scenarios for the West Bank – either as part of Jordan or as an Israeli-controlled area. According to Dayan, one could not divide Bethlehem from Jerusalem or Jerusalem from Ramallah, as those areas had historic and socio-economic ties; he compared this to the ties between Holon,

Tel Aviv and Ramat Gan.[32] According to Dayan, Israel needed to encourage investment and economic development in the territories, while allowing the population to retain their ties with the Arab world, in order to promote coexistence.[33]

Dayan rejected the 'decision not to decide' and demanded a decision on the territorial issue.[34] Dayan was not alone in demanding unequivocal decisions, in this respect he enjoyed the support of Ahdut-Ha'avoda; Allon claimed that 'the decision not to decide on Israel's future map was a mistake'.[35] Allon argued that the fact that the government had acted, 'conceptually', in an incremental way, along the lines of his plan, was insufficient. He called on the party to act in a clear manner and legislate on the matter.[36] Nevertheless, with regard to Israel's economic objectives, Ahdut-Ha'avoda was adamantly against Dayan's idea of economic integration.[37]

Dayan's popularity eclipsed that of any other Israeli politician and his threat to leave the party had an effect on the Mapai elites. A Rafi split appeared an imminent reality, as neither Mapai nor Dayan would back down. Yet the need to maintain unity and find a compromise was not lost on either side.[38] Dayan needed to remain defence minister to have a realistic chance of becoming the next prime minister, while Meir feared being outflanked by the 'doves' in Mapai.[39] Additionally, there was a genuine fear, within Mapai, that Rafi would collaborate with Gahal, in a move that would pose a direct threat to Mapai's hegemonic status: it would have transformed Israel's political structure from a dominant one-party to a genuine two-party system. In the end, the Mapai elites were afraid to 'call Dayan's bluff' and settled on a compromise.[40] Sapir was deeply unhappy about the capitulation to Dayan, having previously threatened to resign if Rafi's and Ahdut-Ha'avoda's amendments were accepted.[41] But, as always, Sapir accepted Meir's decision regardless of his own position on the matter. Sapir was rumoured to have had three prerogatives in life: 'not to fight with Golda, to serve the party and to serve the state, and that what was good for Golda, and the party was good for the state'.[42]

The agreed compromise, written by the Information Minister Yisrael Galili, who was Meir's confidant and close advisor, and Dayan, with some input by Meir,[43] became known as the Oral Law – a non-binding 'optional-unwritten understanding'.[44] This created a situation where the party had proposed two distinct policies: one policy it had formally agreed upon and another 'informal' policy which would accompany the party's electoral platform.[45] The main reasoning behind the Oral Law, other than to satisfy Dayan's demands, was to provide answers to several important questions that the government and the party had been avoiding for years: what was Israel's long-term vision, what were its strategic imperatives and what were its settlement policies?[46] The Oral Law was as follows:

> The government's decisions regarding the issue of secure borders include: Israel views the Jordan River as its eastern border, a secure border fit for the purpose of providing protection from possible invasions. The Golan Heights and the Gaza Strip will remain under Israeli control, while maritime movement through the Gulf of Eilat will remain free and secure by Israeli forces controlling the straits. The latter area will be an Israeli territory, allowing for continuity that would suit its security requirements.[47]

There was nothing in the Oral Law that contradicted the Allon Plan or, for that matter, previous government or party decisions.[48] With the exception of the demand for territorial continuity from Sharm el-Sheikh to Eilat, both the Oral Law and the Allon Plan share the same geographical parameters – a fact acknowledged by Allon.[49] Allon, however, stated that while the Oral Law became part of the party's electoral platform, in reality it was the Allon Plan that was implemented.[50] In order not to alienate Mapam, and under pressure from Mapai's elite, an additional statement was added to the Oral Law reiterating that if a suitable peace partner emerged, Israel would be willing to enter into negotiations without any preconditions.[51]

Labour Party Convention

On 11 September 1969, the Labour Party's Central Committee members, including Mapam's members as part of the Alignment, convened to vote on the party's electoral platform. According to the platform, Israel was ready to hold direct negotiations without preconditions, aimed at achieving peace agreements. These would be based on 'strategically secure borders' so as to ensure Israel's national interests and until such agreements were reached, the current status quo would be maintained.[52] The party preferred not to define Israel's political and economic relationship with the territories, and left the matter in the hands of the government.[53] Because of the Labour Party's political dominance in the Knesset, the decision not to define Israel's economic and political relationship with the OT effectively represented the government's territorial policy. Despite the party's disagreement with Dayan's de facto

implementation of the economic integration programme, it chose not
to challenge him and called for the retention of his Open Bridges policy
(against the wishes of Sapir) and for the raising of the population's living standards.[54]

For the first time, the party made clear its support for the settlement
programme. This, in effect, stood against the party's promise to engage
in negotiations without preconditions. The party's agreed position was
a step towards the acceptance of the Allon Plan and it reinforced the
idea that Israel must define its own borders and security arrangements
by creating facts on the ground. The agreed position read:

> security outposts and civilian settlements should be established
> with more urgency and vigour. Whenever debating over the issue of
> the settlements, be it urban or rural, the government will take into
> account the country's security needs and the current state of affairs.
> Special consideration will be given to the areas essential to Israel's
> national security.[55]

After reading the first chapters concerning settlements and security,
Reuven Barkatt (chairman of the committee responsible for drafting
the platform) informed party members that another additional chapter
'that is not part of the platform but is related to it' would also be put to a
vote. Barkatt explained that, due to 'the lack of time', he had no copies to
circulate and would therefore read it out loud.[56] The additional chapter
was the Oral Law. Dayan – angered by reports in the media about the
'dovish' attitudes among Mapai's elite – demanded the inclusion of the
Oral Law in the electoral platform. The move was in stark contrast to
the understanding reached that it would serve only as a non-binding
guideline. Dayan made it clear that the platform's vague phrasing was
unacceptable to him and threatened – yet again – to leave the party.[57]
Despite being against the move, Sapir agreed to put the matter to a
vote. The Oral Law was put to a vote even though most members were
previously unaware of its contents. Nevertheless, it was approved unanimously,[58] with the exception of Mapam members, who abstained. What
was supposed to be a secret guideline, became the cornerstone of the
party's position on the territories.

The inclusion of the Oral Law clearly signalled a change from the
previous position of the Labour Party; the 'decision not to decide' had
clearly been eroded. This can also be viewed as the party's first attempt
to define the political future of the OT. With regard to Israel's borders,
the vague phrasing of 'secure and recognised borders' had been replaced

by a clear indication of the territories Israel intended to hold, that is, the Golan Heights, the Gaza Strip, the Jordan valley and a strip of land stretching from Sharm el-Sheikh to Eilat. Nevertheless, the agreed position did not define the status of those territories. With regard to the population, the party de facto adopted Dayan's vision of economic integration and 'self-rule' and, as a result, ruled out returning the West Bank to Jordan. This is despite the fact that, with the exception of Rafi, the party was against a Functional Solution.

In short, the Labour Party, in order to maintain unity and appease Dayan, adopted several conflicting ideas. The party had effectively agreed on a policy that blended elements from the Allon Plan and the Functional Solution. Nonetheless, Meir claimed that, despite the adoption of the Oral Law, Israel was still committed to negotiations without preconditions, adding that the government was doing all it could to promote peace.[59] However, by seemingly adopting multiple positions, and preferring unity over clear policies, the party leadership created a situation where no meaningful decision could take place.[60] In other words, while there was a clear shift to the right on the territorial issue, the Labour Party (and, by default, the government) adopted an incoherent policy that blended several conflicting plans, while leaving the long-term future of the OT unresolved.

The adoption of the Oral Law helped to defuse an ideological struggle, but at the same time it also alienated elements within the Labour Party and the Alignment, most notably Mapam, whose members chose to abstain from the vote on the Oral Law. Mapam enjoyed a unique situation in the Alignment in that its members were not bound by the Labour Party's decisions as the members of other factions were.[61] Moreover, the Mapam secretariat expressed concern with the party's settlement chapter and emphasised its support for negotiations without preconditions.[62]

Despite the ongoing 'War of Attrition', and the intense political wrangling within the Labour Party, the period leading up to the elections was devoid of any substantial debate among the political parties.[63] Gahal leader Begin concentrated on brandishing his newly acquired statesman credentials – as a minister-without-portfolio in the national unity government – by publicly supporting the government, and by not challenging Meir and Dayan's leadership. Begin supported the government against what he referred to as the 'dovish' elements within the Labour Party.[64] These, according to Begin, would rather withdraw from the territories than achieve secure borders and therefore could not be trusted with Israel's security.[65] The results of the elections were never in doubt, with the only question being whether the Labour Party would manage to win an outright majority; in the end, the party lost seven seats (it went down from 63 to 56 out of 120 Knesset seats), but kept its position as Israel's dominant party. There were no major changes to the political scene and it was clear that Meir favoured the continuation of the national unity coalition – including Gahal. However, even after offering Gahal four ministerial positions, Begin – citing differences over employment rights – refused to join the coalition. Begin's refusal, however, was about to change with the unveiling of the new American peace initiative.

The Rogers Plan

On 25 September, Meir met with Nixon in Washington to request a stop to the ongoing US–USSR talks.[66] Meir was particularly concerned about the solutions proposed by Rogers. The Israeli government believed that Rogers was proposing an Israeli withdrawal from all the territories. However, Meir was unsuccessful as Nixon refused to stop the talks and was reluctant to distance himself from Rogers' ideas. The only concession Meir elicited was a tacit US acknowledgement of Israel's right to develop nuclear weapons – in itself a major diplomatic achievement.[67] In addition, Meir's request for additional military hardware was met with a US counter-proposal to exchange 'hardware for software', that is, tying the supply of military hardware to territorial concessions.[68] The assurances the Johnson administration had previously provided regarding the supply of military hardware were increasingly dangled as carrots in front of the Israeli government.

On 9 December 1969, Rogers unveiled a new Middle East initiative – referred to as the Rogers Plan. Rogers announced that the US had decided to 'play a direct role' in promoting a solution based on Resolution 242 and the Jarring Mission. The solution was based on the understandings that had been reached with the USSR, and referred specifically to Israel's negotiations with Jordan and Egypt.[69] Rogers called for an Israeli withdrawal from the Sinai Peninsula and the West Bank, with only minor border modifications. However, Rogers made it clear that special provisions would have to be made with regard to Sharm el-Sheikh and the Gaza Strip.[70]

The Rogers Plan had an immediate impact on Israeli politics. Within hours of its introduction, Begin devised a ploy for settling his main disagreements with the Labour Party and joined the coalition. For Gahal, the perceived threat, inherent in the plan, was enough to galvanise the party into action; it made no secret that it decided to join the coalition to work against any withdrawal from the territories.[71] The coalition's immediate response to Rogers was to dispatch Eban to Washington to express Israel's disappointment.[72] Eban demanded to know whether the plan represented US official policy, but did not receive a clear answer. While Eban was awaiting an answer, Rogers circulated a document in the UN (known as the Yost Document), which was a new plan for settling the Israeli-Jordanian conflict.[73] The move was a clear departure by the US from consulting with Israel before launching new initiatives.[74]

The Yost Document (named after Charles Yost, the US ambassador to the UN) called for an Israeli withdrawal from the Gaza Strip and the West Bank to the international border, with minor modifications. Furthermore, the West Bank would be demilitarised and the final status of the Gaza Strip would be negotiated between Israel, Jordan and Egypt. The final status of East Jerusalem was left to be determined by the parties at a later stage; the American idea was not to divide the city but allow for some form of Jordanian religious and municipal jurisdiction.[75]

The Yost Document alarmed many in Israel. For the first time the US administration raised the prospects of Israeli concessions in East Jerusalem and the West Bank. Despite the professed shock, and unbeknown to the US administration, Israel had previously examined possible solutions concerning East Jerusalem, through a special committee headed by Mordechai Gazit (Director-General of the Foreign Ministry). The special committee made several recommendations, among them a joint Arab-Israeli municipal administration in Jerusalem.[76] The fact that the government was willing to examine different scenarios concerning Jerusalem does not indicate whether any of those would have been approved. It does demonstrate, however, that, despite publicly refusing to compromise on the matter, Israel actually examined different possibilities at a sub-ministerial level.

On 22 December, the Israeli government officially rejected both the Rogers Plan and the Yost Document; the plan was also rejected by Egypt. The government explained that it 'would not be sacrificed by any power-policy and will reject any attempt to impose a forced solution on it'.[77] The government was astonished by the perceived pro-Arab stance taken by the US; the plan was seen as an attempt to appease the Arabs at Israel's expense.[78] Meir described the plans as a 'disaster for Israel' and the possible adoption of them by the US as 'an act of betrayal'; she claimed Israel was fortunate that Egypt had rejected the Rogers Plan.[79]

In order to understand Israel's position, it is important to bear in mind the balance of power within the government. Meir used her political capital to avoid and deter any meaningful decisions regarding the territories. On most territorial issues, Meir sided with the hawks, that is, Dayan, Galili and Begin.[80] Ministers not toeing the official line, were labelled internally as 'defeatists' or 'weak doves' and were excluded from the territorial decision-making process.[81] Under the pretext of Nasser's actions and statements, the government gradually abandoned the notion of the territories as bargaining chips, in favour of viewing them as strategically important. Additionally, the Meir government would have been placed in a precarious position of having to choose between appeasing the Americans and maintaining political stability, had Egypt accepted the Rogers Plan. In this respect, the rejection of the plan by Egypt, and the lack of US pressure, convinced Meir, who saw no point in risking the unity of the government and the Labour Party, that Israel did not have viable negotiation partners. According to Israeli assessments, Jordan would not be able to sign an agreement without Nasser, and he would not approve any plan unless it included a full return to the pre-war borders.[82]

Rabin, in a meeting with Sisco and Rogers, accused the US of changing its stance.[83] In response, Sisco claimed that the US had not changed its stance and that in fact it was Israel that had changed its stance 'since November 1967'. Arguably, Sisco was referring to Israel's decision from 30 October 1967, which was never officially conveyed to the US. Even so, Sisco added that the US shared Israel's assessment that the Arab states were 'not interested in peace', but implored Israel not to obstruct the international diplomatic efforts, as this would strain American relations with the Soviet Union and the moderate Arab states.[84]

In the end, the Rogers Plan was rejected by both Israel and Egypt. Egypt's insistence on a comprehensive solution, coupled with the reluctance of the USSR to put pressure on Nasser, doomed the plan. The inability, or unwillingness, of the Soviets to force the Egyptians to make 'specific obligations to peace' meant that the US was not willing to force Israel to make territorial concessions.[85] Nasser's stance allowed Israel to claim that there was no one to negotiate with and push forward the creation of settlements in the Gaza Strip, the Rafah plains and Sharm el-Sheikh.

There are many reasons why the Rogers Plan was rejected by Israel, among them the ongoing 'War of Attrition' and the rejection of the plan by Nasser. Probably the two most important reasons were the lack of US pressure, and the desire to maintain coalition and party unity. The

American administration was speaking in two voices and sending out mixed messages, which contributed directly to Israel's reluctant stance. On the one hand, Rogers asserted that the US was ready to use financial aid and the supply of military hardware as leverage if necessary.[86] On the other hand, Nixon and Kissinger (National Security Advisor) agreed to accommodate some of Israel's military and financial requests, in spite of Rogers' threats.[87] It is, therefore, not a surprise that Israel did not agree with the Rogers Plan, as it knew the administration was not fully behind it. The lack of either an imposed American solution or direct US pressure allowed Israel to avoid controversial decisions and continue its non-policy regarding the OT.

Perhaps even more important was Meir's unwillingness to risk the unity of the coalition and the Labour Party. It is clear that any decision by the government regarding the West Bank, including the formal adoption of the Allon Plan, would have brought down the government, and possibly also split the Labour Party. It was, therefore, important for Meir to avoid any decision regarding the future of the West Bank. Arguably, the Eshkol government would have accepted the Rogers Plan and the Yost Document, as they both provided Israel with more than it initially bargained for.

The Rogers B

At the basis of the Meir government's territorial position was a perverse dichotomy. On the one hand, the government refused to put forward any strategic policies regarding the OT, while claiming to leave all diplomatic options open. On the other hand, it was creating facts on the ground that corresponded to the Allon Plan and the Functional Solution, while also building settlements that matched neither of these plans. The government publicly justified its position by linking it to Nasser's bellicose rhetoric and the continuing hostilities. However, the government's inability to bring an end to the war with Egypt raised questions regarding its approach and tested the patience of the electorate. The general sense of frustration was deepened by the resumption of low-scale clashes with Syria in the Golan Heights and the increasing number of attacks perpetrated against Israeli targets around the world by Palestinian groups.[88]

In order to end the war, Israel decided on deep-penetration bombing raids against Egypt's main military bases. While the initial raids proved highly successful, they failed to achieve the desired effect. Instead of backing down, Nasser requested additional Soviet military aid.[89]

The ensuing military aid was without precedent in Soviet history. Not only were massive amounts of military hardware shipped to Egypt, but Soviet advisors, military instructors and even pilots were also provided. By April 1970, Israeli pilots were reporting Egyptian aircraft flown by Russian pilots, as well as being attacked by Russian-operated surface-to-air missile batteries.[90]

On 19 June 1970, in order to defuse the situation, the US publicly called on Israel and Egypt to accept a short-term ceasefire. This was followed by the unveiling of a new US initiative, a scaled-down version of the Rogers Plan, referred to as Rogers B. The initiative called upon the parties (Jordan, Egypt and Israel) to publicly restate their acceptance of Resolution 242 and their willingness to work towards its implementation. Furthermore, it invited the parties to resume negotiations under UN auspices, based on an Israeli withdrawal from territories occupied in the 1967 war, and recognition by all parties of each other's sovereignty, territorial integrity and political independence.[91] In addition, Israel was informed by the US that future supplies of military hardware were conditional on its decision.[92]

The Israeli government immediately rejected Rogers B, but Rabin – who objected to the 'tone of the message' – on his own initiative decided not to relay the government's response to Nixon. Instead, Rabin advised the government to wait and see how Egypt would respond, before issuing further statements.[93] In order to alleviate Israel's concerns, Nixon assured Israel that any withdrawal would only be to 'secure borders', which was the first time the Americans had used the Israeli term. Moreover, Kissinger stated publicly that it was necessary to maintain Israel's military superiority in face of the growing Soviet intervention. The US also decided to speed up the delivery of military hardware and reassured Israel that the final boundaries would not be imposed on it, but would be left for the parties to negotiate.[94]

On 22 July, and after pressure from the Soviet Union, Egypt announced its unconditional acceptance of Rogers B; Jordan followed suit. The Arab response put the onus on Israel.[95] In order to persuade Israel to make the right decision, and in response to Israeli inquiries,[96] Nixon sent an additional letter to Meir promising that the final borders would have to be acceptable to Israel and that Israel would not be forced to withdraw from the OT before acceptable peace agreements were signed. In addition, Nixon assured Meir that the US would not press Israel to accept a solution to the Palestinian refugee problem that would change the demographic nature of the Jewish state.[97]

Nixon's letter was a turning point; it altered the mood within the government and brought about a week of intense wrangling among the coalition members.[98] On 25 July, Meir convened the ministers closest to her to decide whether to accept Rogers B (and the dissolution of the national unity government) or reject the initiative with the knowledge it would adversely affect Israel–US relations. All ministers – with the exception of Dayan, who did not express an opinion – agreed to accept Rogers B.[99] The decision to accept Rogers B proved to be the final act of the national unity government, as Gahal members withdrew from the coalition. Meir tried to convince Begin to stay, arguing that accepting Rogers B did not mean the acceptance of the territorial demands made in the Rogers Plan, but he refused to reconsider.[100]

On 31 July, Israel informed the US that it accepted Rogers B, based on the assurances given to it by Nixon.[101] When asked, in a meeting with Rabin, whether the US was willing to forgo the Rogers Plan, in return for an Israeli acceptance of Rogers B, Sisco responded that the US could not promise that.[102] In its reply to the US, the government confirmed that it was ready to enter negotiations based on Resolution 242 under UN auspices without preconditions, in order to reach an 'agreed and binding contractual peace agreement between the parties'. It added that Israel's forces would withdraw from the territories held only after secure, recognised and agreed borders were defined by peace treaties.[103] The following week, Meir stated that the acceptance of Rogers B did not indicate a change in the government's territorial policies which, according to her, had been the same since 1967.

The acceptance of Rogers B demonstrated the American administration's influence on Israel. In the first instance of sustained and direct pressure from the Americans, who threatened to withdraw financial and military support, Israel fell into line with the US. Israel's decision to accept Rogers B was in fact a testament to its commitment to Resolution 242 and to withdrawing from most of the territories, in exchange for peace and American security and financial assurances. Israel refused to be bullied into making concessions regarding the territories, but it is clear that, once Egypt and Jordan accepted the US proposals, Israel was left with no room for diplomatic manoeuvring. Arguably, had Egypt accepted Rogers A, Israel would have been put in a tight spot.

In short, the government engaged in a diplomatic process which was based on Resolution 242 and the concept of land for peace. However, at no time during this process did the government put forward clear territorial demands or policies. The Israeli insistence on direct negotiations without any preconditions, on the basis of secure and recognised borders, was clearly aimed at domestic audiences, with the hope that it would contribute to political stability. The government had already stipulated that it would not withdraw from territories it deemed essential for its national security, but it nevertheless refused to decide on their status.

5
Golda's Kitchenette

Israel's secret peace plan

Israel's acceptance of Rogers B signalled a change in the government's stance regarding the Occupied Territories (OT). Begin interpreted this decision as a de facto willingness to withdraw from most of the territories;[1] as if to affirm Begin's assessment, Meir and Allon had prepared a secret peace plan along those lines. The plan, which could be seen as Meir's first attempt at formulating a strategic territorial policy, defined the territories according to their perceived strategic importance, in accordance with the Oral Law and the Allon Plan. The plan – highlighting Israel's diplomatic and territorial 'red lines'[2] – was to be presented to Nixon during Meir's visit to Washington in September 1970. The cabinet was not privy to the plan details as Meir decided not to confer with most ministers.[3] Arguably, Meir based her decision to keep the plan secret on the assumption that she would have little difficulty convincing the government to accept it, if it was approved by the US. In the introduction to the plan, Allon wrote that it would be an accomplishment if the US were to accept the plan, although he doubted that that would happen. According to the plan:

1. Israel would withdraw from the majority of the West Bank according to the Allon Plan.
2. United Jerusalem would remain under Israeli control.
3. Israel would withdraw from the Gaza Strip: it would become a demilitarised area, to be used as a free-port by an Arab state (presumably this referred to Jordan).
4. Israel would retain the Rafah plains and a strip of land stretching from Sharm el-Sheikh to Eilat.

5. The rest of the Sinai Peninsula would be returned to Egypt on the condition that it would remain demilitarised.
6. Israel would withdraw from up to a third of the Golan Heights in exchange for a peace agreement. The rest of the Golan Heights would be retained by Israel in order to protect its water sources and the Upper Galilee area.[4]

The inclusion of the Golan Heights in the plan can be understood as an attempt to pre-empt a possible Syrian acceptance of Resolution 242. It might also be connected to Israeli intelligence reports that indicated a US willingness to discuss the future of the Golan Heights conditional on Syria changing its diplomatic stance.[5] According to Allon, the proposed withdrawal would not include the strategically important areas in the Golan Heights and would not, therefore, endanger Israel's long-term security.[6] Additionally, the areas from which Israel was proposing to withdraw did not contain any settlements.

The plan, however, was neither brought to the attention of the American administration nor was it presented to Nixon. Because of the outbreak of clashes between the Jordanian army and Palestinian groups, discussions on the resumption of negotiations between Israel and its neighbours were postponed.[7] Nevertheless, the fact that Meir prepared the plan attests to the importance Israeli leaders put on gaining American acceptance of their policies and the fear they had of an American-imposed solution.

Black September

In the aftermath of the Six Day War, and in particular from mid-1968, the Palestine Liberation Organisation (PLO) came to dominate Palestinian politics and refugee camps in Jordan; in the process, it slowly eroded the authority of the Jordanian state and its king.[8] From their bases in the refugee camps, member groups of the PLO, such as Fatah and the Popular Front for the Liberation of Palestine (PFLP) orchestrated cross-border incursions into Israel and a world-wide campaign of plane hijacking to highlight their cause. On 16 September 1970, as a result of a failed attempt to assassinate him, as well as a humiliating episode of multiple plane hijackings by the PFLP, which directly challenged his authority,[9] King Hussein decided to confront the Palestinian armed groups in Jordan (an event later referred to as 'Black September'). Hussein's decision was welcomed by Israel, which viewed the king's unwillingness to confront the PLO as a weakness and the activity of the

Palestinian groups in Jordan as a security concern. Incidentally, in the months leading up to September, Hussein reached an agreement with Israel that, in the event that he decided to act against the Palestinian armed groups, Israel would not take advantage of the situation.[10] In the ensuing episode, the Palestinian groups were no match for Hussein's professional army.

In an attempt to assist the Palestinian groups, Syrian forces crossed into Jordan; an action that put the whole region on alert. Acting Israeli Prime Minister Allon (Meir was in Washington at the time) informed Hussein that Israel would come to his aid.[11] In consultation with the US, Israel redeployed its forces on the Syrian front, sending a clear message that it was willing to intervene. Arguably, Israel's show of support thwarted the Syrian attack and paved the road for Hussein's victory.

After the event, Hussein and Allon met in what was described as a meeting between friends; Hussein thanked Allon for Israel's support.[12] Allon chose the opportunity to present Hussein with the idea of establishing a Jordanian civil administration, or a Palestinian civil administration linked to Jordan,[13] in parts of the West Bank as an interim agreement, based on the Allon Plan. This would include an Israeli withdrawal from the Gaza Strip in order for the area to be used as a deep-water port by Jordan. It is unclear whether the status of Jerusalem was discussed, although Israel had previously agreed to limited religious and municipal roles for Jordan in the city.[14] Hussein, reportedly, reacted positively to Allon's idea and wanted to 'hear more about it', but was willing to consider the idea only as an interim agreement.[15] Possibly, Hussein was unwilling to commit because it was Allon's private idea and had not yet been approved by the Israeli government.[16]

On his return to Israel, Allon raised the idea with Meir, who convened the kitchenette;[17] according to Allon those present included Meir, Dayan, Galili, Justice Minister Ya'akov-Shimshon Shapira and Police Minister Hillel.[18] Despite Hussein's positive reaction to the plan, the ministers unanimously rejected it – a move considered by Allon to be a mistake. According to Allon, 'everyone was against the idea'; the only reasonable objection came from Dayan, who confessed that he did not 'believe in it'.[19] In a somewhat ironic and remarkable turn of events, after the Yom Kippur War, Meir and Dayan offered Hussein the exact same plan.[20]

For the first time ministers were presented with an opportunity to vote on the Allon Plan, albeit as an interim agreement. The cabinet had previously voted for the creation of settlements and security arrangements based on the plan, despite never officially endorsing it. With the departure of Gahal from the government, one would have expected ministers to vote in favour of Allon's idea; instead, they rejected it. Arguably, Meir feared that the adoption of the plan would alienate Dayan and hawkish members of the Labour Party. It is unclear why the idea was discussed in the kitchenette and was not brought to the attention of all ministers. The idea was consistent with both the Allon Plan and the Oral Law and, as such, it would have presented ministers with an opportunity to vote on these issues. According to Health Minister Shem-Tov, however, most ministers were not privy to the secret negotiations with Hussein.[21] By and large the important foreign policy and security decisions were taken by ministers associated with Meir's internal circle – known as Golda's kitchenette – which included Dayan and Galili, but also Allon and Shapira.[22] This episode clearly indicates that, even when presented with an opportunity to vote on the policies they were implementing, Meir and her close ministers preferred the comfort of not deciding. Time and again, Meir explained that, if faced with suitable peace partners, the Labour Party and the government would formulate a strategic territorial policy. However, it transpired that, even when faced with suitable peace partners, the Meir government chose not to decide.

Sadat

On 29 September 1970, Nasser passed away and was replaced by Vice President Anwar El-Sadat. Sadat's first important decision came in November when he extended the ceasefire agreement with Israel by three months. Sadat claimed that a further extension would be conditional on a precise Israeli timetable for withdrawal, adding that Egypt would not consider itself bound by the ceasefire if this was not produced.[23] On 5 January 1971, Sadat surprised the whole world and proclaimed his willingness to sign a peace agreement on the basis of a full Israeli withdrawal from the territories; Sadat threatened that if Israel did not withdraw he would be left with no alternative but to go to war.[24] Despite his threat, Sadat's proclamation should be seen as a historic breakthrough in Israeli-Arab relations; this was the first time an Arab head of state publicly agreed to recognise Israel and sign a peace agreement with it.

Sadat followed his peace statement by informing the US of his willingness to consider an interim agreement with Israel, borrowing the concept from Dayan. Back in December 1967, Dayan proposed a plan, initially put forward by Meir Amit, to unilaterally withdraw from the Suez Canal – which had remained closed, at great financial cost to Egypt, since the June 1967 – as a gesture of goodwill.[25] Dayan believed an Israeli withdrawal from the canal would promote better understanding between the two states, eliminate friction and legitimise Israel's demand for a military presence in Sharm el-Sheikh. Galili claimed that this would be a dangerous precedent and that Israel should instead prepare for a lengthy stay in the area. The Eshkol government decided to leave the option open.[26] However, the idea was then rejected by the Meir government, with Meir particularly not supportive of it.

The interim agreement proposed by Sadat was slightly different from the one advocated by Dayan. Sadat called for an Israeli withdrawal to the Mitle and Gidi passes (40 km from the canal) and for the 'thinning' of Egyptian forces, up to 40 km from the canal on its western bank. This would create a semi-demilitarised area to allow for construction work to reopen the canal. After a period of six months the canal would reopen for shipping, and would include free passage for Israeli vessels. Sadat claimed this was not a tactical ploy but a sincere attempt to reduce tensions and avoid a future war.[27]

Following on from Sadat's proposal, on 8 February, UN envoy Jarring presented Egypt and Israel with a step-by-step approach – the Jarring Document – for resolving the conflict. Working outside the narrow remit of his mandate, and with the consent of the US, Jarring proposed a framework for a comprehensive settlement 'in accordance with the provisions and principles of Resolution 242'. Jarring called for an Israeli withdrawal from occupied Egyptian territories to the international border. He proposed practical security arrangements for Sharm el-Sheikh and for demilitarised zones. In return, Egypt was required to sign a peace agreement based on: the termination of all claims of belligerency; maritime freedom and mutual respect for each side's sovereignty; territorial integrity; and political independence.[28]

Dayan, while welcoming Sadat's offer and the Jarring Document, argued that Israel should emphasise the differences between the sides' positions, in particular Israel's refusal to withdraw to the international border. He argued that Israel should not make any unnecessary territorial concessions unless forced to do so by the Americans and Russians.[29] According to Dayan, the presence of the Israeli Defence Force (IDF) in Sharm el-Sheikh was the only acceptable security arrangement. Dayan argued that, until an acceptable agreement was reached, the IDF would consolidate its position there: 'At the moment we are sitting there and building.'[30] In contrast, Egypt, by and large, accepted the Jarring Document. Nevertheless, Egypt refused to accept the presence of any forces other than those of the UN in Sharm el-Sheikh, and demanded that Israel withdraw from the Gaza Strip.[31]

While Israel appeared to view the Sinai Peninsula as a bargaining chip and publicly stated its desire to negotiate with Egypt without preconditions, it was continuing to consolidate its presence there. This was done through increased investment in the extraction of oil and other natural resources,[32] as well as through the establishment of outposts and civilian settlements. Israel's policies towards the Sinai Peninsula seemed to be in accordance with the Allon Plan and the Oral Law and based on its security needs, that is, securing maritime freedom and ensuring strategic depth. In practice, and with the exception of the Rafah plains (which will be discussed later in the chapter), Israel's actions in the Sinai Peninsula followed a different route.

The first Israeli settlements in the Sinai Peninsula (Nahal Yam and Nahal Sinai) did not correspond to Israel's security needs or the parameters of the Oral Law. Colonel Netzer (the head of the Nahal) acknowledged the problematic location of these settlements and the fact that they were not part of any particular plan.[33] It is true that the majority of settlements were established by the Inter-Ministerial Committee for the Development of the Shlomo Region[34] in the Sharm el-Sheikh–Eilat region in accordance with the Oral Law. However, despite Israel's stated desire to remain in Sharm el-Sheikh, the development of the region did not match the diplomatic rhetoric; in 1972 there were only 300 settlers in the region.[35] Moreover, Israel continued to invest in the establishment and development of settlements outside the remits of the Oral Law.

Israel's muddled policy towards the Sinai Peninsula was to some extent because of logistical issues but mostly because it was following two separate and contradictory plans. In his diary, Ra'anan Weitz (the head of the Settlement Department) listed several concerns regarding Israel's future policy in the Sinai Peninsula; one of the most important, other than the lack of proper planning, was the lack of adequate water resources,[36] an issue also listed by the Ministerial Settlement Committee (MSC).[37]

On the one hand, Galili[38] and the Settlement Department called for investment in projects and establishment of settlements within the government's stated parameters. On the other hand, Dayan and the IDF were pushing for the establishment of outposts and civilian settlements outside the parameters, in northern (near El-Arish) and south-western Sinai (At-Tur). According to Dayan, Israel's strategic line in the Sinai Peninsula needed to be drawn from El-Arish to Sharm el-Sheikh, and not, as envisioned by the government, from the Rafah plains. This, Dayan maintained, would strengthen Israel's grip on

Sharm el-Sheikh. Despite attempts by Galili to restrict the establishment of settlements outside the government's parameters,[39] Israel – not surprisingly – proceeded to establish settlements according to both Galili's (Oral Law) and Dayan's maps. Thus, in 1973, Israel transformed the Nahal Sinai outpost into a civilian settlement and established a second settlement near the city of El-Arish – the only heavily populated area in Sinai. This came despite concerns raised by Tourism Minister Kol that this went against the 'current policy'.[40] Additionally, Israel established a Nahal outpost in At-Tur, which Netzer admitted was controversial and not in accordance with Israel's plans.[41] In conclusion, Israel's settlement activities in the Sinai Peninsula were neither directly related to its stated objectives nor to Sadat's diplomatic stance. In fact, even those officials entrusted with the implementation of Israel's settlement policy (Galili, Netzer and Weitz) were unable to articulate the reasons behind some of the decisions.

Arguably, because of Israel's muddled policy towards the Sinai Peninsula, the Foreign Ministry, and in particular Eban, proposed that Israel use a 'non-committal formulation' in its reply to Jarring and Egypt. This would include welcoming Egypt's response and agreeing to withdraw to secure, recognised and agreed borders, which would be determined during the negotiations. The government agreed to use this formula but, under pressure from Dayan, Galili and Rabin, it added a 'decisive qualification' that Israel would not withdraw to the international border.[42] In addition, Israel made it clear to the US that it would require suitable security arrangements in Sharm el-Sheikh,[43] and that it would not accept minor border changes.[44]

Israel's reply to Jarring put it in a difficult position vis-à-vis the American administration. Sisco informed Rabin that the American administration was disappointed with Israel's actions and that it might re-examine their relationship. According to Sisco, the US had always accepted the idea of a territorial compromise, by which Israel would be required to withdraw from most of the territories. He called on Israel not to miss this opportunity and to offer to withdraw from the canal, as part of an interim agreement.[45]

On 16 March 1971, possibly in response to US queries, Meir outlined Israel's territorial position. According to her, the final borders would be determined by peace negotiations, but Israel would not return to the ceasefire lines. She reiterated that the Gaza Strip would not be returned to Egypt, that the Sinai Peninsula must be demilitarised and that Sharm el-Sheikh would remain under Israeli control.[46] Meir also claimed that the government had not adopted any particular plan regarding the territories and was considering several different options. Meir's map 'neither appealed to Sadat nor comforted the state department'.[47]

The gap between Meir's stated and actual positions regarding the Sinai Peninsula was demonstrated by her response to Dayan's new initiative. Dayan, in a meeting with Sisco, suggested that Israel demonstrate its peaceful intentions by withdrawing to the Sinai passes, while destroying its canal fortifications and allowing a symbolic Egyptian presence on the eastern bank. In return, Egypt would end its state of belligerence and agree to leave the final borders to be determined in negotiations between the sides.[48] Meir was furious when she found out that Dayan had presented the US with a different position to that of the government, and rejected it. Dayan sent the head of AMAN Brigadier-General Yariv, one of Meir's favourite generals, to convince her. Yariv brought maps and spent several hours trying, but to no avail. Meir claimed that 'nothing would come out of this initiative and the public would not understand the need for an Israeli withdrawal from Sinai'.[49] Eban suggested bringing Dayan's proposal to the government for a vote, claiming that there might be enough votes to approve it. Dayan replied that if 'Golda does not support my position, then I do not support my position!'[50]

The kitchenette

Israel's territorial actions appeared contradictory. Israel was engaged in the creation of settlements in the Rafah plains, the Gaza Strip and Sharm el-Sheikh, based on the Oral Law and the Allon Plan, stating that these areas would remain under Israel's control. This was based on Israel's desire to define its own borders and its fear of international security arrangements. At the same time, however, Israel refused to define the future status of these areas, expressed its willingness to engage in direct negotiations without preconditions, and established additional settlements and outposts outside of the scope of the Oral Law and Allon Plan.

The majority of Israel's decisions regarding the OT were dictated, to a large extent, by the kitchenette. Therefore, in order to understand Israel's approach towards the territories, during the Meir period, it is important to understand the views of the main members of the kitchenette (Meir, Galili and Dayan). In the midst of the interim agreement negotiations, the Labour Party held its annual convention. During the convention Meir, Galili and Dayan put forward their views on Israel's territorial approach. Meir described the Arab states as consisting of one united front which still harboured some desire to destroy Israel.[51] She accused the Jarring Mission of attempting to return Israel to the pre-Six

Day War situation, and questioned the need to risk Israeli lives by accepting this idea.[52] Meir made it clear that Israel would never agree to rely on others to provide for its security needs.[53] She claimed that Sadat was not sincere in attempting to reach peace. Because of her distrust of Sadat, she considered a withdrawal from the Suez Canal as a prelude to withdrawal from the Sinai Peninsula and the Gaza Strip. According to Meir, Israel should not be made to pay merely because Sadat wanted to reopen the Suez Canal.[54]

Dayan criticised the claim that Israel should withdraw from all the territories. Dayan also challenged the view that Jordan was a credible peace partner, stating that Hussein had not changed and that dealing with Jordan also meant dealing with the likes of Yasser Arafat (the leader of the PLO); this was despite the fact that he proposed offering the Functional Solution to Jordan. He raised the question of who would control the Gaza Strip and the West Bank once Israel has left, 'Egypt, Jordan or the PFLP [which Israel accused of being a terrorist organisation]'.[55] For Dayan, only the continued presence of the IDF along Israel's strategic lines would ensure long-term security and force the Arab world to accept Israel's new borders.[56]

Regarding the Palestinians, Dayan explained that they understood that Israel was aiming for 'mutual and beneficial lives together'. He argued that the Palestinians were more willing to find ways to accommodate Israel than they were to 'settle with the terrorist organisations'.[57] Dayan concluded his remarks by stating that, 'despite Resolution 242, the Rogers Plan, the Allon Plan and other plans', the strongest guarantees for Israel's long-term security were 'the return of the nation of Israel to its homeland and the presence of the IDF along the Jordan River'.[58]

Galili claimed that the Labour Party was not entrusted with the right to relinquish the historic right of the 'Jewish people to the land of Israel', and that the party had agreed to establish settlements 'not in Uganda or some undefined state, but in the historic land of Israel'.[59] According to Galili, the Labour Party had won the trust of the nation because of its commitments to the realisation of the Jewish aspirations of settling the land of Israel, as well as its sincere desire to pursue peace.[60] Galili explained that he was happy the party did not draw any maps, 'when the time comes and there is a real chance for peace we will submit our map'. Galili, in his usual verbose style, claimed that Israel wanted 'secure and recognised borders' corresponding to its 'geographical, topographical, strategic, security, historical and political considerations', and in accordance to Israel's 'Zionist and security' needs as well as 'the political realities'.[61]

These remarks, by Meir, Dayan and Galili, raise several important issues. First, it is clear that, despite the great importance they assigned to Israel's strategic and security needs, these were strongly modified by their views on Zionism and the history of the Jewish people and the land of Israel. Second, their willingness to accept territorial concessions was directly related to the degree of trust they had in Arab leaders and their proposals. With regard to Jordan and Hussein, Dayan in particular raises the concern that a peace agreement with Jordan based on Israeli territorial concessions will lead to a PLO state in the West Bank. Lastly, it is apparent from their stated views that Meir and Galili did not attach a great deal of importance to formulating a strategic policy and therefore did not have an end-game in mind. This was in contrast to Dayan, who was pushing for the Functional Solution.

Israel's continued contradictory approach

On many occasions Meir stated Israel's willingness to negotiate with Egypt in order to achieve a peace agreement based on secure and recognised borders. However, despite agreeing, in principle, to withdraw from the majority of the Sinai Peninsula, in practice, the Meir government argued with the American mediators over every inch, while constantly adding new 'strategically important' areas from which Israel could not withdraw. Israel's professed strategic aims of retaining control over the Rafah plains and Sharm el-Sheikh could have only been realised with American diplomatic support. Israel's stated reasons for demanding these territories were purely strategic-military. However, when the American administration addressed Israel's security concerns, Israel refused to change its stance and refused to define its future relationship with these territories.

Israel's contradictory approach towards the Sinai Peninsula and the OT was made amply apparent during a series of meetings with Sisco and Yevgeny Primakov (the Deputy Director of the USSR's Institute of World Economy and International Relations). According to Sisco, the US was willing to provide Israel with long-term financial and military guarantees in order to ensure its security, after it withdrew as part of an interim agreement.[62] Sisco reaffirmed that in the final agreement Sharm el-Sheikh would remain under Israel's control.[63] Nevertheless, even though the US was willing to address Israel's security concerns and ensure that Sharm el-Sheikh remained in Israeli hands, Israel refused to budge. Meir informed Sisco that Egypt was unwilling to enter into negotiations without preconditions and that, in her opinion, Sadat was not ready to sign a peace agreement with Israel. Israel, according to Meir, did not want the resumption of hostilities and was therefore willing to work towards an interim agreement, as long as this was consistent with its security.[64]

Following Sisco's visit, at the behest of the Soviet leadership, Primakov came to Israel for a series of secret meetings with Meir, Dayan and Eban. Primakov informed Eban that the USSR was willing to discuss all of Israel's security concerns although, to Primakov, Israel's policies appeared to have little to do with security concerns and more to do with the acquisition of territories.[65] Primakov stated that Arab recognition of Israel, and its territorial integrity, was more important to security than territorial changes.[66] Sadat, he claimed, was willing to sign a peace agreement with Israel. Furthermore, he added that Israel's demand for direct negotiations without preconditions was not consistent with its stated desire to retain the Golan Heights, Sharm el-Sheikh, parts of Sinai and Jerusalem.[67] Eban replied that Israel's main concern was security, but that some territories were essential for its national security.[68] Primakov explained that in his view the Arabs had shown a great deal of diplomatic flexibility and Israel should now dispel the notion that it was happy with the status quo and was bent on territorial acquisition. He reassured Israel that the Arabs were no longer interested in destroying it and that the USSR was willing to provide help to ensure the success of the negotiations.[69] Dayan inquired about the Soviet position regarding the territories. Primakov asserted that the USSR agreed with Sadat's demand for a complete Israeli withdrawal to the international border, but was willing to consider different scenarios for the Gaza Strip, none of which would involve an Israeli presence there.[70] Israel, however, had already decided to include the Gaza Strip in its secure borders and was making arrangements to tighten its grip over the area.

The Rafah plains

In January 1972, several Bedouin tribes petitioned the Israeli Supreme Court, claiming that the army had expelled them from their homes in the Rafah plains. The petition was supported by members of Hashomer Hatz'air,[71] who helped uncover the incident. Chief-of-Staff David El'azar claimed the orders did not emanate from him and established a fact-finding commission to investigate the incident.

On 15 March 1972, members of Hashomer Hatz'air presented Mapam's Central Committee with their report into the incident, including the lands that had been appropriated, the numbers of dispossessed (around

5000), and maps showing existing and planned settlements in the Rafah plains and the Gaza Strip.[72] They claimed that the government was creating an Arab-free area, south of the Gaza Strip, in order to separate the Strip from the Sinai Peninsula. This, they suggested, was part of a plan to clear certain areas before settling them, and linking or annexing them to Israel. The areas cited by Hashomer Hatz'air were the same areas in which Allon and Dayan had previously proposed to establish security outposts. The report also uncovered details of a possible planned city in the Rafah plains. Referring to the existing settlements in the Gaza Strip, members of Hashomer Hatz'air asked 'how was it possible that a transitory outpost established by the army, for security purposes, could transform into a civilian settlement?' The report advised the party to examine whether this method of operation was evident in other regions of the OT as well.[73]

As one of the faction's leaders, Health Minister Shem-Tov professed to have had no prior knowledge of the incident and claimed that no decision regarding the subject had ever been taken by the government.[74] He added that from a conversation he had had recently (after the case was brought to light) he concluded that neither Dayan nor Chief-of-Staff David El'azar were involved. Some members of Mapam inquired how it was possible that, despite being part of the Labour Party and the ruling coalition, they were kept in the dark on this matter. Shem-Tov replied, 'How could I know of something I only read a few hours ago in the press?'[75]

The Rafah plains were seen by the IDF and most political parties, including Mapam, as a means of separating the Gaza Strip from the Sinai Peninsula and providing Israel with strategic depth, and thus vital for Israel's national security.[76] The first proposal to establish settlements in the area came from Allon in December 1968.[77] Allon based his proposal on a survey done by the Settlement Department, which included a detailed plan for four settlements. In its report the Settlement Department clearly stated that parts of the area were inhabited and cultivated by Bedouin tribes.[78] Additionally, Israel, in its response to Jarring, proclaimed that it would retain a strip of land linking Sharm el-Sheikh with Eilat. This decision opened the door for the establishment of settlements in the Rafah plains, and prompted the Settlement Department to present a revised plan for the creation of six to seven settlements in the Rafah plains.[79] During a cabinet meeting on the issue,[80] Dayan explained that they would need to relocate the Bedouins who lived there. He added that the project should be defined as a military one, and that Israel should strive initially to establish Nahal outposts in the area. Dayan claimed the area was one from which Israel would not with-draw as it was vital for its national security.[81] This raises an important question: was Shem-Tov part of that meeting or were 'dovish' ministers like him excluded from discussions and decisions of this nature?

Arguably, Israel's policies in the Rafah plains were an attempt to compensate for its lack of a clear approach towards the Gaza Strip,[82] and to provide an answer to the strategic and demographic problems posed by the territory, in particular the perceived 'terrorist' threat.[83] On the one hand, Israel could not afford to annex the Gaza Strip, because of the demographic implications. On the other hand, it feared its with-drawal would lead to the use of the area as a base by a foreign army.[84] In other words, Israel's strategic-military needs regarding the Gaza Strip, dictated, to a large extent, its settlement activity in the Rafah plains.[85]

The idea of settling the Gaza Strip was first suggested by Allon in 1967 as part of his plan. Nevertheless, the decision to establish settlements in the area would only be taken in September 1970. This decision came as a result of Galili's proposal to establish two Nahal outposts in the Gaza Strip (Kfar Darom and Netzarim), in order to assert Israel's claims to the area.[86] In a discussion in the MSC, prior to the government's decision, the IDF's coordinator of activities in the OT Brigadier-General Shlomo Gazit claimed the settlements were necessary for 'political-psychological', reasons 'to give an electric shock to the residents of the Strip', though he acknowledged they served no 'tactical point'. Major-General Ariel Sharon (head of Israel's Southern Command) went even further, arguing that the settlements would 'wean the Arabs of the Gaza Strip from the illusion that we will eventually get out of there'.[87]

The decision by the government to settle the Gaza Strip had been taken before its long-term future was decided upon. Initially, the Eshkol government avoided taking a decision over the future of the Gaza Strip until it could find a solution to the demographic problem it posed. Several ideas were discussed, among them exchanging the Gaza Strip for parts of the West Bank in order to conclude a deal with Hussein. The Meir government's decision to settle the Gaza Strip therefore not only hampered negotiations with Hussein but also plunged Israel into a demographic conundrum. In fact, a proposal by Dayan to provide the residents of the Gaza Strip with Jordanian passports, in order to strengthen Jordan's ties with Gaza, was rebuffed by Meir and Galili, who expressed fears the move would provide Jordan with a foothold in the territory.[88]

As mentioned earlier, the decision to settle the Rafah plains was clearly in opposition to Israel's professed desire to negotiate with Egypt without preconditions. The creation of facts on the ground clearly hindered such negotiations. Furthermore, the non-transparent appropriation of lands in the Rafah plains discredited Israel's democratic and legal traditions. However, despite these problems, the idea that the Rafah plains would remain under Israel's control became central to its territorial position.[89] This idea was strengthened in May 1973, when Israel's Supreme Court rejected the Bedouin tribes' petition. The court accepted the army's argument that the area was essential to Israel's security needs and that the decision to appropriate lands and 'resettle' the Bedouin population was taken out of 'military necessity'.[90] However, during the court case several Israeli daily newspapers published accounts of a secret plan for the establishment of a large, deep-sea port city in the Rafah plains named Yamit.[91] These detailed plans were drawn up by Dayan and Galili with the assistance of the Settlement Department long before the court case began.[92]

The case of the Rafah plains illustrated the perverse dichotomy inherent in Dayan's concept of the Functional Solution and a 'benevolent occupation'. Dayan was well aware of the economic, political and social problems that existed in the OT, and had urged both the government and the Knesset to do more for the welfare of the Palestinian population.[93] He therefore supported efforts to alleviate poverty and strengthen the economies of the territories in order to promote a long-term Israeli-Arab peaceful coexistence under Israel's rule. At the same time, Dayan also supported the expansion of Israel's settlement activity, which included land appropriation, and its military occupation, which denied political rights to the occupied population. It should have been apparent to Israeli decision-makers that this approach could not be maintained for long. The reason this contradictory approach survived, and that the security and political situation was stable (from Israel's perspective), was that socio-economic and security conditions in the OT were improving dramatically during the first few years of occupation.[94] The lack of a security problem and rising living standards for the occupied population meant that the government was in no hurry to re-assess its approach.

The fact-finding commission established by the army concluded that Major-General Ariel Sharon acted of his own accord and in contravention of procedures, but that neither the government nor the army command was involved. Nevertheless, the committee recognised that the new situation in the Rafah plains was advantageous and therefore advised that no further action be taken, other than to officially reprimand Sharon.[95] Arguably, Sharon understood the importance that the government and the army attributed to the area, and the difficulty they had in making such a decision. He therefore decided to support their efforts and made that decision for them; Sharon later claimed that Dayan 'had been fully aware of what was going on'.[96] Indeed, in a letter to Meir, during the court case, Galili proposed establishing a regional centre in the area, explaining that it was *now* relatively empty. Galili added that the proposal was produced in consultation with Dayan and Gvati.[97] It is therefore clear that while the Israeli government was officially not deciding over territorial issues, this non-decision was used by members of the 'kitchenette' to advance their visions for the OT.

Hussein's federal plan

Israel's contradictory and muddled policies were not limited to the Sinai Peninsula, the Gaza Strip and the Rafah plains; in fact, it was the West Bank which proved to be the epitome of this confused approach. Instead of agreeing on a comprehensive approach, decision-makers appeared content with the implementation of elements of both the Allon Plan and Dayan's Functional Solution. The Israeli government chose to leave the question of defining its long-term relationship with the OT open, even though the establishment of settlements and outposts continued unabated. With the exception of the Jerusalem municipal area, the OT existed in a legal limbo, with Israel unwilling to extend its jurisdiction even to areas it declared would remain under its control. Arguably, the government preferred the status of the territories to be determined through negotiations and did not wish to jeopardise those by taking unilateral action. However, with the Israeli occupation of the territories entering its fifth year, the undefined status of the territories created numerous problems for Israel, not least that of legitimacy.

The idea that Israel would be required to remain in the territories for a long period of time was not new. Back in 1967, Dayan put forward a proposal that would have seen the territories (the West Bank and the Gaza Strip) remain under Israeli control indefinitely.[98] During his time in the Defence Ministry, Dayan worked towards the realisation of this aim with the apparent backing of the government. As noted by Shem-Tov, when it came to the implementation of political, social and economic decisions regarding the OT, Dayan was 'completely and exclusively' in control.[99] This included a drive towards Palestinian 'self-rule' by which Israel recognised and supported local elected officials. Dayan's actions empowered local officials, particularly the mayors, and enhanced their position. Subsequently, the relative financial weakness of the Palestinian municipalities, and their dependence on the military administration for public services and investment, provided Israel with a great deal of control over them.[100] This was in contrast to the Allon Plan, which did not envision the continuation of Israeli control over the Palestinian population centres.

Israel's need to legitimise and empower local officials necessitated holding fresh elections in the West Bank; the previous local elections were held in 1963. The elections were seen by Dayan as a way of empowering local officials in order to strengthen the case for Palestinian self-rule and his Functional Solution, even if they were in contradiction to the Allon Plan, and represented an action against the interests of Jordan, which opposed both. The relative ease with which Israel administered the territories, and the perceived positive economic and social statistics emanating from the military administration,[101] might have increased Dayan's belief in the Functional Solution and the success of his 'occupation model'.

In 1972, elections were held in the West Bank, with the process run and supervised by local officials without Israeli interference. From an Israeli perspective, the elections proved to be a great success (participation levels were above 80 per cent), despite vocal resistance by the PLO, which opposed the idea of self-rule, and unhappiness expressed by Jordan.[102] The elections did not bring about an immediate change to life in the territories. They did represent, however, the first instance in which Palestinians were able to determine their political future, with several prominent members of the old Palestinian establishment losing their seats to up-and-coming young independents. Consequently, the political leadership of the West Bank became split between local independents and those supporting Jordan and the PLO.[103] The fragmentation of the Palestinian political leadership undermined Dayan's Functional Solution and Israel's Jordanian approach.

In March 1972, King Hussein unveiled a new diplomatic initiative 'the Federal Plan', through which he hoped to reaffirm his claim to the West Bank. The plan, timed to coincide with the West Bank elections, was meant to restore Hussein's credentials and support – damaged in the aftermath of Black September – among Palestinians. Hussein proposed linking the West Bank, and possibly the Gaza Strip, with Jordan in a federal agreement, creating an autonomous Palestinian region under Jordanian control with Jerusalem as its capital.[104] The plan was immediately dismissed by the Arab world, with Hussein accused of trying to sign a separate peace deal with Israel. Among Palestinians, support for Jordan was already waning – not surprisingly considering the events of Black September – and many rejected the plan. The PLO issued a statement condemning and rejecting the plan, claiming that the Palestinians should be accorded the right to determine their own future, and accusing Hussein of being an accomplice of America and of Zionism. The plan did not receive much approval in the West Bank either, with only a minority of elected officials welcoming it.[105]

The rejection of the plan by the Arab states was followed by a formal Israeli rejection. The plan prompted a vote in the Knesset, recognising Israel's historic rights to the West Bank. The government, while not rejecting the federal solution outright, did not accept the territorial aspects of Hussein's plan. One of the few to welcome the plan was Allon, who claimed the federal solution was compatible with his plan, even if he rejected some of its territorial aspects.[106] Allon claimed that there was no reason to dismiss the plan. Allon believed there was a 'real possibility' of reaching a solution based on it and the Allon Plan, adding that it offered a good solution to the Palestinian problem. Nevertheless, Allon argued that in order to bring about a solution based on these plans, Israel should continue to create facts on the ground. He called for the establishment of a new city on the Jerusalem–Jericho road (Ma'ale Adumim), and additional settlements in those areas that would remain under Israeli control after a peace agreement was signed.[107]

What might seem surprising is that, despite rejecting Hussein's plan, the Israeli government, with the exception of Dayan, viewed the Jordanian approach as the most suitable for the West Bank. Indeed, on 11 November 1971, during a meeting with Hussein, Meir stated that Israel had no desire to keep the Palestinians under its jurisdiction: 'They belong to you, they are your people.'[108] Meir proposed a solution based on 'substantial changes to the border' along the lines of the Allon Plan,[109] with Jerusalem remaining under Israel's control but with Jordanian administration of the Muslim holy sites.[110] Hussein informed Meir that he had no problems discussing border changes, but that these should be based on reciprocity and a desire for long-lasting peace between the two states.[111]

On 21 March 1972, Meir met with Hussein and Jordanian Prime Minister Zaid Rifai to discuss the Jordanian federal plan. Meir started the meeting by complaining that Israel was not notified prior to the unveiling of the plan. She informed him that his plan disregarded Israel's historic claims to the West Bank, and that any future agreement must be based on substantial changes to the pre-war borders. These, she explained, would be similar to the Allon Plan, though she did not link Israel's historic claims to the parameters of the Allon Plan. With regard to Jerusalem, Meir proposed administrative solutions to the Muslim and Christian holy places but that the city would remain under Israel's control. In response, Hussein stated that he was willing to sign a peace deal but that this depended on Israel's position. He proceeded to explain how his federal plan would work. The West Bank and the Gaza Strip would form the Palestinian part of the federation, but would remain demilitarised and under Jordanian control. Jordan would be willing to accept some minor border changes and a unified Jerusalem as long as it was also the capital of the Palestinian autonomous region. On the matter of Jerusalem, Hussein asked Meir to desist from changing the status quo in Jerusalem irreversibly.[112] Furthermore, Rifai informed Meir that any future peace agreement must be 'acceptable, workable, durable, something we can be proud of, something that his Majesty can present to the Arab nations and to the world'. This meant that Jordan could not agree to an Israeli plan that envisioned major border modifications.[113]

Meir dismissed the federal idea outright, informing Hussein that if this was his position, then they should stop negotiating. In reply, Hussein told Meir not to be despondent and that they should both try, for their next meeting, to find constructive ways to bridge their differences. Meir said that this would not be necessary as the differences between them were too big. She explained that Hussein was basically offering Israel a revised version of the Rogers Plan which Israel had already rejected.[114]

One of the main problems faced by the Israeli government, regarding its negotiations with Jordan, was its lack of an agreed position or negotiator. Caught between two contrasting plans (Allon's and Dayan's), while at times acting in accordance to neither, Israel could not articulate to Hussein its vision of a Jordanian-Israeli peace plan. On 18 June 1972, in a meeting with Allon and Galili to discuss Dayan's planned meeting with Hussein, Meir said that the ministers needed to decide what it was that they wanted. She inquired whether either of them knew what Dayan was going to offer Hussein and asked what they thought he should offer.[115] Allon suggested that Dayan limit himself to security and military issues, and that he should not bring up the Functional Solution. Galili suggested that Dayan should stick with the offers already made and limit himself to listening and reporting back to the government.[116] As it turned out, Dayan did not deviate from the government's position. In the meeting he urged Hussein – who was disappointed that Israel did not come up with any new proposals – not to miss the opportunity and to reach an agreement with Meir.[117] The meeting exposed Israel's inability to put forward a clear plan; Dayan explained Israel's philosophy as 'a formula ... not an expression of exact territory, although it carries territory with it, naturally'.[118]

According to the Israeli press, Hussein had proposed (possibly to Dayan) a revised version of his federal plan.[119] On 23 August, Dayan allegedly said in a closed meeting of Labour ministers, that there was a real chance for peace with Jordan. He explained that Jordan was willing to sign a separate peace agreement with Israel based on: minor border modifications; Israeli military presence in the Jordan valley; and Jordanian control over the Gaza Strip. Dayan explained that Hussein was willing to consider different solutions regarding Jerusalem, as well as leaving the final status of Jerusalem for future negotiations.[120] This appears to be in line with Hussein's remarks in a meeting with Meir on 3 February 1972, regarding border modifications:

> we realised that changes [to the border] must occur. But the point is how significant, and how drastic? When we spoke of a reciprocal basis, it was reciprocal in terms of land, in terms of something that could really be accepted by people. And we have a very open mind.[121]

Nevertheless, Dayan did not accept Hussein's terms. Dayan explained that because Hussein would not accept the Allon Plan, or any plan that would satisfy Israel, Israel should examine its policies in the West Bank, taking into account that it would probably remain there for many years.[122]

During the talks with Jordan, Hussein presented a clear and consistent position while showing a great deal of flexibility to ensure the talks were successful. Hussein went so far as to discuss different administrative solutions for Jerusalem and offered several concessions with regard to Israel's security needs. While rejecting Hussein's proposals, the Israeli government did not clearly express what it was that it wanted other than major border modifications. The only plans presented to Hussein were variations of the Allon Plan – a plan that was never approved and that was previously rejected by the kitchenette as part of Allon's proposed interim plan. Additionally, had Hussein agreed to the Allon Plan, there were no guarantees it would have been approved by the government. If the details reported by the Israeli press regarding Hussein's offer to Dayan are to be believed,[123] then there would have been no reason for it to be rejected by the government. According to the press, Hussein had expressed his willingness to address all of Israel's security concerns, including a provision for an Israeli military presence in the Jordan valley.[124] According to Rifai, Israel was acting in a way that defeated its declared purposes.[125] An examination of Israel's approach during the negotiations with Hussein leaves the impression that Israel was moving in two opposing directions. On the one hand, Israel made it clear that it did not want to control the heavily populated areas of the West Bank (Allon Plan), while at the same time it provided Dayan with the opportunity to implement his Functional Solution. On the other hand, Israel stated that its preferred option with regard to the West Bank was the Jordanian one, while undermining this approach through promoting Palestinian self-rule and offering Hussein a plan it knew he would never accept. In conclusion, the Meir government adopted an incoherent and contradictory approach towards the West Bank, which was based on the partial implementation of two different plans, while actively undermining these plans and weakening its own negotiating position vis-à-vis Jordan.

6
The Grand Debate

The Grand Debate

Between September 1972 and April 1973 the Labour Party held a lengthy debate – known as the Grand Debate – on the future of the Occupied Territories (OT). The debate, the brainchild of party chairman Aharon Yadlin, was held in response to 'mounting pressures'[1] to reconcile the differences among party members prior to the elections (October 1973); instead, it exacerbated them.[2] The debate exposed the growing rift between the leading figures in the party, with Allon, Sapir and Eban on one side, and Galili, Dayan and Meir on the other.[3]

The debate within the party was not so much between factions as between two main groups: those advocating a Functional Solution and those advocating the Allon Plan. But there were also two smaller groups, the first of which included the supporters of a greater Israel, while the other advocated withdrawal from the majority of the territories. The latter included Arie Eliav (the former secretary-general of the party) and Yitzhak Ben-Aharon (Secretary-General of the Histadrut). Eliav called on the party to support an Israeli withdrawal from the majority of the territories and adopt a two-state solution (Israel and Palestine); Eliav was one of the first in the party to publicly acknowledge the existence of a Palestinian nation.[4] Ben-Aharon was particularly concerned about the demographic problem and asked whether party members wanted a Jewish or a bi-national state?[5] Ben-Aharon called for a unilateral withdrawal from the majority of the territories:

> I am not sure that we need to wait for a peace agreement to decide upon the future of the territories. I feel that one day we may realise

that it would be better if a particular area and population was outside of our area jurisdiction without the need of a signature.

Ben-Aharon was concerned that Israel might be left in control of territories and people it did not intend to keep, and that this would become a burden on it.[6] However, despite his demographic concerns, Ben-Aharon was firmly in favour of retaining the Golan Heights and the Gaza Strip, and against any division of Jerusalem.[7] In addition, Ben-Aharon did not rule out a unilateral withdrawal from the West Bank in accordance with the Allon Plan.[8]

Opening the debate, Yadlin reminded members that they were required to discuss and determine not only the party's economic and political policies towards the OT, but also Israel's required borders.[9] However, he added that 'regarding the exact strategic borders', this could 'be left until we enter into meaningful negotiations with the Arab states'.

Finance Minister Sapir claimed that, in the aftermath of the Six Day War, and unlike other ministers, he had reached certain conclusions which events had only helped to strengthen.[10] He maintained that, before entering into meaningful negotiations, Israel should first decide what kind of solution it desired and refrain from engaging in activities that would hinder these negotiations;[11] he provided the example of Yamit to illustrate these types of activities. Sapir questioned the logic behind investing large sums of money in Yamit 'over the next 25 years', and asked whether 'this is what Israel needs at the moment'. He ridiculed party members who argued that these investments would not come at the expense of Israel's development towns ('*Ayarot Pituah*). Sapir asserted that the territories were a financial burden – one that would only increase with time.[12] For Sapir there was 'no difference between a formal decision on annexation and annexation that was not decided upon but creeps up on us [the Functional Solution]'. Referring to Dayan, he said: 'I find it strange that senior political figures, some of whom will enter the history pages, succumb, even if for a short while, to this [Functional Solution] delusion.'[13] Israel, according to Sapir, could ill afford to control the territories without providing – at some point in the future – full legal and economic rights to the population. Sapir asserted that treating the population as second-class citizens would not work in the long run: 'The world will not agree to it, the Arab population will not agree to it … and we, under no circumstances, will agree to it.' Sapir commented that 'the demographic projections are so simple that even a child could calculate them'.[14] Sapir warned that if Israel maintained the status quo it might not be able to extricate itself from the territories; he provided an allegory about 'a boy who ties himself to a tree and then shouts that the tree will not leave him'.[15]

Allon, agreeing with Sapir, claimed that Israel did not need to agree on a final map, but needed to know its parameters. However, fearing a demographic problem, he argued that it was necessary to avoid settling in heavily populated areas. For Allon, guaranteeing Israel's security and preserving its Jewish nature were paramount:

> The discussion should be focused on Israel's strategic long-term peace policy and the correct approach by which to administer the territories until peace arrives.[16] If I am in favour of a territorial compromise, it is from the viewpoint of political-realism and a humanist viewing of Zionism, which requires that we adhere to, and strive for, peace.[17]

Allon argued that what went on in the territories was temporary and could not last. He confessed that assertions made by Dayan, that the local population could live indefinitely under Israeli rule, 'made me wonder'.[18] Allon contended that a Functional Solution would deny political rights to the Palestinian population. He argued that the Jewish people, 'of all people', should not be those to deliver an unjust and deplorable political system: 'Israel should not deny the elementary political aspirations of the local population.'[19] Responding to sniping from attending party members, Allon declared that a Palestinian entity existed, whether or not it was defined as a nation. In his view, Israel should work towards a solution that addressed its needs as well as providing a solution to the Palestinian political problem: 'If Israel does not ignore the Palestinian element, it might prove to be an important element in the march for peace.'[20]

Allon claimed that, for the past five years, Israel's economic relationship with the territories had not been properly scrutinised and that there was a need to redefine this relationship in a manner that would leave Israel with flexibility in terms of its diplomatic options. He asserted that there was a need for two separate economic entities that would cooperate, but not integrate. Allon emphasised that the economic cooperation between the two entities should not lead to the creation of a single economic structure.[21]

> The peace Israel requires, the peace for which Israel should strive and that which can be attained, cannot be any other than a peace based

on compromise. No one should be under the illusion that Israel can achieve peace while holding on to all the territories while, at the same time, no one should delude himself that Israel can achieve security while withdrawing from all the territories.[22]

Speaking several weeks after Allon and Sapir, and in an attempt to heal a growing party rift, Eban argued that the time to resolve the differences and disagreements within the party had not yet arrived. Eban suggested that Israel would be ready to make the necessary territorial compromises when the time arrived.[23] This, he acknowledged, was inherent in the Allon Plan, but he claimed that this was not the only plan available. He proceeded to propose that the party maintain its current policies, as stated in the Oral Law.[24] Israel, according to Eban, should maintain the current 'temporary' situation because that would leave all of the diplomatic options open. Eban argued that, when Israel came to sign a peace agreement, the accord should be based on the establishment of proper relations and on substantial territorial changes that would guarantee Israel's long-term security needs.[25]

In contrast to Eban, Dayan remarked that, after six years of controlling the territories, it was time for the party to decide 'what we should and should not do'. Dayan argued that there was no 'objective need' to tie Israel's policies in the territories with the issue of borders.[26] On the matter of settlements, Dayan stated that Israel would not withdraw from areas it was now settling, even though he conceded that none of the settlements served any security purpose. Furthermore, and in a somewhat contradictory statement, Dayan asserted that there was a difference between areas that served a 'military-security' purpose and those that served a 'diplomatic-security' purpose. He elaborated that the latter were more desirable and, if Israel was in a position to achieve real peace, then it would most probably have to relinquish some of the areas it was currently holding.[27]

He disagreed with the assertions that Israel should only establish settlements for security purposes (Mapam's position) or only in areas it planned to keep (the Allon Plan). Israel, according to Dayan, should expand and strengthen its settlement activity in all the territories; he proposed establishing industrial centres as well as new agricultural, urban and civilian settlements. Furthermore, he proposed regulating the Israel Land Authority (ILA) to allow corporate entities and private individuals to purchase land in the territories.[28] Dayan scoffed at Sapir's fears of annexation. Dayan claimed that Israel was not engaged in a gradual annexation of the territories. Moreover, he made it clear that he was against annexation, claiming he would rather withdraw from the territories than accept the Palestinian population as Israeli citizens.[29] It is clear that Dayan firmly believed that the Palestinians, as a consequence of their improved living standards and greater political freedom (than under Egyptian and Jordanian rule) would accept the idea of self-rule in the context of the Functional Solution.

Dayan agreed that no formal decision was needed over the issue of the final borders, but that the party needed to define its future relationship with the territories. He contended that Israelis and Palestinians could live together under the military administration and that Ben-Aharon and Eliav were wrong to suggest that 'what is west of the Green Line is Israel and what is east of it is Palestine'.[30] Dayan was basing his statement, to an extent, on the Israeli Defence Force's (IDF) assessments regarding the OT. Shlomo Gazit described Israel's relationship with the occupied population in all spheres as 'outstanding'; he attributed the situation to the trust-building measures and activities by the military administration, and to the lack of foreign pressure on Israel.[31] Looking back in retrospect, after retiring from the army, Gazit came to the conclusion that Dayan's approach, even if fully implemented, was doomed to fail.[32]

Taking the middle ground between Allon and Dayan, Galili explained that the party had a 'pragmatic and practical' policy but that it had not yet defined its long-term strategic-territorial aims nor did it agree on 'our final map'.[33] Galili rejected the 'Palestinians' right to self-determinate as a ploy for establishing a Palestinian state over the ruins of Israel'.[34] The future of the West Bank, according to Galili, was within a Jordanian framework, based on significant changes to the pre-war borders. However, 'in the absence of peace, we do not withdraw nor do we leave a void; instead, we create settlements'. Galili maintained that Israel's policy should be defined by what 'is good and necessary for Israel', taking into account the needs of the local population. He defined the main points of this approach: 'continuation of the settlement activities', 'continuation of the Open Bridges policy', the establishment of an 'enlightened [territorial] administration', the need to 'regulate the employment of workers from the territories in Israel' and for the local population 'to live their lives without foreign intervention'. Referring to the demographic problem, Galili asked 'What would be a bigger threat, the population living under an enemy Arab leader or under Israel's control?'[35]

Galili proposed that Israel should take over the Gaza Strip and that the large population areas of the West Bank be handed over to Jordan, 'similarly to what was suggested in the Allon Plan'. He made it clear that the West Bank would be demilitarised and that its population would enjoy 'some of their rights from Jordan and some from Israel'.[36] On the one hand, Galili called on the party not to make unilateral decisions that would block the chances for peace, while, on the other hand, he called for the continuation of the settlement activity and the 'enlightened occupation'.[37] The proposed solution, as suggested by Galili, appeared to be an amalgamation of the Allon Plan with parts of Dayan's Functional Solution. For Galili, the time for peace had not yet arrived and there was no need to make any decisions: 'This was not the hour to decide.'[38]

The last speaker, in the Grand Debate, was Prime Minister Meir. Meir tried to defuse the debate by stating that there was no sign of a 'real chance for peace' and therefore no need to make firm decisions:[39] 'when the time comes', she claimed, the party would need to either reject or support the proposals that would be put in front of it. She admitted that she had a map of her own which would provide Israel with secure borders, but that at that moment it was nothing more than an academic exercise.[40] Meir made it clear that the territories were neither an obstacle for peace nor a recipe for war. She reminded party members that in 1957 Israel withdrew from the Gaza Strip, and from the Sinai Peninsula, 'an act that did not lead to peace', while in 1967 Israel did not hold any territories and yet war broke out: 'We want to be here while they [the Arabs] do not want us to be here.'[41] In order to hide any 'dovish' tendencies, Meir claimed to have never met with Hussein: 'I would have loved to meet him' but 'unfortunately, he did not want to meet'. After stating to the press that Palestinians did not exist, she clarified to party members that it was not for her to determine whether they were a nation or not, but that between Israel and Jordan there was a place for only two states, 'not three'. She added that Israel would never enter into negotiations with the heads of the terrorist organisations that aimed 'to destroy Israel'.[42]

Striving to preserve party unity, Meir questioned the need to make difficult and far-reaching decisions: 'If I am allowed to voice my opinion, there is no need to make decisions or reach conclusions.'[43] Unsurprisingly, the Grand Debate ended without any decisions being taken or resolutions voted on. Despite the debate lasting for over 80 hours, being held over eight sessions and showcasing 80 speakers, the party could not even agree on a concluding statement. Unable to heal the growing rift between its elites, the party, rather than risk a split in its ranks, preferred not to decide.

The Galili Document

On 8 April 1973, and in preparation for the upcoming elections, Dayan, unhappy with the indecisiveness shown by the Labour Party and the government, presented Meir with a plan titled 'The Policy in the Territories in the Next Four Years'. Dayan called for:

- an increase in resources for development and infrastructure in the OT;
- the expansion of Jerusalem's urban and industrial areas beyond the Green Line;
- the development of Yamit as a regional-industrial centre;
- the establishment of an industrial centre in the West Bank and an urban-industrial centre in the Golan Heights;
- the establishment of new settlements in accordance with the Settlement Department;
- allowing private Jewish businessmen to establish industrial enterprises in the territories;
- allowing the ILA to acquire lands in the territories and make them available for settlements, public and private enterprises and 'land exchanges'.[44]

Dayan's radical ideas generated controversy and hostility among ministers, and his plan was rejected by a small majority. The majority of ministers (including Meir) were deeply concerned that Dayan's proposal would close the door to achieving a territorial settlement. It is important to note that ministers agreed with several of Dayan's proposals, such as the establishment of a regional centre in the Golan Heights.[45] Despite the rejection of his proposal, Dayan did not relinquish his drive to influence Israel's territorial policy. On 23 July, he declared that, due to the Labour Party's present territorial policy, he would have to reconsider his position within it,[46] especially after the party mirrored the government and rejected his proposal.[47] Dayan requested that the party reconsider his plan as the basis for its electoral platform. He made it clear that his participation in the Labour Party was conditional on the adoption of his plan.[48] Unwilling to risk a defection by the Rafi faction to the opposition, and taking into account Dayan's electoral appeal, Meir as usual entrusted her close confidant Galili with the responsibility for finding a compromise.[49] The Galili Document, as it became known, eroded most of Dayan's proposals but did not reject them out of hand. In fact Galili, with clever use of elaborate phrasing, managed to produce a document that met most of Dayan's demands while being in accordance with the government's and the party's position.[50]

Yadlin opened the party's debate on the Galili Document by commenting that there was no need for the party to talk about 'winners and losers' since, on this particular occasion, 'the party as a whole won by adopting the document'.[51] After Yadlin's brief introduction, Galili proceeded to explain the document's main points. Galili clarified that the document, if agreed upon, would represent the party's territorial policies 'for the next four years'.[52]

On the matter of settlements, Galili, as Israel's settlement Tsar (head of the MSC), explained that all new settlements were to be established according to government decisions: 'We have a system according to which we shall operate in the future.' The Galili Document referred to the idea of strengthening and expanding the existing settlements programme within the agreed-upon parameters. Within those parameters, and subject to government regulations, there would be some scope for private individuals to take part in the establishment and development of settlements. This last point was an attempt to address one of Dayan's core demands without rejecting it. With regard to establishing Yamit, Galili claimed: 'There could be no mistake when it comes to the government's position with regard to the settlement and development of the Rafah plains.' According to him, the government intended to expand the existing settlements and establish an urban centre [Yamit] by 1977, and establish a deep-sea port in the area for economic as well as political-military reasons. However, he claimed that the final decision on the matter might take two to three years.[53] Galili stated that the 'ILA will be directed by the government to purchase all land necessary for settlement, development, housing and industrial purposes.' However, this would be undertaken only in areas identified by the government and in accordance with its policies. Galili declared that the party was united on the issue of settlements, and that even Mapam agreed with the settlement programme in certain areas, such as the Golan Heights, Sharm el-Sheikh and Gush-Etzion.[54]

The Galili Document gained near-unanimous approval, with only Aliev refusing to vote for it. Aliev declared that the document 'stood against all that I understand to be the values of the Labour movement' and that it gave credence 'to the strangulation of Zionism!'[55] In a written piece published in the press, Aliev went on to provide an allegory about a ship whose navigators were steering it straight into a storm; with the outbreak of the Yom Kippur War, Aliev's allegory proved prophetic!

As part of the Alignment, Mapam did not partake in the debate. Nonetheless, Mapam stated that it did not agree with the Labour Party on this matter and that it 'regretted' the adoption of the Galili Document. Furthermore, Mapam claimed its members would vote against the adoption of the document as the electoral platform of the Alignment.[56] In contrast, Allon, and many other prominent Labour leaders, claimed the document did not fundamentally change the party's policies. The near-unanimous approval of the document proved that Dayan and his supporters, despite being a minority in the party, wielded 'greater actual power' and were able to influence the party's policies in their favour. Dayan, through 'implicit threats' and intimidation, was able to 'constrain' the power of the moderates and overcome their 'numerical superiority'.[57]

The Galili Document was a patched-up solution approved by the party in order to avoid Dayan's more radical ideas.[58] Nevertheless, some of its proposals represented a clear change to the party's position. The document expanded the urban and industrial development of Jerusalem beyond its municipal boundaries. Additionally, the document adopted Dayan's proposal for developing an industrial area in the West Bank[59] – expanding yet again the scope of the Allon Plan.

The Yom Kippur War

The Galili Document was based on a scenario in which war was an unlikely event and Sadat's actions (such as ordering all Soviet military personnel out of Egypt in the summer of 1972) gave no immediate indication of an impending war. But, by not providing Sadat with a diplomatic recourse, Israel had made the war a certainty. On 6 October 1973, Egypt and Syria launched a surprise attack on Israel, catching it completely unprepared, focusing on regaining the territories they lost in the Six Day War (the Sinai Peninsula and the Golan Heights).

It is not the purpose of this book to deal directly with the narrative of the Yom Kippur War, but to focus on those aspects that relate to Israel's territorial policy: the 'Concept'; Israel's tactical decisions during the war regarding the territories; and the changes that came about as a result of this war. The 'Concept' is the term used in the literature to describe AMAN's (the military intelligence unit), and the political leadership's, guiding assumptions about Israel's relations with its Arab neighbours in the pre-war period. It was assumed that Israel's military might, in conjunction with the military and political support it received from the US, was sufficient to deter any Arab attack. The Arab states, it was assumed, would have to come to terms with Israel's demands for new borders.[60] The assumptions and predictions made by AMAN and the political echelons were based on this 'Concept'.

As mentioned earlier, matters of national security and foreign policy were primarily dealt with by the kitchenette, which in 1973 included Meir, Dayan and Galili, as well as (depending on the occasion) Allon, Haim Bar-Lev (Industry Minister and former chief-of-staff) and Justice Minister Shapira. Meir, Dayan and Galili operated in relative isolation and exhibited qualities such as 'self-righteousness and self-assurance', which are normally associated with 'group think'.[61] This is why Israel's leaders, trapped in their own 'Concept', were in no rush to conclude negotiations with either Egypt or Jordan and were in no rush to define Israel's territorial policy. Their belief that time was on their side, and that the Arab states would eventually accept Israel's position,[62] proved to be mistaken. Israel's leaders were well aware of the possibility of signing a peace agreement – or at least an interim agreement – with Egypt, based on withdrawal to the pre-war borders. However, held captive by their own convictions, they chose to overlook these possibilities; for example, a few months before the war, Eban briefed the Knesset that Egypt had reiterated its call for an interim agreement, and acknowledged that Egypt was willing to sign a peace agreement based on the pre-war borders.[63]

Israel's assumptions and predictions led to the rejection of several potential Arab proposals regarding the OT (such as Sadat's interim proposal and Hussein's federal plan), and is clear that the 'kitchenette' in general, and Meir in particular, adopted 'objectionist' and 'obstructionist' attitudes towards these and other suggestions regarding the OT.[64] Meir's dominance was such that, even in those instances where members of the 'kitchenette' were in favour of a solution (e.g. Dayan's interim proposal), they were unwilling to challenge her. This attitude would come back to haunt the government; in the aftermath of the Yom Kippur War, Meir admitted that, at the time, she followed her heart rather than her head, and that she did not fully understand the logic behind Dayan's interim agreement proposal.[65] Arguably, it was Israel's rigid diplomatic stance, its exaggerated self-confidence, based on the 'Concept', as well as its unwillingness to define its territorial policy, that led to the Yom Kippur War.

The majority of assumptions held by decision-makers regarding the territories were also proved wrong. They assumed that, in the unlikely event that the Egyptian army tried to cross the canal, the Bar-Lev line[66] would be sufficient to hold it back long enough for Israeli forces 'to move up and destroy it'.[67] In reality, the Bar-Lev line – from which Meir refused to withdraw during the negotiations for the 'interim agreement' – did not prove an obstacle for the Egyptian army. It was widely believed that it was essential for Israel to control Sharm el-Sheikh,[68] in order to ensure free passage through the Straits of Tiran.[69] This, however, did not prevent the Egyptian forces from blocking the straits further south. Additionally, the perceived wisdom that settlements contributed to security proved to be misplaced. Israel was required to evacuate its settlements in the Golan Heights and the Sinai Peninsula during the war.

It can be argued that only the notion of strategic depth proved to be correct. This, of course, is based on the assumption that Egypt's and Syria's war efforts were not based exclusively on retrieving those territories that supposedly contributed to Israel's strategic depth. Sadat's limited war plan, and his army's limited capability to fight outside the range of its SAM-3 anti-aircraft-missile batteries, are testimony that, at least with regard to Egypt, they were. It is also questionable whether the Syrian forces would have invaded northern Israel had they managed to secure the Golan Heights. This is not to say that both armies would not have expanded the fighting theatre had their initial successes been left unchecked.

Militarily, Israel had managed to secure a resounding victory despite being caught off guard. In addition, its decision to counter-attack in the Golan Heights and advance into Syria, in order to balance the possible loss of territories in the Sinai Peninsula,[70] left Israel in possession of additional territories. On the Sinai front, the Egyptian forces managed to secure several bridgeheads in the first days of the war and control both banks of the canal. Sadat was adamant that parts of the eastern bank should be held at all costs. Israel's initial inability to dislodge the Egyptian forces meant that the war became one of attrition along the canal, until it managed to cross it and surround the Egyptian forces. By the time a US- and UN-backed ceasefire was negotiated, on 23 October, Israel's forces not only encircled the main Egyptian force along the canal but they were also on their way towards Cairo. The outcome of the war was a resounding military victory for Israel, while at the same time also providing Sadat with a surprising much-needed success – his forces were on the east bank of the canal.

More than anything else, the war and its aftermath exposed the degree to which Israel had become reliant on American financial and military support. During the war, the US provided Israel with 22,000 tons of military equipment, one-and-a-half times the combined Soviet military aid to Egypt and Syria.[71] In the aftermath of the war, Israel's military and financial dependence on the US only increased. The military support provided by the US in the period leading up to the war averaged $400 million a year; this sum grew to $1.5 billion a year during the years 1974–75 – 'fully 42% of Israel's defence spending'.[72] This unhealthy state of dependency was not lost on the American administration. It became apparent, in particular to Kissinger, that they could turn this situation to their advantage by bringing Egypt, as well as Jordan, to the negotiating table in the full knowledge that they could secure Israeli territorial concessions.[73]

The Fourteen-Point Document

The Yom Kippur War had a 'traumatic effect on the Labour Party and throughout Israeli society', leading to a crisis of confidence in the party's leadership.[74] The months following the war were characterised by 'shock and recrimination';[75] the deep sense of public anger and frustration were channelled through protest movements, which were initially composed of army reservists returning from the battlefield. The public accused the leadership letting down the nation by being caught off guard, by mismanaging the period leading up to the war and being complicit in the death of thousands of Israeli soldiers, and demanded their resignation. Dayan – more than any other leader – was held responsible for the failures of the war.[76] The protest movements' demands that those responsible for the *'Mehdal'* (the blunder) be brought to justice led to the establishment of an investigative committee headed by Shimon Agranat (the Chief Justice of the Supreme Court). The committee, established in November 1973, would publish its first report in April 1974 – four months after the elections took place.

The growing public resentment was not the only obstacle faced by the Labour Party in the run-up to the 1973 elections. The war had provided discontented members of the party with an opportunity to speak out against policies, in particular those relating to the OT, with which they did not agree. Dayan and the Galili Document were held up as symbols of a party that had lost its way. For the first time since the Lavon affair, senior party members were openly challenged and asked to resign. On 25 October, Shapira called for the resignation of Dayan, blaming him for Israel's 'lack of preparedness' at the outbreak of the war; Shapira later resigned following Meir's decision to support Dayan.[77] Shapira expressed his frustration at the hard-line policies adopted. He blamed the party's leadership for making promises to promote territorial concessions while, in practice, hoping that the territories, 'if not all of them, then at least a large portion of them' would be 'annexed, or integrated, or united with the state of Israel'.[78] A group comprising former army officers spoke for many in the party, when they called for the party's political and military policies to be revised. They referred to the Galili Document as 'irrelevant', and asked whether it was possible 'to go to elections with the present leadership and policy'.[79]

The simmering feeling of discontent in the party finally erupted, during the Central Committee's vote on a new electoral platform – referred to as the Fourteen-Point Document. One after another, senior members of Mapai, as well as several from Ahdut-Ha'avoda, expressed their support for the new document while retracting their support from the Galili Document, claiming they had voted for it only to prevent a split in the party. Haim Tzadok (Chairman of the KFDC), claimed that the Yom Kippur War made it clear that the Galili Document was based on political misconceptions.[80] Allon reminded party members that the Galili Document was adopted in order to 'save' the party from a more radical document which 'Moshe Dayan tried to force upon it'. Allon asserted that the document was not relevant to Israel's needs when it was voted on, and is 'probably irrelevant to our current situation'.[81]

The new platform, drafted by Eban, was an attempt to 'negate the concessions made to Dayan and Galili and redress the balance of power within the party, in the aftermath of the war'.[82] In this respect, the new document represented a clear shift away from Dayan's policies. The document did not – with the exception of Jerusalem – mention any area as being 'indispensable to Israel'.[83] Additionally, it refrained from mentioning any of the urban and industrial centres, which had been planned to be built. For the first time, a document drafted by Israeli decision-makers discussed the rights of the Palestinians and tried to address the Palestinian problem, and, in that sense, broke new ground.[84] Moreover, the document indicated a willingness to offer territorial concessions in exchange for peace.

The Fourteen-Point Document stated, among other things, that:

- Israel would strive towards peace agreements based on territorial compromises that would provide it with secure borders.
- Israel would not return to the pre-war borders.
- 'The Jewish nature of the state of Israel' must be protected 'in order for it to fulfil its Zionist destiny'.
- Israel would strive to achieve a peace agreement with Jordan based on the concept of two independent states.

- Israel rejected the notion of a Palestinian state in the West Bank.
- The rights of the Palestinians to self-determination could only occur within a Jordanian-Palestinian state.
- Israel would continue to establish and expand settlements with particular emphasis on its security needs.[85]

At the end of a particularly fiery session, calls were made for the party to revoke the Galili Document. Sapir, fearing the rejection of the document would create a terminal schism within the party, claimed there was no need to revoke the document. Instead, he decided to leave the party with two contradictory documents. Dayan interpreted the move as neither the sanctioning of the new document nor the revoking of the Galili Document.[86] Meir demanded a vote and accused Sapir of not solving the party's problems with his actions but making things worse. Yadlin, instructed by Sapir to find a bureaucratic loophole, stated that a vote was unnecessary, as the party's Secretariat decision (the Galili Document) could not be changed by the Central Committee (the Fourteen-Point Document).[87] Meir, desperate to cement her position within the party, and clearly upset with Sapir's decision, requested a vote of confidence in her candidacy. Despite requests for a secret ballot, Yadlin decided to have a vote by a show of hands; in the end, 291 voted in favour, 33 opposed and 17 abstained.[88] However, the vote was anything *but* a vote of confidence as half of the 615 members left the meeting before the vote, arguably because of the late hour.[89] The party had once again decided not to decide.

The 1973 elections

The 1973 elections were held later than scheduled because of the Yom Kippur War. The elections were unique in there being two electoral campaigns: a pre-war campaign in which domestic issues dominated the agenda, and a post-war campaign that focused on peace and security.[90] The participation rate – the second-lowest in Israeli history – reflected the fact that the public was still in a state of shock and that many reservists were still on duty. The Labour Party, despite the fact that it was headed by Meir and Dayan, managed to remain Israel's dominant party, albeit with its lowest ever share of the votes.

On the political right, through a series of mergers, a new force emerged: the Likud. The Likud won 39 seats, while the Labour Party won 51 – losing 10 seats over the previous two elections. These results reflected a general shift to the right and indicated a change in Israel's political system from a dominant-party to a two-party system. Labour's loss of seats forced the party to form a government with a nominal majority of two seats – the smallest majority it had ever held.

In addition to its weak parliamentary base, the new government was further constrained in its ability to formulate policies by two important developments: the generational and ideological change within the National Religious Party (NRP), and Israel's growing military and diplomatic dependency on the US. The NRP had been Mapai's, and subsequently the Labour Party's, preferred coalition partner, due to its size and policies, that is, a medium-size moderate religious party with middle-of-the-road views on foreign affairs and security matters. As a result of the changes the NRP had undergone, its new leadership demanded a firm commitment that there would be no withdrawal from the West Bank as a minimum condition for joining the coalition.[91] Meir, after a lengthy negotiation period with the NRP, and in order to secure a working majority, pledged that any agreement on a territorial compromise in the West Bank would lead to new general elections.[92] In reality, this pledge – and the additional ministerial seats procured by the NRP – represented a clear change in the balance of power within the coalition and in the government's approach towards the OT.

The elections were held against a backdrop of 'unprecedented' American involvement in the region. Kissinger, who had taken over as secretary of state, brought with him new diplomatic methods, that is, step-by-step and shuttle diplomacy. The American involvement and Kissinger's new approach yielded early dividends. Kissinger, under the cover of an international peace conference, set the stage for direct talks between Israel and Egypt. These talks culminated in a disengagement agreement signed on 18 January 1974. The agreement proved to be similar in nature to Dayan's interim agreement proposal, with its success highlighting Kissinger's new approach and the magnitude of the American administration's previous diplomatic failures. It also demonstrated that when the US applied sustained pressure, while providing enough incentives, it could alter Israel's policies. One could only guess what would have happened had the US put its full weight behind the Israeli-Egyptian interim agreement in 1971 or the negotiations with Jordan.

Meir's meeting with Hussein

In the aftermath of the Yom Kippur War, Jordan hoped to be rewarded for its neutrality and diplomatic stance: Hussein had refused to join

Egypt and Syria and personally warned Israel of the impending attack (Israeli leaders chose not to heed his warning). Yet, lingering doubts persisted on the Jordanian side regarding Israel's willingness to negotiate and the real purpose of a peace conference organised by the Americans. The conference, they believed, was a cover for American efforts to bring about an Israeli-Egyptian agreement.[93] In order not to be left out of the diplomatic process and keen to reach an agreement with Israel, Hussein and Prime Minister Rifai met with Meir and Dayan. The meeting (held on 26 January 1974) revolved around Jordan's proposal for a parallel disengagement process and the return of Jordanian civil administration to those areas vacated by Israel.[94]

Hussein warned that Israel would be left to negotiate with the Palestine Liberation Organisation (PLO) if it failed to reach an agreement with Jordan. Rifai explained that Jordan was taking a risk by trying to secure a peace agreement with Israel. Instead, it could just 'disassociate' itself from the process and support the PLO, which had received the backing of most Arab states; this, he added, would 'please the Arabs and get everyone off our backs'.[95] Meir challenged the Jordanian assertion that the Palestinians would come to view the PLO as their representatives. Hussein replied that they might not do so at present, but if Jordan disengaged from the West Bank 'it will not be Israel that they will look to'.[96] Meir's comments indicated that Israeli leaders were generally out of step with the desires of the people they occupied.

Rifai proposed a step-by-step disengagement that would be negotiated 'as we went along'. Rifai called on Israel to withdraw parallel to the Jordan River, which would include dismantling settlements and military positions along the river and the setting up of a Jordanian civil administration. According to Rifai, this plan would 'put an end to any possibility of the theory of a Palestinian state'.[97] Dayan, after questioning Rifai's plan, inquired 'If we asked for the proposal for the real and sincere and final peace settlement, what would it be?' Rifai suggested two kinds of agreements: a contractual peace agreement based on the pre-war borders with some 'rectifications' and including Arab sovereignty over East Jerusalem 'but with a new status to it'; or another agreement based on phases, where the line 'can vary from month to month' without a need for contractual agreement and based on a de facto peace. Meir questioned whether the second suggestion would eventually lead to 'the reestablishment of the 4 June Line', to which Rifai answered: 'Yes!'[98]

Unhappy with Rifai's suggestions, Meir proposed the Allon Plan as a framework for the disengagement process, initially only in the Jericho area. She explained that even this would be difficult for her to implement, as she was in the midst of coalition negotiations, which might lead to new elections. Dayan, expounding on the idea, suggested that 'the Allon Plan or something like that' would be the maximum the Labour Party could agree to.[99] The plan suggested by Meir and Dayan was the same as that proposed by Allon (in October 1970) which they rejected. However, it is reasonable to believe that, even if Hussein had accepted the basic tenets of the proposal, Meir – because of the NRP, the internal divisions within the Labour Party and her weak parliamentary base – would choose not to approve the agreement for fear of fresh elections. This raises the question of what kind of agreement Meir and Dayan would have been willing to risk new elections for.

Dayan asked whether Jordan could envision a situation in which Israel maintained its military positions in the West Bank. Meir quickly added that Israel would be willing to lease the land for the military bases. Rifai suggested that Jordan might be able to agree to some limited military presence, but what was important was the purpose behind it.[100] Hussein added that he could live with an Israeli radar position, or something of that sort, on some hill tops: 'In a state of peace, this is something we can live with.'[101] Rifai articulated Jordan's position: 'If Israel wants territory, expansion, corridor here and corridor there and positions and settlements ...' then 'it [will be] impossible for His Majesty and for us to accept any settlement on those lines'. He explained that if Israel did not withdraw, it would eventually be stuck with Arafat.[102]

Dayan suggested that Israel withdraw from the Jericho area, which would provide Jordan with a corridor into the West Bank, to which Rifai asked, 'What is your hang-up on the river itself. It isn't much of a barrier, you know.' Rifai proceeded to explain that he did not see 'any great cost to Israel if it withdraws 5 or 10 or 15km from the Jordan Valley'.[103] Hussein, unable to understand Dayan's fixation with the river, asked whether Israel had in fact any military bases there to which Dayan replied, 'Very, very close to it.'[104] In fact, Israel had established its military bases in accordance with Dayan's plan on the mountain ranges. Meir suggested allowing Jordanian civil administration to be exercised over some of the West Bank population centres. Hussein and Rifai agreed, provided that it was linked to the first stage of the disengagement process. Both refused to 'be sucked into' a plan that had all the hallmarks of the Functional Solution. Meir tried to explain that she could not go to the government and suggest a disengagement plan when both sides were not engaged in any fighting: 'People would laugh at me.' Rifai, in a jovial manner, asked Meir, 'Must we go to war in order to be taken seriously? Do you want us to fight so that you can with-draw?'[105] Towards the end of the meeting, Dayan once again explained that the Allon Plan was the most Israel could agree to. Rifai explained that Jordan would not consider the Allon Plan:

> if we are going to start playing with the West Bank and we give you one part of the valley and we keep this here and this here ... We would much rather, honestly, have you keep the whole lot. And there won't be any peace, there won't be any settlement.[106]

The meeting with Hussein summed up Meir's approach towards the OT in general, and the West Bank in particular. After five years in power, Meir was unable to articulate Israel's preferred approach towards the OT. While Hussein appeared to acknowledge and address Israeli con-cerns, Meir and Dayan were fixated on plans they had either previ-ously rejected or had never approved, and which they knew Hussein could not accept. On the one hand, Meir and the kitchenette pursued a Jordanian approach based on the Allon Plan; while, on the other hand, they allowed Dayan to implement his Functional Solution and promote Palestinian self-rule, thus undermining Jordan's position in the West Bank and the Allon Plan. It is interesting to note that Meir once claimed to favour a Functional Solution over a territorial solution with Jordan.[107] The Israeli government under Meir did not only take a decision not to decide, it was also undermining its own initiatives and plans. This is why 'disjointed incrementalism' offers the best characterisation of ter-ritorial decision-making under Meir. It is evident that the Meir govern-ment was incrementally creating facts on the ground and altering the status of the OT; this did not add up to a coherent policy, however.

On 2 April 1974, the Agranat Committee published its provisional report on the Yom Kippur War. In its report, the committee criticised the conduct of AMAN and called for the dismissal of its senior ranks. More importantly, the committee held Chief-of-Staff El'azar directly responsible for the blunders. However, in a move that provoked widespread condemnation, the committee absolved Meir and Dayan of responsibility.[108] On 10 April, Meir – standing in front of party members, and in response to growing criticism[109] – announced her resignation, 'I cannot bear this yoke any longer ... I have reached the end of the road.'[110]

7
Hand Picked

Yitzhak Rabin

The collapse of the Meir government left the Labour Party in a difficult situation. Its popularity had diminished as a consequence of the war and the reputation of its veteran leadership was tarnished. In order to fill the leadership vacuum, and fearing new elections and a renewed succession battle, the party needed to find a compromise candidate behind which to unite.[1] The party's main candidate, Sapir, had made it clear that he would not accept the nomination. Due to Sapir's unwillingness, several names were mentioned: Allon, Eban and Transport Minister Shimon Peres – who had the backing of Rafi. Both Eban and Allon were informed that the party would not support their nomination: no faction would back Eban and nominating Allon could have caused Rafi to withdraw from the party. In the absence of a unifying figure, Sapir and Mapai turned to Yitzhak Rabin – whom Allon and Ahdut-Ha'avoda agreed to support.[2] Rabin appeared to be the perfect candidate – from Sapir and Mapai's perspective. The reputation of the former chief-of-staff, and ambassador to the US, was not tainted by the war, and he had managed to maintain his national hero status for his role in the Six Day War. Moreover, Rabin received wide support among the electorate and was seen as one of Labour's most promising politicians.

For the first time in its history, the Labour Party put forward two candidates: Peres and Rabin. Both had known each other for many years but had little respect for one another. Peres, during his time as deputy defence minister, successfully blocked Rabin's appointment as chief-of-staff. He viewed Rabin as an unsuitable future prime minister because he lacked any political experience.[3] Rabin's attitude towards Peres did not differ by much; he suspected that Peres was behind Ben-Gurion's early decision not to promote him to chief-of-staff. Additionally, he resented the fact that Peres was not a military man and considered him unsuitable to lead.[4] The Central Committee convened on 22 April to vote for its new party leader and future prime minister by a secret ballot. The primary contest was marred by allegations regarding both candidates' character. Rabin won the nomination, albeit by a small majority of 298 to 254; Rabin's narrow victory put him in a difficult situation within the party. Based on Peres' strong showing, Rafi threatened to withdraw its support for the new government if Peres was not chosen as the next defence minister; Rabin had initially nominated Allon,[5] and he would later claim that he reluctantly accepted Peres.[6] In order to placate Allon and Ahdut-Ha'avoda, Rabin made him foreign minister, while deposing Eban, with whom Rabin did not have a good working relationship during his term as ambassador to the US.[7] This may explain why some of Mapai's veterans, most notably Eban, supported Peres in his battles with Rabin.

Rabin's first task was to form a coalition government. The National Religious Party (NRP) – influenced by its young guard – decided against joining the government. Thus, the Alignment (the Labour Party and Mapam) was forced to settle on a minority government, which included the centrist Independent Liberal Party (headed by Tourism Minister Kol) and the new left-wing Citizens' Rights Movement (headed by former Labour Party member Shulamit Aloni). Holding only 58 seats (in a 120-seat parliament), Rabin's government was the weakest in Israel's history. In order to address his weak parliamentary base, Rabin announced that, at some point in the future, the NRP would be invited to join the government.

The Rabin government, without a working majority and with a neophyte for prime minister, was at a disadvantage from day one. It lacked veteran political heavyweights, with the exception of Allon and Minister-without-Portfolio Galili, as most of the Labour Party's founding generation withdrew: Sapir decided to retire from politics and passed away the following year. Additionally, Rabin was not a member of a party faction and therefore suffered from the lack of a solid party base.[8] This lack of support meant that Rabin could not count on any of the factions and had to operate on the basis of consensual politics.[9] The government's decision-making process was bound to be fragmented because of the uneasy working relationship between Rabin, Peres and, to a lesser degree, Allon. The relationship among the triumvirate (Rabin, Peres and Allon) threatened to return the government to the decision-making immobilisation that reigned under Eshkol.[10] The ability of this new government to agree or decide on the future of the Occupied Territory (OT) was thus severely hampered from the start.

Syria and the Golan Heights

On 31 May 1974, Israel and Syria signed a separation-of-forces agreement, in what was to be the last act of the outgoing Meir government. The agreement included an Israeli withdrawal from Syrian territories it had conquered during the Yom Kippur War and several smaller areas it had held since the Six Day War.[11] Israel's acceptance of the separation-of-forces agreement created a precedent with regard to the Golan Heights. Until that moment, Israeli politicians of all political persuasions accepted the notion that Israel would remain indefinitely in the Golan Heights. The driving force behind Israel's acceptance of the agreement with Syria was US mediation. But it is also true that Israel's acceptance of the agreement was due to its desire to stop the war of attrition that broke out on its northern border in the aftermath of the Yom Kippur War, and its desire to conclude a prisoners of war exchange deal with Syria[12] – Syrian President Hafez al-Assad tied in the exchange of prisoners to the agreement. However, in order to conclude the agreement, Israel required the assistance of Kissinger and American assurances and guarantees.[13] Furthermore, Israel only agreed to sign the agreement once it was told by Kissinger that Assad had sent him a secret letter agreeing to prevent attacks from Syrian territory into Israel.[14] According to Allon, the agreement had more to do with Israeli relations with the US than with Syria.[15]

From Israel's perspective, it became apparent that Assad would not sign a peace agreement for less than a full Israeli withdrawal from all the territories occupied and a solution to the Palestinian refugee problem.[16] This was a price Israel was not willing to pay. Kissinger made it clear that the US did not view the new line (the separation-of-forces agreement line) as the final border between the sides.[17] However, Israel concluded that it could not afford to withdraw from large parts of the Golan Heights without risking Israel's national security. Because of the perceived belligerent and radical nature of the Syrian regime, ministers were advised to put the idea of negotiating with Syria on hold, and shift their attention to negotiations with Egypt and Jordan instead.[18]

Since the 'War of Independence', Israel had viewed Syria as its most belligerent enemy. Leading up to the Yom Kippur War, Syria had refused to negotiate with Israel either directly or through mediation. Therefore, the future status of the Golan Heights did not come up during either the

Jarring Mission or Israeli-American discussions. Israel initially viewed the Golan as a bargaining chip in its 19 June decisions. Its subsequent reluctance to withdraw can be attributed to Syrian intransigence and changes to Israel's perceived strategic imperatives. It was widely believed that Israel's position, on top of the Golan mountain ranges, 60 km from Damascus, provided strategic depth and a constant deterrent.[19] In addition, it provided Israel with the ability to protect its main water sources and its northern region from Syrian and Palestinian attacks.[20] Syria's refusal to negotiate and its activities against Israeli interests, coupled with Israel's strategic imperatives, meant that public and political opinion in Israel was steadfast against making any concessions in the Golan.[21]

Early development plans for the Golan set very ambitious targets, presupposing the area would remain under Israel's control. The plans estimated a Jewish population of about 45,000–50,000 within ten years, in addition to the development of industrial and tourist centres.[22] However, these plans never materialised. By 1973 the total population of the Golan Heights was only 1300, including several hundred Nahal soldiers, concentrated in three main settlement clusters in the southern region of the Golan. These were small agricultural-based settlements, in an area rich in resources and close to the settlers' base of the Upper Galilee region. Outside the southern region there were only six settlements, of which only one was in the central region – the most important area strategically.[23] Furthermore, the settlements suffered from a lack of adequate funding; this problem was brought up by the settlers[24] and by Knesset members.[25] In short, despite the fact that there was both a national and a political consensus about keeping the Golan Heights, Israel's settlements policy neither matched its rhetoric (its desire to remain in the territory indefinitely) nor its strategic needs (controlling the central region).

There are two main reasons why the development and settlement of the Golan Heights did not match the political rhetoric. First, settlement activity in the region was beset by many logistical and technical problems, for example, the lack of water supply, scarcity of suitable agricultural land, harsh topographical conditions and lack of infrastructure.[26] The second and most important factor was the American diplomatic stance towards Syria. Israel could neither annex the Golan nor heavily develop the region without drawing the ire of the US. An example of US influence on Israel in this matter can be found in Meir's secret peace plan of 1970. As a consequence of US pressure during the Rogers talks, Israel was willing to agree, in principle, to withdraw from up to a third of the territory.

In the aftermath of the Yom Kippur War, the government came to the conclusion that it had to anchor its presence in the Golan Heights. It was therefore concluded that Israel must increase the number of settlements and allocate more resources to the development of the region.[27] In addition, Israel feared that the US would use the fact that the central region was largely empty to demand concessions there.[28] This prompted new development plans which aimed to settle the central region and increase investment.[29] In its first few weeks in office, the Rabin government agreed to expand and strengthen Israel's presence in the Golan by constructing an urban centre (Katzerin), an industrial area and an additional agricultural settlement in the central region.[30] Yet, despite these efforts, the government had to scale down its plans because of logistical problems, the ongoing negotiations with Syria, Egypt and Jordan, and its desire to avoid antagonising the US. Additionally, most politicians assumed that the Golan would remain under Israel's control and therefore saw no need to hasten settlement activity there, 'There was no need to create facts on the ground.'[31] It did not help that Israel's housing minister at the time, Avraham Ofer, was known as a moderate and as one who was against large-scale works that would harm peace negotiations.[32] Another important factor inhibiting Israel's policy was the local Druze population. The precedent created by the disengagement agreement with Syria and Egypt changed irrevocably the attitude of the Druze population towards Israel, who expected the region would return to Syria in the near future. Once seen as natural allies – at one stage its leaders even appeared to support the idea of an Israeli annexation[33] – the Druze community became vocal, though non-violent, opponents of Israel's occupation.[34] It is therefore not a surprise that, despite the government's intentions, the population and development of the Golan Heights did not increase much under Rabin. Nevertheless, despite refusing to annex the territory and vowing to keep its diplomatic options open, the incremental decisions taken by successive governments – in particular the increased development of the central region by the Rabin government – were moving Israel towards a de facto annexation of the region.

Jericho First

In June 1974, the new government stated its foreign policy approach: it declared its willingness to hold direct negotiations without preconditions in order to bring about peace agreements. These agreements would be based on territorial compromises that would provide Israel with secure and recognised borders. Until such agreements were reached, Israel would continue to remain on the ceasefire lines.[35] The government also made clear its intentions with regard to Jordan; it concluded that an agreement with Jordan was the only viable solution for the West Bank, and would be based on an Israeli state, with Jerusalem as its capital, and a Jordanian-Palestinian state, where the political aspirations of the Palestinians would be fulfilled. Furthermore, it decided not to negotiate with 'terrorist organisations [Palestine Liberation Organisation – PLO] whose sole purpose is the destruction of the state of Israel'.[36]

In reality, Israel's intentions towards Jordan were slightly different. It sought to normalise relations with Jordan in order to reach a de facto peace, which would include a nominal Jordanian presence in the West Bank (as long as it did not infringe upon Israel's security) in order to limit the influence of the PLO. Israel believed that, if this objective was met, the possibility of peace between the two states, whether based on a Functional Solution or a territorial compromise, would be enhanced.[37] The resumption of the debate on Israel's intentions for the OT, which had been stifled under Meir, once again exposed stark differences among ministers regarding Jordan and the West Bank, and illustrated the problems it faced in formulating a strategic policy: Allon favoured an agreement based on his plan; Peres pressed for a Functional Solution; and Rabin favoured a combination of elements from the two plans.[38] In light of this, it is not a surprise that the government adopted a tentative approach towards Jordan.

Allon believed that the best way to advance relations would be through an interim agreement based on his plan. This, he thought, would lead to a permanent peace between the two states and would link the West Bank with Jordan.[39] This idea is referred to as the Jericho First plan, because Allon envisioned that it would be initially implemented in the Jericho area.[40] The idea was supported by Kissinger, who pressed Jordan and Israel to accept it. According to Kissinger, Israel had two choices with regard to the West Bank: either negotiate with the Jordanians or deal with the Palestinians; he favoured the former.[41]

In a meeting on 28 August, King Hussein, accompanied by Prime Minister Rifai, proposed to the Israeli triumvirate a disengagement plan along the Jordan River – similar to what he had proposed to Meir in February; Rabin and Peres rejected this. Peres proceeded to propose an agreement along the lines of a Functional Solution. Hussein expressed surprise that, after conducting so many meetings, Israel would come up with an offer 'like that'.[42] Allon, in an attempt to rescue the talks, suggested an Israeli withdrawal from the Jericho area as an interim agreement and the establishment of a Jordanian civilian administration there. Hussein was against that idea; Rifai explained that Hussein would settle either for a disengagement-of-forces agreement along the Jordan River or a complete Israeli withdrawal from the West Bank.[43]

On 19 October, a second meeting between Hussein and the Israeli triumvirate took place. There is some controversy over what exactly occurred during this meeting, as its content has not yet been made public. It is unclear whether Hussein, growing anxious because of an upcoming Arab League summit in Rabat, was willing to reconsider the Jericho First plan. According to Allon, Hussein was inclined to settle for the plan but, because of the proximity of the meeting to the Rabat Summit, chose not to. Allon claimed to have told Hussein that, he would only advise the government to support the plan if Hussein agreed to commit to the plan, regardless of the summit's outcome.[44] According to Shulamit Aloni, however, Hussein agreed to the plan because he wanted to prove, before going to the summit, that he was still the rightful representative of the Palestinian people. The merits of the Jericho First plan were debated in the cabinet, with some uncertainty as to what actually happened during this debate. According to Aloni, ministers debated the plan and then voted to reject it: only Aloni, Transportation Minister Gad Ya'akobi and Information Minister Aharon Yariv voted in favour.[45] This has been denied by Police Minister Shlomo Hillel and Education Minister Aharon Yadlin, who stated that the government did not hold a formal vote on the plan and that the debate never reached the stage where a decision had to be made.[46]

However, ministers agreed that the main reason the plan was not accepted was due to Rabin's desire to include the NRP in his coalition.[47] When asked why the plan was rejected, Rabin replied that a promise had been made to the NRP that any territorial concessions in the West Bank would necessitate either new elections or a referendum. Aloni expressed her amazement that 'a promise made by Meir [who had since resigned] during coalition negotiations [as part of a government that had since resigned] to the NRP [who were not part of the current coalition] should be honoured'.[48] There is some evidence to support Aloni's version of events. Rabin, in a meeting with Mapam members, expressed hope that Hussein would be accepted as the representative of the Palestinians in Rabat, but that he would not call for elections over Jericho. Rabin stated that an agreement with Jordan was not feasible at the time, and stressed the importance of focusing on Egypt, believing that doing so would also lead to a breakthrough with Jordan.[49]

In the ensuing summit in Rabat, the Arab League passed a resolution accepting the PLO as the sole representative of the Palestinian people. The resolution was passed unanimously – even Hussein resigned himself to supporting it – despite considerable American pressure on several Arab states to support Jordan's position.[50] The summit elevated the international stature of the PLO and helped to highlight the Palestinian question. It is unclear whether or not Hussein pursued an interim agreement based on the Jericho First plan. It is also unclear whether an agreement with Israel would have changed the outcome of the summit. However, it is clear that Rabin had decided to pursue an interim agreement with Egypt first and deferred negotiations with Jordan to a later stage. This decision was taken with a desire to broaden his parliamentary base in mind, and was possibly due to the lack of American pressure for an interim agreement with Jordan. It could be argued that Kissinger could have applied pressure on Hussein to lower his expectations and on Israel to show more flexibility, but Kissinger was more interested in the Egyptian track.

The government was also deeply divided on the subject of territorial compromises in the West Bank. The doves were in favour of territorial compromises beyond the Allon Plan, the majority of the ministers favoured a territorial compromise along the lines of the plan, while others – most notably Peres – were arguing for a Functional Solution. The inability of the government to reach a common position on the matter, regardless of whether it would have been accepted by Hussein, attests to its lack of a policy towards the West Bank. As if to confirm this, Allon claimed that Rabin's promise to the NRP was not as big a problem as Rabin imagined it to be and could have been easily overcome.[51] Additionally, the missed opportunity highlighted the continual failure among dovish politicians to have any influence on Israel's territorial policies.

The NRP

One of the main reasons behind Rabin's rejection of the Jericho First plan, and his government's lack of policy, was his desire to include the NRP in the coalition. On 30 October 1974, and on the heels of the Rabat Summit, the NRP joined the government, which prompted the resignation of Aloni's Citizen's Rights Movement. Rabin's decision to broaden his parliamentary base followed months of negotiations with the NRP and the other coalition members, to which Aloni was not invited.[52] This explains why Mapam and the Independent Liberal Party, which favoured the Jordanian track, did not push the government on the

Jericho First plan, even though Mapam's leaders stated that a settlement with Jordan was necessary.[53] Negotiations between the Labour Party and Mapam regarding the NRP shed light on the relationship between the government's handling of the territorial policy and its inner politics. Rabin explained to Mapam that he had reached an agreement with the NRP and, as a result, could not make any substantial decisions regarding the OT. Rabin added that, with regard to the West Bank, he did not foresee any serious developments taking place before the next general elections.[54] Rabin promised the NRP that the government would allow settlements in all the land of Israel, while assuring Mapam and the Independent Liberal Party that they could abstain or vote against any such decisions.[55]

The coalition negotiation process revealed deep anxieties within the Alignment regarding the NRP. The NRP was presented as a 'Trojan horse' that would sideline Mapam and the peace process while serving the interests of the Likud.[56] However, others within the Alignment called for the inclusion of the NRP in order to heal a growing national rift over religious matters, and as a way of avoiding the possible future collaboration between radical nationalism [Likud] and a radical religious movement [NRP].[57] The fears expressed regarding the inclusion of the NRP – a former perennial coalition partner known for its diplomatic and religious pragmatism – were a result of the changes that occurred within the NRP during the previous decade.

In the aftermath of the Six Day War, Israel had witnessed a period of religious revivalism. This manifested itself in the growing importance attached to religion in everyday and political life. However, this change was not a result of the war, but built upon demographic and institutional changes that had been brewing for many years, among them the growth of religious education; high birth-rates among religious communities; and the influx of Jewish immigrants from Arab countries with a religious attachment.[58] These changes also brought about the inclusion of new factions in the NRP – already preoccupied with faction-based politics – and in particular the emergence of a young guard led by Zevulon Hammer. Within this competitive system the emergence of the young guard proved to be a deciding factor.[59] The young guard demanded a more active role in the management of the party, and a change to the party's traditional policies of alliance with Mapai, religious status quo and neutrality in foreign affairs. In addition, the growth of religious nationalism and a general shift to the right among the electorate forced the NRP to secure its electoral base against the incursions of the Likud, which, in turn, strengthened the young guard.[60]

The generational debate within the NRP took on a new dimension with the acquisition of the OT, in particular the West Bank.[61] The territorial issue thus became entangled within an evolving religious debate.[62] The young guard refused to support a Labour Party that was willing to withdraw from the West Bank.[63] Therefore, in order to avoid alienating the young guard and wishing to preserve unity, the old guard avoided making decisions on the territorial issue.[64] Although not a major factor, the unwillingness of the NRP to make controversial decisions on the OT also contributed to Israel's lack of clear policy under both Eshkol and Meir.

The Yom Kippur War further strengthened the religious sentiment among the young guard that it was necessary to retain the OT.[65] As a result, in the 1973 elections, the NRP tied in its participation in the coalition with the government's territorial policies. Interestingly, this represented the first time that Religious Zionism or, for that matter, nationalist or religious sentiments, were presented as the main reason for supporting a particular position regarding Israel's territorial policy. Moreover, the party's decision to join the Rabin government was only approved by a narrow margin. The decision was severely criticised by the young guard, who decided to remain in the opposition, essentially splitting the party, and by many of Israel's leading rabbis, despite Rabin's promises regarding the West Bank.[66] The young guard's identification with the concept of greater Israel and with the settlers' movement was most apparent in the formation and activities of Gush Emunim – 'the Bloc of the Faithful'.

Gush Emunim

Gush Emunim has been characterised as the 'tip of the iceberg': a small, radical, ideologically motivated group that arose out of a larger social context and therefore enjoyed broader public support than was initially apparent.[67] It is not the intention of this book to either explain or define Religious Zionism, or to rationalise the resurgence of nationalist and religious fervour during the period researched; what is of interest is the effect that individuals and groups associated with Religious Zionism had on Israel's territorial policy.

The outcome of the Six Day War was a predictable one for Rabbi Tzvi Yehuda Cook, the son of Avraham Hacohen Cook, Israel's first Ashkenazi chief rabbi and leader of the Religious Zionist movement. His father had compared the establishment of the state of Israel to the beginning of the time of redemption. The Six Day War was seen as a direct validation of this process.[68] For Cook, it was the beginning of the messianic age, the return of the Jewish people to the land of Israel: 'We have just returned to the elevations of holiness and our holy city. We shall never move out of here.'[69] The immediate manifestation of this revelation was most apparent to a small group encompassing the young guard of the NRP and the students of Cook's 'Merkaz Harav' *yeshiva* – from where most of the Hebron and Gush Etzion settlers came. They believed that the government was not fulfilling its role in this era of redemption and took it upon themselves to do so, first in Gush Etzion and Hebron and later in Kiryat Arba. They found that the government – torn apart internally – was standing in their way. The group perceived Zionism as being associated with the creation of settlements on the land of Israel, as did early Labour Party members. However, for them the notion of settling the land of Israel was not only a Zionist mission but also a religious imperative; by settling the land of Israel they were redeeming their souls.[70] Thus, they attributed the Yom Kippur War to the government's insufficient settlement drive, which led them to found Gush Emunim.[71]

Gush Emunim considered the territories, in particular the West Bank, as part of the land of Israel. This view attributed neither a strategic nor a bargaining value to the OT.[72] For Gush Emunim there was no reason to negotiate with an Arab world bent on destroying Israel. This fear of annihilation by the Arab world, combined with a sense of religious justification, resulted in a rejection of the politics of the 'gentile world'.[73] The group rejected the internal Israeli political system as a force for a change, arguing instead for a bottom-up grassroots approach. They were supported in their endeavours by many politicians from the opposition, including Begin and Sharon. In addition, they were supported by followers of Tabenkin, who admired them for being the pioneers of a new generation and shared much of their Zionist zeal.[74] Moreover, even prominent left-wing politicians admired their zeal, which reminded them of the early Zionist pioneers.[75]

Gush Emunim initially tried to lobby the government for more settlements across the West Bank but with little success.[76] Rabin stated that settlement projects would only correspond to government policies. Attempts by Gush Emunim to settle independently in the West Bank, and once in the Golan Heights, were unsuccessful. The government's refusal to allow the group to settle, and their forced eviction from sites, caused the group to view the government as illegitimate and immoral. For them, the actions of a government that deprived its people of their 'God given right' to settle were akin to those of the British Mandate's 'White Book' policies.[77]

For the first time since the attempt by Rabbi Levinger's group to settle Hebron, the government faced a group that was bent on influencing its settlement policies. Gush Emunim not only offered an alternative to the government's policy, they actively implemented one.[78] The government was thus faced with a determined and growing movement, which opposed its settlement policy and which was encouraged and supported by a broad section of society, opposition politicians and even members of the Labour Party. The group took upon itself the task of expanding settlement activities to areas outside of the mandate of the Allon Plan. Outside the publicised settlement attempts by Gush Emunim, several low-key attempts were made; two of them proved highly successful and signalled the end of the Allon Plan as the government's rough settlement concept.

Ma'ale Adumim

Ma'ale Adumim represented the first clear example of Gush Emunim's impact on the government's settlement plans. The idea of establishing a settlement in the area of Ma'ale Adumim had first been raised by Allon in 1968, but the exact location of the project had remained obscure and was described as being in the vicinity of Jericho.[79] Although Allon had described the project as one which would help fulfil Israel's diplomatic and security objectives,[80] it was still rejected by the Eshkol government. One of the main issues regarding Ma'ale Adumim was that establishing a settlement in the area would divide the West Bank by narrowing the strip of land in the Jerusalem–Jericho corridor. Therefore, the decision over whether to establish a settlement in the area was not taken lightly by either the Eshkol or the Meir governments.

As part of a discussion regarding the expansion of Jerusalem's municipal boundaries under Meir, an ad hoc committee had been established to look at future industrial sites. The committee advised the government to appropriate lands to the east and north of the city, because these represented suitable sites for future industrial areas.[81] The committee decided to start development in one of those areas – a site to the east of the city named Ma'ale Adumim. In addition, Galili advised the government to allow the Israel Land Authority (ILA) to support the effort by purchasing additional lands in the area.[82] Allon, being the head of the Ministerial Committee for Jerusalem and in charge of land appropriation, wrote that most ministers had already gathered that the area would eventually become an urban settlement.[83] He went on to say that this was the reason why several ministers were against the project, but supported the government's decision to establish an industrial area nonetheless. [84]

On 28 August 1974, during a Ministerial Settlement Committee (MSC) meeting, Galili raised again the idea of settling in the Ma'ale Adumim area. Galili explained that the government had not yet decided what to do with the area, but was considering using it as an industrial area for Jerusalem. According to Galili, the area would initially serve as a storage facility for the army, but would be later transformed into an urban settlement. He told the committee that several private investors were willing to invest money in the project at a minimum cost to the taxpayer.[85]

The idea of creating an industrial area in Ma'ale Adumim infuriated Yehiel Admoni, who succeeded Weitz as the head of the Settlement Department. From Admoni's perspective, the project was outside the scope of the Allon Plan. However, because the exact parameters of the plan were never agreed upon and remained vague, it allowed for the inclusion of areas that were not originally part of the plan, in particular in the Jerusalem region.[86] Allon, therefore, interpreted the project as being within the scope of his plan. The fact that the head of the Settlement Department was unsure about the exact parameters of the plan highlights the fact that the Allon Plan was more of a rough guideline or concept than a detailed plan or policy.

One of the most important facts behind the creation of Ma'ale Adumim was the level of collaboration between Galili and Gush Emunim. Demant argues – and this is backed by reports in the Israeli press – that Galili and the head of the ILA, Meir Zore'a (a supporter of the Land of Israel Movement), had extensive dealings with Gush Emunim. It is important to note that Galili did not always disclose this fact.[87] Arguably, these dealings between Galili, Zore'a, the NRP and Gush Emunim attest to the growing impact individuals and groups associated with Religious Zionism ideology were having on Israel's territorial policies. Demant goes on to argue that the decision to establish an industrial site in the area, and the subsequent decision to allow members of Gush Emunim to settle there, was the product of deals struck with the NRP and Gush Emunim.[88] He also alleges that the project was promised to the NRP by Rabin as part of the coalition bargaining process.[89]

On 24 November, the government agreed to develop Ma'ale Adumim as an industrial area for Jerusalem. Hillel explains that the decision was taken in light of the need to create facts on the ground in response to the Rabat Summit.[90] It was decided that the site would not be used as a civilian settlement and that only those employed in the construction could reside there.[91] This was followed by a decision of the MSC, in consultation with Peres, to establish a work camp in Ma'ale Adumim.[92]

The Ma'ale Adumim project was beset by problems from the start. The most pressing problem was the lack of funds for it.[93] In addition, several prominent politicians were either against the project or were actively undermining it. Housing Minister Ofer was doing his best to delay the project while Labour Member of the Knesset (MK) Yossi Sarid was publicly stating that the government, by investing in the project, was neglecting Israel's developing towns. On top of that, the government was forced to restrict the Settlement Department's involvement in the project after it became apparent that Admoni was acting against it.[94] Admoni's reluctance to support the project may have been due to the project's location or to the involvement of Gush Emunim.[95]

In order to address some of the problematic issues raised by the Ma'ale Adumim project, a special ad hoc ministerial committee was established. In its first meeting in January, Finance Minister Yehushu'a Rabinowitz asked how the government could have authorised a project and made financial commitments when no budget had been allocated and there was a lack of clear plans. Ofer went on to claim that, although the committee was discussing the creation of an industrial site, there was a suspicion that this was intended to be a civilian settlement.[96] It is unclear whether Ofer was aware of Galili's meetings with Gush Emunim and the fact that he allowed them to reside in the area while helping with the construction.[97] Galili explained that, if the government did not develop the area, the far right would. Galili claimed that developing Ma'ale Adumim was an 'ingenious' move to quell some dangerous domestic developments. Rabin backed Galili by stating that, although Sarid was making a fuss, he would only be able to bring tens of people to protest, while the NRP would bring hundreds to support it.[98] These statements by Galili and Rabin raise questions regarding the exact purpose and necessity of the project. Additionally, it further demonstrates that prominent decision-makers were influenced not only by political considerations, but also by individuals and groups associated with Religious Zionist ideology. Furthermore, it would appear that the project was a result of political deals and was not done in response to the needs of the city of Jerusalem.

In a subsequent meeting, ministers continued to debate the project's budget and appeared genuinely unsure as to who was responsible for it. Rabin informed the committee that the Finance Ministry would, 'by hook or by crook', find the appropriate funds. Rabinowitz insisted that the main problem with the settlement was political, and that is why there was a great deal of confusion. Nonetheless, he added, as the decision had been taken by the government, he would comply with it.[99] In the end, the committee decided to establish 25 residential units for 100 settlers/workers at the site.[100] In one particularly revealing episode, Galili – struggling to find money for the project – urged Rabinowitz to allocate funds for the project.[101] Mapam alleged that Galili and Zore'a had allocated money to the project without receiving the government's approval. Leaks of revolts within the government on this issue exposed the complexity of decision-making within a fragmented government.[102]

On the one hand, several ministers, in particular Mapam's, were working to undermine the project.[103] On the other hand, Rabin and Galili were working hard to satisfy the NRP's demands for the project. While Galili claimed that ministers supported the decision to include Ma'ale Adumim in the future boundaries of the state of Israel, the decision to build residential units on the site only passed by a slim majority (11 to 8).[104] The decision – to build a number of residential units for the site workers – appeared to be an attempt to satisfy both the NRP's demand for a civilian settlement and Mapam's opposition to it.[105] The government's inability to agree on a comprehensive settlement policy, and the need to reach a consensus within a divided coalition, forced the government to revert to an incremental mode of decision-making. Thus, the weakness of the dovish ministers, and the growing influence of Gush Emunim and the NRP, contributed to the fact that this far-reaching decision was taken as a political compromise.

Ofra

The growing threat from Gush Emunim was a source for concern within the government. On 26 January 1975, Rabin, Peres, Galili and Hillel met to discuss the illegal activities of Gush Emunim. They agreed to use all means necessary to restrict the movement of its members in the OT and stop any attempts by them to create facts on the ground. Rabin acknowledged that the political reality in Israel had changed as a result of Gush Emunim. He stated that it was a political movement that would not be placated by giving in to their demands. Rabin feared that the government might be unable to deter Gush Emunim from future actions.[106] The meeting also represented the second occasion at which officials mentioned the concessions made to Gush Emunim in Ba'al-Hatzor. This fact was first revealed during the ministerial meeting regarding Ma'ale Adumim, where Peres informed the committee of 700 would-be settlers waiting to settle on the site. Rabin sarcastically replied that he could settle them in the Galilee as opposed to Ba'al-Hatzor.[107]

Ba'al-Hatzor is the highest peak of the Samaria mountain range and was designated as a new army base (in accordance with the Dayan Functional Solution). Under orders from the Defence Ministry, lands were appropriated in the area and construction began in late 1974. Several members of Gush Emunim contacted Moshe Netzer (Peres' settlement advisor and former head of the Nahal) and requested permission to establish a working camp on the site in order to help with the construction. Netzer, acting under the direction of Peres, authorised the request.[108] Peres authorised the move despite the fact that Ba'al-Hatzor was in the midst of a heavily populated area and clearly outside of the parameters of the Allon Plan.

By April 1975 the settlers had established themselves next to the army base and were effectively living on the site; they named their camp/settlement Ofra. According to Netzer, Peres authorised the settlers to remain at the site as a way of cooling Gush Emunim's settlement fervour.[109] Rabin, who was rumoured to have been upset by the incident, authorised Galili to find a solution to the problem. Galili's solution appeared to have been a compromise by which the settlers could remain at the site as long as they supported themselves and their numbers did not exceed 24.[110] This compromise was taken without consulting the cabinet and in full knowledge that most ministers would vote against it.[111] Rabin's actions did not make much sense, unless he shared Peres' assertion that the move would help dampen the settlement zeal of Gush Emunim. As it turned out, Rabin, whether by design or by default, authorised the establishment of the first settlement clearly outside the scope of the Allon Plan.

In June, due to inquiries made by Sarid, knowledge of the settlement became public. Sarid asked how a settlement could be established without a government decision and without anyone knowing anything about it.[112] The truth of the matter is that the decision to allow the settlers to remain in Ofra was taken by Peres[113] – who also ordered the Defence Ministry to support the settlers' effort.[114] Peres had previously met with members of Gush Emunim and had expressed some support for their ideals;[115] he also believed that by supporting Gush Emunim he was acquiring potential political support.[116] Additionally, believing in a Functional Solution, Peres saw no problem with Jews settling in the OT.

Peres' decision to allow Gush Emunim to establish a working camp in Ofra proved to be a turning point for Gush Emunim and for the government. It signalled the first time that a settlement was created without the government's approval or knowledge. In addition, it was the first settlement established outside of the government's supposed parameters, in a heavily populated region of the West Bank. Peres' decision shattered the concept that the government had a comprehensive settlement or territorial policy based on the Allon Plan. According to an assessment by the US embassy, 'the rational decision-making process, with regard to settlement creation, operates creakingly if at all'. This 'policy vacuum' allowed Peres to have the opportunity of 'keeping one foot within official guidelines and one in the pro-settlement camp on the right'.[117]

8
Submission to Gush Emunim

Interim agreements

The Rabin government's lack of strategic planning with regard to the Occupied Territories (OT) did not inhibit it from trying to pursue a second interim agreement with Egypt, which was supported by most ministers.[1] However, despite broad ministerial support, and before being asked to do so by Kissinger, the government was unable to take a firm decision on the matter. In a secret memo, Galili pointed out that an interim agreement with Egypt was both feasible and desirable. He explained that such an agreement would usher in a period of de facto peace and ensure that psychological and political conditions, which are essential for peace, were attained. Only after a sustained period of stability was achieved could Israel examine the possibility of pursuing a permanent peace agreement. Until such an agreement was signed, Galili advised the government to hold on to as much of Sinai as possible in order to provide Egypt with an incentive to strive for peace.[2] Ministers raised concerns regarding a second interim agreement. They wanted to ensure that the agreement would include an end to the state of war between the sides and act as a prelude to peace agreements.[3] Additionally, they feared that Israel might be required to withdraw from the strategically important Sinai passes and from Abu-Rhudeis – the main oil field in Sinai.[4] Lastly, some were sceptical about the real value of the American and international security guarantees.[5]

Israel's main objectives were to ensure an end to the state of war, secure free naval passage and a non-belligerency agreement. In return, Israel was willing to withdraw to a strip of land 30–50 km wide, not including the Gaza Strip. In addition, Israel would continue to hold a continuous strip of land from Sharm el-Sheikh to Eilat.[6] The negotiations with Egypt proved harder than expected as Sadat was unwilling to sign a non-belligerency agreement. As a result, Israel refused to pursue an interim agreement based on an Israeli withdrawal from the Sinai passes and Abu-Rhudeis.[7] Kissinger, acknowledging that Rabin was in a difficult position domestically and within his coalition, offered extensive American guarantees.[8] However, Kissinger also warned Israel that its refusal to sign an agreement would result in delays to its military and financial aid.[9]

The US agreed to provide Israel with military assistance, economic aid, oil supplies and diplomatic assurances. These assurances included: a US agreement not to recognise or negotiate with the Palestine Liberation Organisation (PLO), an assurance not to press Israel for an interim agreement with Jordan and an assurance that it had not adopted a position regarding the final border between Israel and Syria.[10] Additionally, Kissinger elicited an agreement from Sadat to provide Israel with free non-military naval passage through the Suez Canal. Only after the US agreed to provide Israel with these extensive guarantees and assurances did the government agree to sign a second interim agreement. Some members of the coalition remained sceptical, however; in the Knesset vote on the agreement several Rafi members, including Dayan and the young guard of the National Religious Party (NRP), voted against.

The second interim agreement with Egypt revealed the extent to which American pressure affected Israel's decision-making process, and how important American guarantees and assurances were. Arguably, the main driving force behind the diplomatic effort was the American administration. The interim agreements with Egypt and Syria shared similar characteristics: the agreements were in line with American Middle East policy and Israel only signed them in response to US incentives and under American diplomatic pressure.[11] In other words, despite the importance of the agreements to Israel, the government was unable to work towards its own objectives, and overcome its internal divisions, without direct US involvement. Furthermore, due to its fragmented decision-making process, domestic constraints and weak leadership, the government was unable to take the necessary decisions without being pressured, provided with incentives, and rewarded with guarantees and assurances by the American administration.

The interim agreement was in line with Israeli interests, as it did not require it to withdraw from areas it regarded as essential for its national security. Despite agreeing to negotiate with Egypt without precondi-tions, successive Israeli governments had agreed to hold certain areas in

Sinai indefinitely.[12] This stemmed from Israel's desire to maintain strategic depth and ensure free naval passage through the Straits of Tiran.[13] Therefore, successive Israeli governments concluded that they could ill afford to withdraw from the Rafah plains and Sharm el-Sheikh. Instead, they chose to invest in settling and developing these areas in anticipation that they would remain under Israel's control.[14] Under Rabin, Israel strengthened its presence in the Rafah plains by creating a dense and continuous line of settlements from Yamit to the Eshkol region east of the Gaza Strip,[15] which helped Israel to control the Gaza Strip by surrounding it with Jewish settlements. The idea of controlling the Gaza Strip was directly linked to Israel's presence in the Rafah plains; Israel had no intention of holding the former without the latter.[16] The Gaza Strip was the price Israel was willing to pay in order to secure strategic depth in the Sinai Peninsula.

In the run-up to the second interim agreement with Egypt, the Rabin government appeared to be willing to consider further territorial compromises with Syria and Jordan. This was partly the result of a change in public perception. After the initial interim agreement with Egypt and Syria, and according to the polls, a majority of Israelis were in favour of territorial compromises, though not a return to the 1967 borders.[17] The government envisioned further interim agreements with Jordan and Syria, based on an end to the state of war and further Israeli withdrawals. The interim agreement with Jordan would have been based on Israel's continued presence in the Jordan valley and on the West Bank mountain ranges. On the matter of Jerusalem, Israel was only willing to discuss religious and administrative arrangements. Additionally, any agreement with Jordan would have necessitated either new elections or a referendum, as promised to the NRP. With regard to Syria, Israel was willing to withdraw from an area encompassing up to a third of the Golan Heights. Further Israeli withdrawals from the Golan Heights would have depended on an extended period of calm of 10–15 years, and would have been based on the signing of peace agreements.[18] In March 1976, the government voted to accept the idea of interim agreements with Jordan and Syria based on a territorial compromise.[19] However, although the government decided in favour of interim agreements, it did not specify the exact nature of the territorial compromise it was proposing or its future relationship with the territories it planned to hold,[20] so as not to create a schism within the coalition.

Israel offered an agreement that included an end to the state of war and an additional Israeli withdrawal, albeit a small one.[21] According to Yadlin, the government discussed several different approaches, including leaving Israeli settlements under Syrian control, however, he confirms that Syria was not interested in an interim agreement with Israel.[22] Israel pursued an interim agreement because it knew Syria would not agree to a peace agreement for less than a full Israeli withdrawal from all the OT and a solution to the Palestinian problem.[23] According to Kissinger, there was no progress on the diplomatic front because of: internal Arab divisions; the Lebanese civil war; reservations about what Israel could deliver; and the fact that nothing could happened until after the American elections of 1976.[24] In addition, the Labour government was unable to push for far-reaching and extensive interim agreements without risking its narrow parliamentary base. Israel was thus left with territories – parts of the Golan Heights and the areas in the West Bank not included in the Allon Plan – which it did not plan on holding and from which it was willing to withdraw. This provided Gush Emunim with an opportunity to hijack the government's territorial policies and ensure Israel did not withdraw from those territories.

Sebastia

The international stature of the PLO increased dramatically after the Rabat Summit. It was invited to join discussions in the UN as a permanent observer. In the UN, the PLO supported efforts to denounce Israel and banish it from the organisation.[25] On 10 November, the attempts by the PLO and the Arab states to de-legitimise Israel reached their pinnacle with a General Assembly resolution equating Zionism with racism. In response to the resolution, Galili called for the establishment of 30 new settlements in 18 months.[26] Nevertheless, it was Gush Emunim that took the opportunity to protest against the resolution by settling in a heavily populated area of the West Bank.

Back in October 1974, Gush Emunim had presented Galili and Rabin with their settlement plans. They requested that the government allow them to settle in the central region of the West Bank (Samaria), in the vicinity of Nablus. After being refused permission, the group attempted to settle illegally in the area, only to be forcibly removed by the army. On 29 November 1975, hundreds of Gush Emunim supporters arrived at the old railway station in Sebastia – the location of the capital of the biblical kingdom of Israel – about 10 km from Nablus. According to Gush Emunim, their settlement attempt was in response to the Rabat Summit and the resolution equating Zionism with racism.[27] The government voted unanimously to remove the settlers, but ministers decided to wait until after the conclusion of a meeting of the leaders of the Jewish faith. The meeting, a show of solidarity with the Zionist cause by leaders of world Jewry, opened in Jerusalem on 3 December.[28]

In parallel, on 3 December, in a meeting of Mapam's Political Committee, members argued that, by not removing the settlers immediately, the government was effectively legitimising their attempt. There were calls for an ultimatum to be given to Rabin regarding Mapam's participation in the government. In the end the committee decided to provide the government with more time to deal with the situation.[29]

The government's pause was exploited by thousands of Gush Emunim supporters who joined the would-be settlers in Sebastia; among them were members of the NRP, MKs from the opposition, leading rabbis and even Rabin's Special Security Advisor Ariel Sharon. Sharon appeared to be supporting the project while advising Rabin on how to deal with it.[30] Because of the large number of supporters, and the delicate nature of the situation, concerns were raised by ministers and the army regarding the possibility of bloodshed.[31] This prompted ministers to search for a solution that would remove the settlers without violence.[32] Additionally, the NRP exerted intense pressure on Rabin to find a compromise.[33] While ministers debated, Peres took it upon himself to negotiate a compromise, without consulting the government.[34] Peres' compromise was later approved because it was assumed that once the demonstration subsided, the government would gradually remove the settlers.[35] The compromise allowed for 30 men – this later became 30 families – to relocate temporarily to the Kadom army base nearby, and be employed by the army, until the government decided on their fate.[36]

On 10 December, Mapam's Political Committee agreed on a resolution describing the Sebastia incident as an attempt to create facts on the ground in order to realise the dream of Greater Israel and hinder peace. It called the compromise with the settlers a dangerous precedent of yielding to illegal acts. Mapam criticised the government's lame attempt to remove the settlers and concluded that the whole incident had hurt its credibility and authority.[37] Nevertheless, Mapam chose to remain in the coalition.

It took the government almost six months to decide not to establish a settlement in the Sebastia area. The decision called for the relocation of the settlers to a suitable site in accordance with government decisions elsewhere in the West Bank. Furthermore, it decided that no action should be taken to imply the transformation of the temporary camp in

Kadom into a permanent one.[38] This decision was prompted by the fact that the settlers were doing just that. In an official report, the Defence Ministry listed 23 families, 30–40 single people, and 45 children living in the camp. The report stated that the Defence Ministry was willing to establish several small factories in order to employ the settlers in jobs related to the defence industry.[39]

On 1 June, Rabin requested that all of the settlers' activities in the Kadom camp be in accordance with the government's decision.[40] Earlier that day, Galili had notified Rabin that some of the activities in the camp 'might be' contravening the government's decision.[41] In response, Peres claimed that the activities alluded to, for example, new structures being built, employment by the army, building of a synagogue, were all done in the period before the government's decision and therefore did not contradict its decision.[42] Despite Peres' response, Galili informed Rabin that activities contravening the government's decision were still being carried out.[43] Galili authorised Admoni to offer the settlers alternative settlement sites, among them Mescha, a site not yet approved on the western edge of the West Bank that was not near any large Palestinian population centre.[44] The settlers, however, refused to relocate; they explained that there were other members of Gush Emunim who would be glad to settle there. Admoni wrote back to Galili informing him of the settlers' negative response and claimed that there was nothing more he could do.[45]

On 20 July, Health Minister Shem-Tov wrote to the government's secretary demanding to know whether the government had invested any money in the camp and whether or not a factory was established there that employed the settlers. Additionally, he inquired whether any of these actions contradicted the government's decision.[46] On 27 July, Netzer replied to Shem-Tov detailing what had happened in Kadom. The settlers were initially moved into a prescribed area in the camp and several tents and sheds were provided. At the request of the defence minister and the prime minister, 30 caravans were borrowed from the Jewish Agency to provide temporary accommodation. An area within the perimeter of the camp was allocated to the caravans and several additional 'temporary structures' to serve as study rooms and toilets. These structures were connected to running water, sewage and electricity. The entire operation was done by the army and the settlers, and was paid for by the Defence Ministry. Additionally, the settlers requested permission to establish several additional 'temporary structures', for example, a mess hall, a synagogue and a small factory. The settlers were given permission to establish these on condition that it was done at their own expense.

The Defence Ministry did not provide any funds for these additional structures.[47]

On 9 August, Tourism Minister Kol wrote to Rabin to inquire when the government was planning to implement its decision to relocate the settlers.[48] This was followed by a letter from Aharon Barak, the Attorney General, who wrote in response to the settlers' demand for access to state education. Barak argued that the government should provide education for the settlers' children. However, he added, because Israel's law did not apply to the OT and as there was no legal settlement in the area, the government was not obliged to provide for education at Kadom, since this might imply the transformation of the settlement into a permanent one. He concluded, therefore, that Israel should provide access to state education outside of the OT. In this way the government could fulfil its obligation to the settlers' children without changing its stance.[49]

Unable to resolve the problem and unwilling to confront the settlers or risk the dissolution of the coalition, the government decided not to decide and instead to postpone the debate until after the elections.[50] The story of Kadom illustrated the difficulty of operating on the basis of consensual politics, within a narrow coalition, on issues relating to the OT. It also demonstrated the political power held by Gush Emunim. According to Yadlin, the Sebastia/Kadom episode demonstrated 'the government's submission to Gush Emunim'.[51]

The episode also provided clear indication of the hostile relations between Peres and Rabin, which helped to further fragment the government's decision-making process. On the one hand, Rabin could not afford to dismiss Peres because of factional politics, even though the latter was undermining the government. On the other hand, Peres' behaviour was partly in response to the disrespect shown to him by Rabin, in particular Rabin's decision to bypass Peres by appointing a special advisor on security matters, former Major-General Ariel Sharon.[52] The Kadom episode was followed by mutual recriminations. Rabin blamed the UN resolution, the fear of bloodshed and Peres;[53] he went as far as hinting that Peres served as a Trojan horse for Gush Emunim.[54] Most ministers, with the exception of the NRP, also blamed Peres for the government's capitulation.[55] Peres, however, blamed Rabin for undermining him – Rabin was apparently negotiating with the settlers through Sharon at the same time[56] – and the chief-of-staff for not wanting to remove the settlers; the army, in turn, blamed the police.[57] More than anything else, Sebastia/Kadom exposed the inability or unwillingness of the dovish ministers – Mapam's in particular – to hold the government to account. Shem-Tov described his experience during the affair as a 'lone voice in the wilderness'.[58] Yet, according to Police Minister Hillel, during cabinet debates Shem-Tov would deliver his condemnatory speeches, ministers would pretend to listen and then the meeting would proceed as normal.[59]

Settlement policy under Rabin

Israel's early settlement approach was loosely based on a military-strategic concept inherent in the Allon Plan. The government perceived the OT, with the exception of Jerusalem, as serving a strategic function. Therefore, territories were designated either as dispensable or indispensable; the Allon Plan served to distinguish the latter from the former. The indispensable territories included the Jordan valley, the Rafah plains, the Golan Heights and Sharm el-Sheikh. This view of the territories changed with the establishment of Gush Etzion, and later Hebron and Kiryat Arba, and their inclusion in the Allon Plan, as these settlements did not serve any strategic purpose. This change was further enhanced with the arrival of Gush Emunim and the growing ideological importance attached to the territories by the NRP and the Likud.

The Israeli settlements and army bases in the Jordan valley provide a clear example. The Jordan valley was perceived as a strategically important area and as integral to the Allon Plan. During negotiations with Jordan, successive governments refused to compromise over this area. According to Netzer, the clearest indication of the Israel's settlement approach was with regard to the Jordan valley.[60] In reality, however, the settlements established in the Jordan valley were not as extensive or developed as intended; these were small agricultural settlements with 44 residents each on average.[61] It is unlikely that Israel based its security concept on these settlements. Even on a strategic level, the main army bases and troop concentrations were not in the area but on the mountain ranges, in accordance with Dayan's 'Mobile Defence' concept. Additionally, Rabin made it clear that Israel would not relinquish its military control over those mountain ranges.[62] In essence, Israel was holding on to both the Jordan valley and the mountain ranges, even though it stated that, from a military-strategic perspective, it needed only one of these. In short, it seems that the government was not acting purely on the basis of the Allon Plan's settlement and strategic requirements. This lack of strategic planning was acknowledged by Galili. In June 1976, Galili informed the Ministerial Settlement Committee (MSC) that he did not intend to present a comprehensive settlement plan. Instead, he proposed that the committee discuss and decide on settlement issues in an incremental manner, as and when required.[63] This lack of strategic planning, or the lack of a clear decision, however, provided an opportunity for interested individuals and groups to push for new ideas and plans.

The most important plan to be considered was Peres' idea of thickening Israel's settlements on both sides of the green line, in order to 'enlarge Israel's tight hips'.[64] The areas along the green line were mostly uninhabited and it was agreed that these were areas Israel should continue holding on to indefinitely.[65] Additionally, by controlling these areas, Israel controlled the region's main water aquifers, which affected the water resources of both Israel and the West Bank.[66] Several new Nahal outposts were created towards the end of 1976 and the beginning of 1977 in accordance with this new approach. It was widely understood that these would be transformed at a later stage into civilian ones.[67]

The idea of settling along the green line was raised by Gush Emunim and was supported by the NRP. A group associated with Gush Emunim lobbied the government and the NRP for the right to settle there for several years.[68] Additionally, Galili and Admoni supported these efforts as part of Israel's efforts to thicken the green line. Galili explained to Gush Emunim that, once a decision has been taken by the government and the logistical problems had been overcome, they would be allowed to settle there.[69] Under pressure from Gush Emunim and from the NRP to authorise this settlement, Galili wrote to Zevulon Hammer explaining that attempts to forcibly settle in the area were unnecessary as the delay in settling the area was due to technical and logistical problems. Galili asked Hammer not to publicise the arrangement as this would hinder the project.[70] The Mescha outpost was established two weeks before the elections and settled by the group; the new settlement was called Elkana.

Elkana was not the only place in which the government either gave in to or cooperated with Gush Emunim. In late 1976, following a request by Peres, and supported by Allon and Galili, the government approved the creation of a working camp in Ofra, a move reminiscent of the early settlement period of the Golan Heights. Furthermore, Galili informed the government of a proposal to transform Ma'ale Adumim into a permanent settlement.[71] The Allon Plan was clearly no longer the driving force behind Israel's settlement activities and even Allon was supporting projects outside of its scope.

The settlement activity of the Rabin government during its final year resulted from three developing trends. First, due to the lack of meaningful negotiations and international pressure, areas that were previously outside of the national consensus were labelled 'vacant' by the MSC. Some of these were incorporated into the national consensus because of political pressure from the NRP and Gush Emunim as well as the growing ministerial appetite for redefining Israel's future borders unilaterally.[72] Second, dovish ministers – in particular ones within Mapam – appeared unable to influence the decision-making process and were also unwilling to weaken the government. Thus, in an effort to bolster Rabin's government, Mapam was allowing it to act with impunity. Lastly, it became clear that the US would not put undue pressure on the government regarding the creation of settlements. This was despite the fact that the American administration was fully aware of Israel's settlement activities,[73] and that it viewed these activities as illegal under international law.[74]

The Palestinian option

Despite the Rabat Summit resolution, Israel continued to view the Jordanian option as the most desirable one for the West Bank. However, Jordan's weakness in the diplomatic arena, as a consequence of the Rabat Summit, and the growing international clout of the PLO, prompted the government to re-examine its approach towards the West Bank. The solution favoured by officials was the establishment of limited Palestinian self-rule in line with the Allon Plan.[75] This limited self-rule would be implemented by expanding the role of the mayors and by creating additional administrative roles in the West Bank and, to a lesser degree, in the Gaza Strip.[76] The move towards Palestinian self-rule was also influenced by international pressure and growing calls from within the American administration for Israel to pursue a Palestinian-based approach. A prime example was a report presented to the US Congress, regarding the centrality of the Palestinian problem to the Arab-Israeli conflict, by the Deputy Assistant Secretary of State Harold Saunders.[77] The report was taken very seriously in Israel as it was feared it might entail a change in US policy.[78] Israel's concern was not misplaced; the report was later adopted by the Carter administration.

According to Shlomo Gazit, Israel's decision in late 1975 to move towards Palestinian self-rule was too little too late due to a number of social changes that had occurred in the territories.[79] These were reflected in the changing attitude of the Palestinian population towards

Israel. The new Israeli-Palestinian relations were directly linked to the prolonged occupation, the worsening economic situation in the territories and Israel's settlement policies.[80]

Israel's officials believed that the most effective way to promote limited self-rule would be through new local elections. It was hoped that these would promote a new leadership among Palestinians. This was despite growing fears among the intelligence services that the new elections would be used by the PLO to strengthen its grip on the West Bank and remove pro-Jordanian notables. Indeed, the intelligence services accurately predicted the outcome of the 1976 elections; it was a resounding victory for the PLO: long-serving pro-Jordanian mayors were replaced by younger pro-PLO nationalists.[81] The elections caused great distress in Israel and Rabin was quick to lay the blame at Peres' door.[82] On 28 December 1976, a report by the former head of AMAN (military intelligence unit), Yehoshafat Harkabi, stated that it was very unlikely that a new Palestinian leadership acceptable to Israel would arise.[83] Despite the election result, the government was unwilling to consider a Palestinian option based on the PLO. The government went so far as to make it an offence for Israeli citizens to contact members of Palestinian 'terrorist' organisations.[84] Additionally, attempts, by Mapam and the Independent Liberal Party, to leave all diplomatic options open by promoting dialogue with any Palestinian group that was willing to recognise Israel's right to exist and renounce terrorism – as defined by Israel – were not successful.[85]

Approaching the 1977 general elections, the government was left in a difficult situation. Violent incidents and civil disobedience in the West Bank and the Gaza Strip were on the rise, and Israel's settlement policies were only worsening the situation; in other words (and in contrast to Dayan's principles of non-intervention and non-visibility), the occupation was increasingly visible and Israel was increasingly intervening in Palestinian economic, social and political life. Israel's lack of a strategic policy towards the territories only made the job of maintaining a stable and 'benevolent' occupation more difficult.[86]

Israel supported limited Palestinian self-rule in the hope that a new leadership might emerge. However, this was undermining Jordan's position in the West Bank and, as a result, complicated Israel's negotiations with Jordan. Nevertheless, negotiations with Jordan continued on the premise of a territorial compromise based on a variant of the Allon Plan. This in turn was in complete contradiction to the activities of Peres in the OT. While Israel debated the merits of the Palestinian and Jordanian options, Peres was busy implementing Dayan's Functional Solution.

Thus, in the absence of a guiding policy, Israel was advancing simultaneously in three different directions.

The 1977 elections

On the eve of the 1977 elections, the Labour Party held a series of discussions to decide on its new electoral platform. Party Chairman Danny Rosolio called for a meaningful debate on the merits of the Fourteen-Point Document as the basis for the new platform. However, party members rarely discussed the document; instead they used the occasion to debate Israel's policies towards the OT. Several issues were discussed and debated: interim agreements, future borders, the preferred West Bank approach, coalition promises made to the NRP and the party's platform. According to Rabinowitz, the main issue facing the party was what to offer in return for an interim agreement and whether this should be included in the platform.[87] There was a realisation within the party that further territorial compromises would be required. Housing Minister Ofer called on the party to face up to the fact that it needed to take very hard decisions.[88] Rabin declared that the party was willing to accept territorial compromises, but would not agree to return to the 1967 borders. He went on to say that the main reason peace had not been achieved was due to 'the other side' not being ready.[89] The party's reluctance to return to those borders was, according to Yariv, based on the perception that the Arab world wanted a return to the situation that prevailed before the Six Day War, with the addition of a Palestinian state in the West Bank and the Gaza Strip.[90] Dayan proposed that the party inform the electorate that the Arab states were offering peace agreements in return for a full Israeli withdrawal – a price the Labour Party was refusing to pay. Dayan, therefore, proposed asking the electorate directly whether they approved of this approach.[91]

The main areas of disagreement were the political future of the Golan Heights, the Sinai Peninsula and the West Bank. There was hardly any reference to the future status of Jerusalem or the Gaza Strip, even though the party never adopted a clear approach towards the latter. While the party was moving towards accepting a territorial compromise in the Golan Heights and the Sinai Peninsula, albeit without agreeing on the scope, it remained deeply divided over the political future of the West Bank, so much so that it could not even define its approach. Therefore, there was a fear, according to Galili, that, because of factional politics and the controversial nature of the territories, the final platform would not be accepted by the entire party.[92]

The Sinai Peninsula

Some members appeared unconvinced by Sadat's drive for peace and the need for substantial territorial compromises. Meir referred sarcastically to Sadat as a moderate: 'We give him the oil fields – he takes, we move beyond the passes – he takes, what a man of peace!'[93] However, it was apparent that most members supported a third interim agreement with Egypt based on further Israeli withdrawals. The main question was the scale of these withdrawals and whether or not Israel intended to hold on to certain areas. Hillel complained that he did not know the party's position on Sinai. He added that 'we must say that there are areas [in Sinai] from which we will not withdraw, in which we plan to continue settling and developing'.[94] Rabin stated that Israel would be required to withdraw from a large portion of Sinai in order to achieve peace, but would not agree to return to the 1967 border. According to Rabin, the new borders should include the Rafah plains and a continuous strip of land from Sharm el-Sheikh to Eilat. However, Rabin caused some confusion when he stated that Israel 'could leave open for interpretation what exactly is meant by territorial continuity'.[95]

It is clear that the views expressed were based mainly on the strategic value of the Sinai Peninsula and were consistent with the idea of further withdrawals. In addition, disagreements over the extent of future Israeli withdrawals were directly linked to the level of confidence members had in Sadat's commitment to peace. According to Yadlin, the second interim agreement proved to most ministers that Sadat was bent on peace.[96] It was apparent that, after the second interim agreement, more party members were willing to consider territorial withdrawals beyond the scope of the Allon Plan.

The Golan Heights

There seemed to be a realisation among party members that further withdrawals would be necessary in the Golan Heights. Bar-Lev, speaking for many, did not see an opportunity for reaching peace agreements with Syria, but did not rule out the possibility of an interim agreement, which would include territorial concessions in return for a non-belligerency agreement.[97] Allon argued that Israel should advance talks on an interim agreement, since waiting for peace agreements and full normalisation was tantamount to ending diplomatic negotiations.[98] The consensus within the party, as outlined by Rabin, was that Israel 'will not withdraw from the Golan Heights, but this does not necessarily mean sticking to the current line'.[99] The party was able to reach a consensus on the necessity of pursuing an additional interim agreement, but not on the extent of the territorial compromise. The difference in this approach from that towards the Sinai Peninsula reflected a greater level of suspicion of Syria. Nevertheless, and as with the Sinai Peninsula, the party did not outline the future status of these territories.

The West Bank

More than anything else, the subject of the West Bank exposed the widespread differences within the party, with different ministers and factions pulling in different directions. The ideas expressed and the solutions offered cannot simply be categorised as being based on the Allon Plan, a Functional Solution, and a more extensive Israeli withdrawal from the West Bank. Within the party, and even within the different factions, these solutions acquired different interpretations. Nowhere was this more apparent than in Ahdut-Ha'avoda. On the one hand, Ahdut-Ha'avoda affirmed its support for the Allon Plan and for the continuation of the settlement activities as the only method of realising the socialist-Zionist ethos. On the other hand, it called for negotiations without preconditions with all Arab states on the basis of territorial compromises.[100] Additionally, and for the first time, prominent dovish members (Sarid, Eban, Ben-Aharon and Yariv), representing all of the party's factions, joined forces to propose an alternative peace plan based on further territorial compromises.[101]

In contrast to the Golan Heights and the Sinai Peninsula, the debate regarding the West Bank did not relate purely to strategic considerations; the debate was complicated by the invocation of ideological, psychological and religious images. The debate related to members' perceptions of the land of Israel, the Jewish state, and Zionism and Palestinian nationalism. Peres – the main proponent of the Functional Solution – stated that, while Israel required secure and defensible borders, neither international guarantees nor 'a 14 km wide strip of land' would be able to provide these.[102] Peres explained that the Arabs would never agree to a territorial compromise that did not include Jerusalem. Because Israel would never accept this, he claimed 'I do not believe there is a territorial compromise that will be acceptable to the Arabs'; 'In my view, it is better to pursue a functional and political compromise than a territorial compromise.'[103]

The need to elaborate on what was meant by the term 'Functional Solution' prompted Meir to request a draft that would define 'what we mean when we say a Functional Solution',[104] and that such a draft be circulated among members.[105] Peres' concerns over the security merits of a territorial compromise were also raised by Hillel. According to

Hillel, territorial compromises were necessary in the Sinai Peninsula and the Golan Heights, but not in the West Bank: 'There is not enough strategic depth ... any withdrawal from the Jericho region will allow hostile elements into the area.' He argued that the solution to the Palestinian problem 'was not east of the Jordan River but west of it' and the party should stop stuttering on the issue of territorial compromises.[106]

Nonetheless, concerns were raised regarding the Functional Solution. Allon maintained that a Greater Israel solution would necessitate providing full rights to the Palestinian population, which would turn Israel into a bi-national state. However, if Israel decided to annex the territories without providing Palestinians with full rights it would cease to be a democratic state. Allon added that 'in my opinion, this kind of [Functional] solution is a new edition or version of the South African approach' and 'the worst of all possible solutions'.[107] Allon asked how it was possible that the party was talking about territorial compromises with Syria but not with Jordan.[108] By agreeing on the need for a territorial compromise with Jordan 'we are freeing ourselves of a great burden'.[109] Allon stated that Israel did not want a third state between itself and Jordan and therefore had to agree to a territorial compromise.[110]

Allon's disdain for the Functional Solution was shared by Galili. 'The main reason we favour a territorial compromise in the West Bank' is because 'we do not want to force the population to live under our control'.[111] Galili asked Peres whether he would consider putting the idea of a Functional Solution to a vote, in order to clarify the party's position.[112] He questioned why the party would not publicly state its willingness to strive for peace with Jordan based on a territorial compromise.[113] However, the need to placate Peres, and his large group of supporters, meant that the party could not afford to reject the Functional Solution altogether. Bar-Lev acknowledged that there were two options and, although he did not believe a Functional Solution was a realistic one, he argued that discounting it completely was unnecessary. He added that it would be good if Israel could reach an agreement with Jordan based on a territorial compromise. However, 'if we can reach an agreement based on a Functional Solution, which, I think, is unlikely, that would be even better'.[114]

This desire to avoid precise definitions and policies appeared preferable. Rabin stated that there was no reason to define the scope of any territorial compromise, 'it is unnecessary in my opinion to draw maps'.[115] Justice Minister Haim Tzadok concluded the meeting by reminding the party that there was no need to include specific plans or proposals in the electoral platform. He stated that the decision on whether or not to accept a particular plan or not should be left to the government.[116] The proposed platform reiterated the party's commitment to pursuing a peace agreement based on territorial compromises. The main difference between the new platform and the Fourteen-Point Document was in nuance. The new platform added that Israel was committed to territorial compromises with *each* of its neighbours,[117] but the paper was approved by only a small margin. Entering the 1977 elections, the Labour Party, unable to clearly define its territorial approach and unwilling to risk party disunity, decided in effect not to decide.

In the wake of Meir's resignation, Rabin had been hand-picked by Sapir to lead the Labour Party. As the head of a minority government, lacking a solid factional base and without much political experience, he was at a disadvantage from day one. In its three years in power, the Rabin government initially based its approach loosely on the Allon Plan. Nevertheless, at no time was it able to define or agree on the exact parameters of the territories it regarded as essential for its national security. Moreover, the establishment of army bases, and the invest-ment in infrastructure and settlement did not correspond directly to the Allon Plan, or, for that matter, to any particular plan or concept. The clearest indication of this muddled approach was the West Bank. On the one hand, the government half-heartedly pursued a settlement with Jordan based on the Allon Plan. On the other hand, it was under-mining Jordan's position in the West Bank by promoting Palestinian self-rule. The government's uncertain approach provided Peres with a blank cheque to implement a Functional Solution in the West Bank. In short, the government was arbitrarily pursuing and implementing three different policies.

The reasons for this lack of clear policies are rooted in Israel's domestic sphere. Rabin was a novice prime minister, constrained by the factional politics of the Labour Party, undermined by Peres and forced to include the NRP in the coalition in order to broaden his narrow parliamentary base. The need to operate on the basis of consensual politics forced him to resort to an incremental and ad hoc strategy of decision-making based on improvisation. The government's political weakness and lack of clear policies were effortlessly exposed by Gush Emunim. The sole exception to the government's ineptitude was its second interim agreement with Egypt. This, however, had more to do with American diplomatic pressure, coupled with the extensive military and financial aid it was giving Israel.

It can be argued that, had the Labour Party won the 1977 elections, it would have been pressured by the Carter administration to commit to further interim agreements with Syria and Egypt, and possibly also Jordan. Additionally, by winning the elections it would have received a public mandate to pursue these agreements. These would have been based on Israel's willingness to withdraw from most of the Sinai Peninsula, up to a third, but possibly more, of the Golan Heights, and from the populated areas of the West Bank with an option of turning the Gaza Strip into a Jordanian or a Palestinian demilitarised area. However, non-decisions and the lack of clear policies were the party's downfall and one of the reasons it lost the elections.[118]

Conclusion

This book proposed to deal with the complex reality that dawned on the Middle East in the aftermath of the Six Day: Israel's occupation of territories three and a half times its own size, and their people, the overwhelming majority of whom were Palestinians. The book raised the question of whether successive Israeli governments, under the leadership of the Labour Party, had a strategic policy with regard to the Occupied Territories (OT): a policy that addressed Israel's national interest and the various challenges posed by the occupation.

As demonstrated throughout the book, successive Israeli governments did not have such a policy towards the OT. This is not to say that decisions were never taken or that the process of formulation, approval and implementation of short-term policies was completely non-existent. Indeed, actions taken by successive governments, interest groups and individuals included establishing settlements and army bases, occasionally in contravention of Israel's own procedures, annexing areas unilaterally, integrating the economies of the territories with that of Israel, negotiating with Arab states over the territories as well as establishing a military administration. These decisions were based on a number of competing, and at times contradictory images, plans and approaches, such as annexation, the Allon Plan and the Functional Solution. However, these decisions, when put into context and viewed as a whole, did not amount to a strategic policy or a coherent long-term approach. At no time during the period did an Israeli government reach a formal decision on the long-term future of the OT.

More specifically, there is little to support the claims that successive Israeli governments had a strategic policy, a specific long-term approach, a settlement plan or map for the OT. It is true that the Allon Plan was widely supported and promoted by ministers. However, the plan was never formally approved and at no time was it the official policy. Additionally, the plan, which fluctuated between a Palestinian and a Jordanian orientation, was only implemented partially and even then only in conjunction with other plans. There were many instances in which the government, and even Allon, acted in ways that contradicted the plan, for example, pursuing Palestinian self-rule and economic integration, and establishing settlements outside the plan's remit, such as Kiryat Arba, Kadom, Ofra and Elkana. The fact is that successive governments employed a variety of different, and at times contradictory, approaches towards the territories. The story of the West Bank provides the clearest example of this.

From the onset of the territorial debate, the government was unable to reach a consensus over the future of the West Bank; it was neither able to define its main objectives nor reach an agreement over its preferred approach. In the absence of a guiding approach, successive governments decided not to decide over the long-term future of the West Bank. The need to reach a consensus on such a controversial issue proved to be difficult within the confines of the national unity government. On the one hand, decision-makers felt a historic-religious attachment towards the West Bank as part of the biblical Jewish homeland; this is particularly true with regard to Hebron. On the other hand, they viewed certain areas of the West Bank as strategically important, for example the Jordan valley.

The debate over what was required, from a strategic-military perspective, and what was desirable, from an ideological-religious perspective, was further clouded by the fear of annexation. Successive governments' approach towards the West Bank was based on the realisation that they could ill afford to annex the heavily populated Palestinian urban centres without jeopardising Israel's Jewish majority and nature. The two main plans proposed by ministers (the Functional Solution and the Allon Plan) were designed to provide a solution to this very problem. These plans, while acknowledging both a Palestinian and a Jordanian element, depended on two distinct approaches. The Allon Plan was based on the principle of static defences, control over military-strategic areas, agricultural settlements and withdrawal from the heavily populated areas, while the Functional Solution advocated mobile defences, urban settlements, economic integration and an administrative self-rule solution. Despite the fact that neither of these plans was officially adopted, parts of both were still implemented. The implementation of the Allon Plan and the Functional Solution simultaneously undermined both plans, as well as the Palestinian and Jordanian approaches.

Israel's settlement activities in the West Bank compounded the problem by deviating from both these plans. It is true that the majority of Israel's settlements in the West Bank were established in accordance with the Allon Plan. However, and especially during the Rabin period, settlements were established in areas outside the scope of the plan. The establishment of settlements outside the scope of the Allon Plan was in contradiction to Israel's stated strategic and demographic objectives. Moreover, Israel's settlement activities outside the scope of the plan contradicted its professed aim of reaching a negotiated settlement with Jordan over the future of the West Bank.

It was not only Israel's settlement policy that made little sense. Israel's political and economic decisions regarding the West Bank did not correspond to its stated objectives. Israel sought, in accordance with the Functional Solution, to empower local officials and implement Palestinian self-rule in the West Bank. This went hand in hand with Dayan's objectives of raising living standards and economic integration. However, Dayan's, and later Peres', political and economic decisions stood in contrast to the Labour Party's desire to avoid economic integration and de facto annexation. Additionally, the economic integration and empowerment of local officials was in contrast to Israel's stated aim of reaching a negotiated settlement with Jordan, as these actions undermined Jordan's position and authority in the West Bank. On the subject of Jordan, time and time again, Israeli leaders rebuffed King Hussein's peace overtures and offers. This was particularly striking due to the fact that the king took Israel's security needs in the West Bank seriously and his position was backed by the US. In short, successive governments did not have a strategic policy towards the West Bank. Instead, Israel's actions could best be categorised as disjointed incrementalism: decisions were taken on an ad hoc basis based on a muddled approach without a clear long-term aim.

Many factors affected Israel's territorial decision-making process. Arguably, it is an impossible task to chart the exact events, and pinpoint the precise factors, which led to Israel's lack of a strategic policy. In trying to explain why successive governments failed to put forward a strategic policy, three major contributing factors stand out: the faction-based politics of the Labour Party; the US position vis-à-vis Israel; and the actions of successive prime ministers. The book acknowledges that there were many other factors involved, and that these played an important role with regard to a particular government, but do not apply to all three governments.

In the introduction I alluded to the fact that Zionism, or the images of Zionism held by specific policy-makers, was not an important factor in

Israel's non-decision and lack of a strategic policy, even though Zionism was an important factor in shaping and forming the worldviews of particular decision-makers. As I have demonstrated throughout the book, the indecision shown by successive governments regarding whether to pursue the Allon Plan or the Functional Solution, or whether to follow a Palestinian or Jordanian approach, had little to do with Zionist ideology and more to do with internal and external political factors. Nonetheless, successive governments' indecision was exploited by individuals and groups to create facts on the ground that were in line with a resurgent Zionist ideology.

The Labour Party

The unification of the Israeli Labour parties (Mapai, Rafi, Ahdut-Ha'avoda and Mapam) was the lifelong ambition of Labour leaders. The main historical points of contention between the parties surrounded the role of Ben-Gurion and the young guard (*tze'irim*), as well as Mapai's internal bureaucratic system and its abuse of political patronage. The acquisition of the territories in 1967 brought to the fore a political debate which focused on the future borders of Israel and the nature of its polity, and which had been left dormant since the acceptance of the UN partition plan and Israel's 'War of Independence'. This debate crossed party and faction lines and threatened to derail the success of the unification process.

Successive Labour governments failed to produce a substantive and coherent territorial policy; they postponed making crucial decisions and decided 'not to decide' because of the improbability of reaching a consensus within governments, which were divided by party and factional loyalties. This problem has been and still is endemic to Israel's proportional-representation parliamentary system. Politicians regularly displayed their inability, or unwillingness to overcome factional differences and inter-factional competition for power and influence. Beilin attributes the party's, and subsequently the governments', policy immobilisation to the 'price of unity'. The need to maintain party unity, and avoid a split among the factions ensured that the unified party was unable and unwilling to take a clear and unequivocal stand on the issue of the OT. The examples of the Oral Law and the Galili Document clearly illustrate this point. In response to Dayan's demands for clear policies, the party tried to find a formula that would fulfil most of Dayan's demands, while not committing the party or alienating its dovish members. In other words, the party's need to formulate a strategic territorial policy became secondary to its need to maintain unity.

The US position

The Israeli government was certain, in the aftermath of the Six Day War, that it would be required to relinquish control over most of the territories it occupied. It is therefore not a surprise that the government had agreed, in its 19 June decisions, to withdraw from the Sinai Peninsula and the Golan Heights to the international border in exchange for peace. However, this decision was taken, first and foremost, for the purpose of pacifying the American administration. Early on, decision-makers understood the prominent role played by the American administration. The US became, in the aftermath of the Six Day War, Israel's most important diplomatic, financial and military supporter. Subsequently, its influence on the decision-making process was such that Israel could ill afford to take a decision that went against US interests without some trepidation. However, the US, in its own interests and for its own reasons, chose, for most of the period, not to put pressure on Israel on the matter of settlements and the territorial concessions.

The lack of a strategic policy did not come directly as a result of the lack of US pressure; nevertheless, the lack of US pressure exacerbated the problem. On the one hand, the ability of Israeli decision-makers to formulate a long-term policy was restricted by the stated position of the American administration, that is, the Rogers Plan and Johnson's Five Principles. On the other hand, Israeli indecisiveness was compounded by the mixed messages it received from the US; this was true with regard to both the Johnson and Nixon administrations.

One of the main reasons articulated by Israeli decision-makers for pursuing certain policies was the position of the American administration. There are many examples of this behaviour, for example, Israel's decision against annexing and implementing a vigorous settlement plan in the Golan Heights; Israel's timid settlement activities during the Eshkol and Meir governments; as well as the government's insistence, even if it was meant only as lip-service, that it had accepted the notion of a territorial compromise. Furthermore, the extent of Israel's settlement activities and territorial ambitions was directly linked to the limits set out by the Rogers Plan and Johnson's Five Principles, that is, the recognition that Israel could annex certain areas in order to fulfil its military-strategic needs. It is true that Israel continuously tried to push these boundaries, but had the American administration rebuked Israel publicly, the Israeli government would have probably come into line with the US position. Israeli decision-makers remarked on many occasions that, as long as the US had not put its foot down, Israel was free to continue with its actions. The US position, that is, at times constraining decision-makers, sending mixed messages and not putting pressure on Israel, helped to exacerbate existing divisions, and – borrowing the historical metaphor – provided a yellow light to those who argued against taking clear decisions, while creating facts on the grounds. In short, while it is true to state that Israel decided not to decide, as I have demonstrated, when Israel was forced to decide, because of US pressure, it found the courage and means to do so.

The prime ministers

There is no doubt that Eshkol, Meir and Rabin led very different governments in their time in office. They also brought with them different sets of experiences, skills and images. Eshkol and Rabin were seen as weak prime ministers, who struggled to control their party and were undermined by their respective defence ministers. In contrast, Meir dominated Israel's decision-making process. The three of them also faced different sets of international and domestic circumstances. Nevertheless, it is clear that each prime minister, for their own reasons, advocated against the formulation of a strategic policy; this was done, at times, against the advice of ministers and advisory committees. There are, of course, many mitigating circumstances but, ultimately, it was the responsibility and imperative of each prime minister to rise to the challenges they faced. Unfortunately, successive prime ministers chose, for reasons of self-preservation and political convenience, not to pursue a strategic policy.

The Eshkol-led national unity government had a wall-to-wall coalition that contained the right, the left and the National Religious Party (NRP). The government was under no US or international pressure and, with the exception of King Hussein – who, it was thought, was internally weak and who could not act without Nasser – it believed it had no suitable peace partners. Under these circumstances, Eshkol, unable to find common ground and undermined by his ministers, chose not to pursue a strategic policy. Any attempt by Eshkol to pursue such a policy had the potential to split the Labour Party and bring down the coalition. In other words, the Eshkol government agreed on the non-decision not by desire but by default.

Eshkol's position within the Labour Party and within the national unity coalition was severely weakened in the aftermath of the Six Day War. Eshkol was actively undermined by Dayan and his margins for political manoeuvring were constrained by the national unity coalition and the Labour Party's unification process. Eshkol initially favoured a practical approach towards the OT that took into account Israel's strategic-military needs. However, due to the perceived lack of suitable peace partners, and owing to his weakened political standing and his dithering and indecisive character, Eshkol decided not to decide and opted for a muddled and ad hoc approach.

In contrast, Meir monopolised and dominated the decision-making process through her kitchenette. Unlike Eshkol, Meir, especially after Gahal left the coalition in 1970, enjoyed an unprecedentedly strong parliamentary base. With Meir, it was not the ministers or coalition partners that undermined her; on the contrary, it was Meir herself who undermined efforts to reach a clear long-term policy, either by interfering with the formulation process or by avoiding taking important decisions. Meir's distrust of the Arab side, her belief that time was on Israel's side and her determination to maintain party unity, led her to favour a non-committing approach to the OT. Meir appeared to be more preoccupied with risk aversion than with defining Israel's long-term approach towards the territories.

Meir, who aligned herself with Galili, Dayan and the hawkish elements in the Labour Party and the coalition, chose to overlook the demographic and social costs of the occupation in pursuit of 'secure and recognised borders' – a term she never fully defined. Meir refused to consider Israel's long-term relationship with the OT and the Palestinian people, whom Meir claimed did not exist. In fact, under Meir, Israel established settlements in the Rafah plains and the Gaza Strip without ever taking into account the long-term implications of such acts. Bacharach and Baratz's concept of non-decisions as devices used by decision-making elites to preserve their power and authority applies to Meir and Eshkol. However, Meir's decision not to decide was her policy of choice and came from a position of political dominance, while Eshkol's decision was not a desired one and came from a position of relative weakness. Additionally, unlike Eshkol, or for that matter Dayan and Allon, who feared the lack of policy would be to Israel's detriment, Meir did not see any danger in leaving the matter of the OT undecided – a fact that led directly to the Yom Kippur War.

Of the three prime ministers, Rabin's political situation was the most precarious; he did not have the unqualified support of the Labour Party or, for that matter, any of its factions. Rabin's position was further weakened by the Labour Party's weak parliamentary base and its increased reliance on the NRP in the aftermath of the Yom Kippur War. Similarly to Eshkol, Rabin was actively undermined by his defence minister. Peres' support within the Labour Party was such that Rabin could not afford to dismiss him. Rabin's position and his government's political base were further weakened by the actions of Gush Emunim and the coalition promises made to the NRP. Unlike Meir and Eshkol, even if Rabin decided to pursue a coherent and comprehensive long-term policy, because of his weak party and parliamentary position, the political risks were greater than his chances for success. In other words, Rabin's decision not to decide was simply a reflection of the political reality, and the lack of necessary votes, rather than a political strategy. Nonetheless, and referring back to the role of the US, when push came to shove, and Kissinger applied enough pressure and provided enough incentives, even the Rabin government found the necessary political capital and courage to act.

In the ten years following the Six Day War, successive Israeli governments, under the leadership of the Labour Party, did not have a strategic policy with regard to the OT. There were many factors that contributed to this lack of clear long-term policy. The OT posed demographic, military, economic, diplomatic and political problems for the state of Israel. The Labour Party, undermined internally by its faction-based politics, grappled with the issue but was ultimately unable to provide a long-term solution to the problem. The failure to find a solution was further complicated by the lack of American pressure on Israel. Under no substantial American pressure, being distrustful of the Arab world and unable to clearly define the nature of the problem and the required solutions, decision-makers were in no hurry to pursue a long-term policy. This situation was welcomed by several ministers, in particular Dayan and Allon. These ministers publicly stated their demands for clear long-term policies, while using the policy vacuum to implement their own designs for the OT.

Final thoughts

One of the most important prerogatives of any government is to identify the state's strategic interests and formulate and implement its policies accordingly. None of the governments examined managed to define their strategic interest, other than to state a broad desire for secure and recognised borders. Whereas one might be willing to absolve the Eshkol government of its responsibility to put forward a strategic policy in the aftermath of the Six Day War – a war the government did not plan for and initially tried to avoid, the same cannot be said for subsequent governments. These governments' aversion to clearly defining Israel's relationship with the OT was not only irresponsible it was also reckless. As a consequence of their non-decision-making, they rejected potential peace agreements with Jordan, Egypt and, to a lesser extent, with the Palestinians, arguing that there was no one to talk to. This behaviour led directly to the Yom Kippur War and to the charge, levelled by Arab states and Palestinian organisations since, that Israel only responds to force and coercion.

The failure to formulate a strategic policy, however, is only part of a greater problem in Israeli politics and decision-making. Israel's non-decision-making was compounded by the impunity with which individual ministers and interest groups were allowed to operate. Key decision-makers, such as Allon, Dayan and Peres, were provided with the space to implement their own plans, advance their own agendas and create facts on the ground that at times contradicted the government's own plans. Had this been part of a flexible government policy that would be one thing, but the actions of these ministers were, on many occasions, in opposition to the stated interests and objectives of the governments they served. The fact that this impunity was also afforded to interest groups, in particular Gush Emunim, whose own statements made it amply clear they were acting in direct opposition to the state, is even more shocking.

What is striking, when everything is taking into account, is that the actions of key decision-makers and interest groups, coupled with non-decision-making and the lack of a strategic policy, have pushed Israel towards the only option almost all political parties, ministers and interest groups have rejected and warned against: annexation and a one-state solution.

Epilogue

At the time of writing news of more violence, including the brutal murder of one Palestinian and three Israeli teenagers, and a new war between Israel and Hamas – the Palestinian Islamic resistance movement which rules the Gaza Strip – emerges from the region. This new round of violence comes on the heels of yet another failed diplomatic initiative, this time spearheaded by US Secretary of State John Kerry, to broker an agreement between Israel and the Palestinians. As with previous peace initiatives, this diplomatic initiative failed because the US leadership is reluctant to spend the necessary political capital and is unwilling to apply sustained pressure on both sides, but in particular on Israel. The failure of the peace initiative makes it clear that the US government, as the only mediator acceptable to both sides, and the only power capable of bringing Israel to the negotiating table, is unable to adequately address the concerns of and bridge the gap between the Israeli and Palestinian sides. By Palestinian side I am referring to the Fatah-dominated Palestinian Authority in the West Bank headed by President Mahmoud Abbas (also known as Abu Mazen), who has publicly stated his commitment to peace with Israel based on a two-state solution on numerous occasions.

The Palestinian negotiating position, which has been leaked to the press, is clear. Though they are unhappy with making concessions that they believe are not based on international law, they have accepted that most of the large Jewish settlements established in the West Bank will be annexed by Israel as will the Jewish settlements (referred to by Israel as neighbourhoods) of East Jerusalem, including the Jewish quarter of the Old City. All in all they accept that some 2 per cent of the West Bank will be ceded to Israel in return for land swaps of equal value and a passage that will connect the West Bank and the Gaza Strip. With regard to the Palestinian refugees, they have privately acknowledged that few will be allowed to return to Israel proper; though it is clear that they will publicly concede this only at the final stages of the negotiating process. Nonetheless, they still demand that any future solution addresses the needs and rights of the refugees, provides for adequate compensation and deals with the issue of Israel's responsibility for creating the refugee problem. The main stumbling points, as far as the Palestinians are concerned, have been Israel's demand to include particularly controversial settlements, such as Ma'ale Adumim, which Palestinians claim make achieving a contiguous Palestinian state impossible; the future sovereignty of the Temple Mount in the Old City of Jerusalem (a site holy to both Jews and Muslims that is currently under Israeli sovereignty); Israel's demand to control the Jordan valley; and its insistence on a Palestinian recognition of Israel as a Jewish state – a move that would make life harder for Palestinians living in Israel and would make the negation of the Palestinian refugees' 'right of return' a precondition rather than a concession at the end of the negotiations.

The Israeli position is less clear; this is to a large extent the result of its historic non-decision and the fact that it has had no strategic policy towards the Occupied Territories (OT) since. On the one hand, Israel claims that no peace agreement can take place while the Palestinians are politically divided; even though Israel has helped derail Palestinian attempts at reconciliation and is unwilling to talk to Hamas. On the other hand, there are some indications, based on leaks to the press that Israel is willing to withdraw from up to 93 per cent of the West Bank, including the Jordan valley (though the withdrawal there would occur in stages and might involve leaving behind permanent Israeli military bases) and parts of East Jerusalem. However, even as the Israeli government expresses its support for a two-state solution and its willingness to withdraw from parts of the West Bank, it has continued to expand and strengthen its settlements and military control there. In addition, Israel has also continued to appropriate land in the West Bank, some of which is claimed for security purposes and for the building of its controversial separation wall/barrier; in addition to appropriating land, Israel has also expelled Palestinians from areas in and around East Jerusalem, along the Jordan valley and the route of the wall. The question of what is Israel's strategic plan with regard to the Palestinians in general and with regard to the West Bank in particular, or whether indeed it has a plan, is therefore still very relevant. Recent statements by leading Israeli ministers, for example, Foreign Minister Avigdor Liberman and Finance Minister Yair Lapid, expressing their frustration with the lack of direction, as well as with the lack of an overall plan, illustrates this point. Thus the questions of whether Israel has a clear vision of what it wants, whether indeed it has a strategic policy and the implications of not having a strategic policy are as pertinent today, probably even more so, than they have been in the past. This makes the relationship between Israel's historic non-decision and lack of a strategic policy, and its current actions an important avenue for examination.

In order to assess Israel's policy towards the OT today it is necessary to understand and note some of the changes that have occurred since 1977 and their relation to Israel's historic non-decision and lack of a strategic policy. For the sake of current relevance and clarity I will focus on the Gaza Strip and the West Bank.[1] Since 1967, no Israeli government has ever managed to put forward a coherent policy towards the Gaza Strip; this has been amply demonstrated by recent events, in particular the three Gaza wars since 2005. After the Six Day War, the Labour Party initially decided to annex the Gaza Strip, but only after the majority of its population were resettled elsewhere; for logistical and diplomatic reasons, this decision was never implemented. As a consequence, the strategy shifted from annexing to controlling the area; this strategy was based to a large extent on a strong Israeli presence in the Rafah plains. After the Likud government's decision to withdraw from the Sinai Peninsula, including the Rafah plains, Israel's position in Gaza became more tenuous. Israel was thus stuck with an area it did not want to withdraw from but could not annex and for which there were no agreeable – from Israel's' perspective – negotiating partners. In hindsight, Israel should have examined King Hussein's offer to take over the Gaza Strip more seriously.

What, then, would explain Israel's insistence on continuing to occupy until 2005 an area with limited strategic value – especially after signing a peace agreement with Egypt – no religious-normative value, with few settlers and which was perceived to be inhabited by a mostly hostile population? I would argue that the main reasons behind Israel's insistence on holding on to the territory were its lack of a strategic policy; its view of the Gaza Strip as a security threat, especially with the rise of Hamas; and the growing impact of the settler movement and its idea of Greater Israel. As a result, Israel continued to invest in settlement creation and controlling the territory without ever formulating, let alone implementing, a coherent long-term policy. To stress this last point, even when, during and after the Oslo Accords negotiations in the 1990s, it allowed Palestinians to exercise administrative autonomy in the main cities of the Gaza Strip, Israel continued to control most of the area militarily, including Gaza's border with Egypt, and invest in settlements there. This muddled approach towards the Gaza Strip should not surprise us. This has been the result of not adequately addressing the future status of the territory for over 40 years. The story of the Gaza Strip, Israel's subsequent unilateral withdrawal from it in 2005 – though it still controls its borders, air and maritime space, and has imposed a blockade since 2007 – and the several wars that have occurred since, between Israel and Hamas, demonstrates the futility of viewing the lack of a strategic policy as beneficial – in providing flexibility – and shows what happens when a non-decision and lack of a strategic policy is allowed to continue for such a long time.

In contradistinction to the decision to annex the Gaza Strip that was unanimously agreed upon in 1967 – though never implemented – ministers from the outset struggled to agree on the future of the West Bank. During the first ten years of occupation, the Labour government pursued a number of different and at times contradictory aims and plans with regard to the West Bank, these included the Allon Plan, the Functional Solution, and both a Palestinian and a Jordanian approach. Nonetheless, and at the same time, the government also established settlements that were not part of any particular plan.

With its coming to power in 1977, the Likud government formulated, agreed upon and implemented what appeared to be a strategic policy of controlling and transforming the West Bank. The Likud settlement policy of the early 1980s – based on a plan by Ariel Sharon, first as the agriculture minister and then defence minister, and Matityahu Drobles, the head of the Settlement Department, set very clear aims in terms of investment, number of settlements and rationale: the eradication of a possible future Palestinian state. The plan called for massive investment in settlement creation, and considerable subsidies and financial incentives to would-be settlers, thus eliminating the vague boundaries of the Allon Plan. It provided a substantial increase in investment per settler with the overall aim of changing the West Bank's demographics – the plan envisioned around 1.5 million Jewish settlers by 2010 (as of 2014 there are slightly over half a million Jewish settlers). In addition to the plan, the Likud Party also transformed the military administration that governed the OT into a civilian administration headed by an eminent Israeli orientalist. This move, which bore the hallmarks of historic colonial regimes, signalled Israel's intention to retain the West Bank indefinitely.

It is true that the Likud Party initiated a clear settlement policy; this policy was coherent in terms of its aims and rationale, it was agreed upon formally and was partially implemented. However, while the Likud Party had a clear settlement policy, this policy was not linked to any coherent overall strategic policy towards the West Bank. The most important issues – the future status of the West Bank and of the Palestinians – were never properly addressed in the Likud's settlement plans. In fact, the Likud Party appeared to assume that the Palestinians living in the West Bank, and the Gaza Strip, would emigrate, disappear or simply accept the changes brought about by Israel – an apartheid-like system of increased marginalisation and discrimination that denied them basic political rights.

Either the Likud Party had a strategic policy, which meant to impose an apartheid-like system, or they went ahead with their settlement plan without considering its long-term implications. Due to the lack of access to the necessary archival documents, it is impossible to answer this question. Another interesting fact to note is that, even though the Likud Party invested in and created many new settlements, the largest new settlements were mostly along the lines of the Allon Plan, particularly in and around Jerusalem. As of 2014, over 80 per cent of all settlers live in the main settlement blocks, which are roughly based on the Allon Plan. Lastly, the Likud-led settlement initiative did not, in the words of Drobles, help settlers and Palestinians to learn to live together. The growth in settlers and settlements, the increased military presence as well as land appropriation and expulsions, directly led to more instability and violence, for settlers and for Palestinians. The Likud's response to the violence was to further restrict Palestinian freedoms and political and economic rights, a recipe that eventually led to the outbreak of the first Palestinian popular uprising: the Intifada. The Likud Party, and the Israeli public, should have heeded the words of Allon in 1972 that treating the Palestinian population as second-class citizens is morally wrong and that the Jewish people 'of all people' should not be those to deliver an unjust and deplorable political system that denied 'the elementary political aspirations of the local population'.

Israel's disjointed approach towards the West Bank, and the Gaza Strip, continued even after the election of Yitzhak Rabin as prime minister and the return to power of the Labour Party in 1992. The following year, Rabin, alongside Foreign Minister Shimon Peres, signed a series of agreements with the Palestine Liberation Authority (PLO) known as the Oslo Accords. The accords paved the way for the creation of a Palestinian Authority in parts of the West Bank and the Gaza Strip and were seen as precursors to ending of the Arab-Israeli conflict; on the back of the accords Israel and Jordan signed a peace agreement in 1995 and Jordan relinquished its claim to the West Bank to the PLO. Despite the optimism these accords generated, they did not deal with *any* of the main issues: Jerusalem, refugees, borders, settlements and sovereignty. The hope was that these would be resolved at some point in the future. It was, therefore, not surprising that the accords failed to produce the desired peace, and instead ushered in a new and more violent stage in the conflict. Israel has mostly placed the onus for the failure of the accords on the Palestinians, and in particular on Hamas and its use of terrorism, which included suicide bombing and the indiscriminate firing of rockets. Nevertheless, it is clear that the accords were deeply flawed. They provided Palestinians with administrative autonomy over, depending on the period, between 3 per cent and 18 per cent of the West Bank, and limited Palestinian administrative control over a further 20 per cent, resulting in islands of Palestinian limited autonomy within an overall Israeli-controlled West Bank. Additionally, Israel's own actions directly sabotaged the accords: several large new settlements were created and settler numbers doubled during the Oslo period; for most Palestinians, Oslo came to signify more rather than less occupation.

At the end of 2014 Israel has returned a full circle back to 1967 with most ministers and political parties still unclear about what to do. Israeli decision-makers are still mulling over the same old formulae: annexation of the West Bank with limited Palestinian autonomy (Functional Solution), annexation of the settlement blocks with the remaining areas forming a Palestinian state (the Allon Plan), or withdrawal from most of the West Bank. Israeli decision-makers have neither defined the future status of the West Bank, and to a lesser extent the Gaza Strip, nor how they intend to deal with the millions of Palestinians who live there.

The impact of the non-decision-making and lack of a strategic policy are most apparent when examined in relation to the opportunities Israel has rejected. As discussed in the book, King Hussein of Jordan offered Israel what would now be considered a generous peace that was also given the blessing and backing of the US. Hussein warned Israel that a failure to negotiate with him would leave Israel stuck with Yasser Arafat and the PLO. During the same period, and leading up to the Oslo Accords, Israel ignored moderate Palestinian elements in the West Bank and Gaza Strip, leaving the PLO as the only relevant interlocutor. When it did finally negotiate with the PLO it failed to put forward its view of how the conflict would end. At the time, it was warned that a failure to provide the Palestinians with a road map to independence and secure peace with the PLO would lead to the strengthening of more extremist elements, in particular Hamas. This is particularly glaring with the emergence of Arafat's successor, Mahmoud Abbas. Abbas has gone out of his way to reassure Israel of his sincerity and has made far-reaching and generous offers to end the conflict. However, Israel has refused to move towards him, thus helping to strengthen Hamas. Israel's current refusal to negotiate with Hamas or accept a united Palestinian government, comprising Fatah and Hamas, not only strengthens even more extreme elements, but raises the question of whether Israel would ever be happy with any Palestinian partner. It also makes it clear that Israel has been a particularly poor partner to those Arabs and Palestinians who have come forward to make peace with it, which has strengthened Hamas' argument that only through violence and armed struggle will Israel ever withdraw or make concessions. Jordanian Prime Minister Zaid Rifai's question to Golda Meir in 1974 is therefore particularly prescient: *'Must we go to war in order to be taken seriously? Do you want us to fight so that you can withdraw?'*

Thus, with Israel's unwillingness to define the future status of the West Bank and the Gaza Strip, and the fact that it has gone out of its way to undermine the two-state solution, only four other alternatives remain: unilateral annexation of parts of the West Bank and withdrawal from the rest, creating in turn a number of isolated Palestinian Bantustans – a solution that would not solve Israel's security problems and which the international community opposes; annexing the West Bank and ethnically cleansing it of Palestinians – a solution the world would never accept; annexing the West Bank without providing Palestinians with equal rights – a suggestion put forward by several far-right Israeli Memebers of the Knesset (MKs), which will lead to a formal apartheid system; and a one-state solution – a solution that most Israelis reject and fear. In short, through its own actions Israel has managed to limit its margins of manoeuvre and bring about policy options it does not desire and which are unpalatable to its population and to the international community.

Israel's historic and current relationship with the OT should therefore be compared with Barbara Tuchman's *March of Folly* – though this analogy has been used before, I feel it best sums up Israel's muddle and contradictory approach – a situation in which an actor, in this case the state of Israel, behaves in a way that goes against its best interests and, while knowing or being aware of the folly of its actions, nevertheless continues.

Notes

Introduction

1. I use the term 'Occupied Territories' to describe the areas occupied by Israel after the Six Day War; these include the Golan Heights, the Sinai Peninsula and what are now commonly referred to as the Occupied Palestinian Territories, that is, the Gaza Strip and the West Bank.
2. See, for example: Gazit, Shlomo. *Trapped* (Tel Aviv, Zmora-Bitan, 1985) [in Hebrew] p. 137.
3. See, for example: Cohen, Avner. *Israel and the Bomb* (New York, Columbia University Press, 1999).
4. Sasson, Moshe. *Talking Peace* (Or Yehuda, Ma'ariv Book Guild, 2004) [in Hebrew] pp. 274–275.
5. Isaac, Rael Jean. *Israel Divided: Ideological Politics in the Jewish State* (Baltimore, Johns Hopkins University Press, 1976) p. 105.
6. Tzur, Tzvi. *Settlements and the Borders of Israel* (Tel Aviv, Yad Tabenkin, 1980) [in Hebrew] p. 20; Admoni, Yehiel. *Decade of Discretion: Settlement Policy in the Territories 1967–1977* (Tel Aviv, Yad Tabenkin, 1992) [in Hebrew] pp. 188–189.
7. Admoni. *Decade of Discretion*, pp. 70–71.
8. Bacharach, Peter and Morton Baratz (1963) 'Decisions and Nondecisions: An Analytical Framework' *The American Political Science Review* 57(3) pp. 632–642.
9. Hill, Christopher. *The Changing Politics of Foreign Policy* (Basingstoke, Palgrave Macmillan, 2003) p. 103.
10. Pedatzur, Reuven. *The Triumph of Embarrassment: Israel and the Territories after the Six Day War* (Tel Aviv, Yad Tabenkin, 1996) [in Hebrew] p. 161.
11. Shlaim, Avi. *The Iron Wall: Israel and the Arab World* (London, Penguin Books, 2000) pp. 316–318.
12. Hill, *The Changing Politics of Foreign Policy*, p. 103.
13. Van Arkadie, Brian. *Benefits and Burdens: A Report on the West Bank and Gaza Strip Economies since 1967* (New York, Carnegie Endowment for International Peace, 1977) pp. 37–38.
14. Gazit, *Trapped*, pp. 32–33.
15. Hill, *The Changing Politics of Foreign Policy*, p. 103.
16. Heywood, Andrew. *Politics* (New York, Palgrave Foundations, 2002) p. 401.
17. Hagan, Joe D. 'Domestic Political Explanations in the Analysis of Foreign Policy'. In: Neack, Laura, Hey, Jeanne and Haney, Patrick J. (eds) *Foreign Policy Analysis Continuity and Change in its Second Generation* (Upper Saddle River, NJ, Prentice Hall, 1995) pp. 122–125.
18. Klieman, Aaron S. *Israel and the World after 40 Years* (New York, Pergamon-Brassey, 1990) p. 73.
19. Beilin, Yossi, interview (5.06.2007 Tel Aviv). Beilin, Yossi. *The Price of Unity: The History of the Labour Party to the Yom Kippur War* (Tel Aviv, Revivim, 1985) [in Hebrew] pp. 215–216.

20. Beilin, Yossi, interview.
21. Izhar, Uri. *Between Vision and Power: The History of Ahdut-Ha'avoda-Poalei-Zion Party* (Tel Aviv, Yad Tabenkin, 2002) [in Hebrew] p. 424.
22. Medding, Peter. *Mapai in Israel: Political Organisation and Government in a New Society* (London, Cambridge University Press, 1972) pp. 225–226.
23. Lochery, Neill. *The Israeli Labour Party: In the Shadow of the Likud* (Reading, Ithaca Press, 1997) pp. 12–13.
24. Teveth, Shabtai. *Shearing Time/Calaban* (Israel, Yish-Dor, 1992) [in Hebrew] p. 477.
25. Yania, Natan. *Political Crises in Israel* (Jerusalem, Keter, 1982) [in Hebrew] pp. 173–174.
26. Lochery, *The Israeli Labour Party*, pp. 56–57.
27. Yishai, Yael. *Land or Peace, Whither Israel?* (Stanford, Hoover Institution Press, 1987) p. 196.
28. Medding, Peter. *The Founding of Israeli Democracy 1948–1967* (New York, Oxford University Press, 1990) p. 3.
29. Shapiro, Yonathan. *Democracy in Israel* (Ramat Gan, Massada, 1977) [in Hebrew] pp. 186–190.
30. Beilin, *The Price of Unity*, p. 45.
31. Shapiro, Yonathan. *Politicians as a Hegemonic Class: The Case of Israel* (Tel Aviv, Sifriat Hapoalim 1996) [in Hebrew] p. 111.
32. Oren, Michael B. *Six Days of War: June 1967 and the Making of the Modern Middle East* (New York, Oxford University Press, 2002) p. 309.
33. Segev, Tom. *Israel in 1967* (Jerusalem, Keter Books, 2005) [in Hebrew] p. 104.
34. Seliktar, Ofira. *New Zionism and the Foreign Policy System of Israel* (London, Croom Helm, 1986) p. 154.
35. Lustick, Ian. *Unsettled States: Disputed Lands* (Ithaca, NY, Cornell University Press, 1993) pp. 387–390.
36. Sella, Amnon and Yael Yishai. *Israel: The Peaceful Belligerent* (London, Macmillan in association with St Anthony's College Oxford, 1986) p. 167.
37. Harris, W.W. *Taking Root: Israeli Settlements in the West Bank, the Golan Heights and the Gaza Strip 1967–1980* (New York, Research Studies Press, 1980) pp. 135–138.
38. Aronoff, Myron J. *Power and Ritual in the Israel Labour Party: A Study in Political Anthropology* (New York, M.E. Sharpe, 1993) pp. 242–243.
39. Izhar, *Between Vision and Power*, p. 394.
40. Segev, *Israel in 1967*, p. 145.
41. Shapiro, *Politicians as a Hegemonic Class*, p. 108.
42. Segev, *Israel in 1967*, p. 52.
43. Segev, *Israel in 1967*, p. 267.
44. Karbo, Juliet. *Coalition Politics and Cabinet Decision Making: A Comparative Analysis of Foreign Policy Choices* (Ann Arbor, University of Michigan Press, 2012) pp. 33–35.
45. Freilich, D. Charles (2006) 'National Security Decision-Making in Israel: Processes, Pathologies, and Strengths' *Middle East Journal* 60(4) pp. 635–663.
46. Brownstein, Lewis (1977) 'Decision Making in Israeli Foreign Policy: An Unplanned Process' *Political Science Quarterly* 92(2) pp. 259–279.

47. Ben-Meir, Yehuda. *National Security Decision-Making: The Israeli Case* (Tel Aviv, Hakibbutz Hameuchad, 1987) [in Hebrew] pp. 85–86.
48. Nisan, Mordechai. *Israel and the Territories: A Study in Control 1967–1977* (Ramat Gan, Turtledove, 1978) p. 22.

1   Early Days

1. Dayan, Moshe. *Story of My Life* (London, Weidenfeld and Nicolson, 1976) pp. 380–381.
2. Eshkol served as both prime minister and defence minister from 1963 to 1967.
3. Interview with Aharon Yadlin (29.9.2007 Kibbutz Hatzerim).
4. Herut's Central Committee Meeting, 2.6.1967, ZA/18/2-1e, p. 2.
5. Dayan lost his eye in the allied invasion of Vichy-held Lebanon in 1941.
6. Bowen, Jeremy. *Six Days: How the 1967 War Shaped the Middle East* (London, Simon and Schuster, 2003) p. 86.
7. Safran, Nadav. *Israel: The Embattled Ally* (Cambridge, The Belknap Press of Harvard University Press, 1981) p. 245.
8. Morris, Benny. *Righteous Victims: A History of the Zionist-Arab Conflict 1881–2001* (Tel Aviv, Am Oved Publishers, 2003) [in Hebrew] p. 304.
9. Shlaim, *The Iron Wall*, p. 243.
10. Dayan, *Story of My Life*, p. 331.
11. Goldstein, Yossi. *Eshkol: Biography* (Jerusalem, Keter Publishers, 2003) [in Hebrew] p. 569.
12. Bleaney, Heather and Richard Lawless. *The First Day of the Six Day War* (London, Dryad Press, 1990) pp. 10, 16.
13. Goldstein, *Eshkol*, p. 569.
14. Yigal Allon Oral History (YAOH). Meeting 4, p. 21.
15. Cabinet meeting, 5.6.1967, ISA/8164/6-a.
16. Cabinet meeting.
17. Benziman, Uzi. *Jerusalem: City without a Wall* (Jerusalem, Schocken, 1973) [in Hebrew] p. 15.
18. This would have included the cities of Bethlehem, Ramallah and Nablus.
19. Teveth, Shabtai. *Moshe Dayan: The Soldier, the Man, the Legend* (London, Weidenfeld and Nicolson, 1972) p. 385.
20. Interview with Meir Amit (June 2007 by correspondence).
21. Oren, *Six Days of War*, p. 225.
22. Goldstein, *Eshkol*, p. 571.
23. Oren, *Six Days of War*, p. 262.
24. Gorenberg, Gershom. *The Accidental Empire and the Birth of the Settlements, 1967–1977* (New York, Times Books, 2006) p. 54.
25. Segev, *Israel in 1967*, p. 378.
26. Goldstein, *Eshkol*, p. 571.
27. Gorenberg, *The Accidental Empire*, p. 37.
28. Goldstein, *Eshkol*, p. 574.
29. Segev, *Israel in 1967*, p. 390.
30. Segev, p. 407.

31. Interview with Shlomo Hillel (23.9.2007 Ra'anana).
32. Interview with Shlomo Hillel.
33. Goldstein, *Eshkol*, p. 575.
34. Interview with Hillel.
35. Oren, *Six Days of War*, pp. 298–300.
36. Seliktar, *New Zionism*, p. 156.
37. Mapai's and Ben-Gurion's animosity towards Begin went back to the 1940s when the latter was head of the notorious paramilitary organisation, the Irgun. This animosity increased in 1952 when Begin led a violent demonstration to the Knesset in opposition to Ben-Gurion's decision to sign a reparations agreement with West Germany.
38. Cabinet meeting, 11.6.1967, ISA/8164/6-a, p. 6.
39. Cabinet meeting, p. 4.
40. Nadel, Chaim. *Between the Two Wars: The Security and Military Activities to Achieve Readiness and Alert in the IDF* (Tel Aviv, Ma'arachot, 2006) [in Hebrew] p. 21.
41. In the aftermath of the Suez Crisis 1956–7.
42. Teveth, Shabtai. *The Cursed Blessing: The Story of Israel's Occupation of the West Bank* (London, Weidenfeld and Nicolson) pp. 10–11.
43. Gazit, Shlomo. *The Stick and the Carrot* (Tel Aviv, Zmora-Bitan, 1985) [in Hebrew] pp. 46–47.
44. Teveth, *The Cursed Blessing*, pp. 97–98.
45. Gazit, *The Stick and the Carrot*, pp. 48–49.
46. Teveth, *The Cursed Blessing*, p. 25.
47. Teveth, p. 54.
48. Nadel, *Between the Two Wars*, p. 14.
49. Gazit, *Trapped*, pp. 138–139.
50. Sasson, *Talking Peace*, p. 91.
51. Bavly, Dan. *Dreams and Missed Opportunities 1967–1973* (Jerusalem, Carmel, 2002) [in Hebrew] pp. 247–251.
52. Bavly, pp. 247–251.
53. Sasson, *Talking Peace*, p. 274.
54. Dayan, *Story of My Life*, pp. 490–491.
55. Bavly, *Dreams and Missed Opportunities*, pp. 35–36.
56. Gazit, *Trapped*, pp. 140–141.
57. Gazit, *The Stick and the Carrot*, p. 129.
58. Gazit, *Trapped*, p. 141.
59. Pedatzur, *The Triumph of Embarrassment*, p. 117.
60. Pedatzur, pp. 34–35.
61. Pedatzur, p. 36.
62. Cabinet meeting, 11.6.1967, ISA/8164/6-a, p. 43.
63. Cabinet meeting, p. 43.
64. Cabinet meeting, p. 38.
65. Cabinet meeting, p. 50.
66. Gazit, *The Stick and the Carrot*, p. 223.
67. Goldstein, *Eshkol*, pp. 580–582.
68. Pedatzur, *The Triumph of Embarrassment*, p. 96.
69. Korn, David A. *Stalemate: The War of Attrition and Great Power Diplomacy in the Middle East, 1967–1970* (Boulder, Westview Press, 1992) p. 13.

70. Interview with Danny Halperin (6.9.2006 Jerusalem).
71. Interview with Danny Halperin.
72. Benziman, *Jerusalem*, pp. 37–40.
73. Gorenberg, *The Accidental Empire*, p. 44.
74. Segev, *Israel in 1967*, p. 422.
75. The Islamic endowment trust that had traditionally managed the site.
76. Teveth, *The Cursed Blessing*, pp. 104–105.
77. Gorenberg, *The Accidental Empire*, p. 45.
78. Cabinet meeting, 18.6.1967 (morning session), ISA/8164/7-a, pp. 61–65.
79. Cabinet meeting, p. 18.
80. Cabinet meeting, 18.6.1967 (afternoon session), ISA/8164/7-a, pp. 96–103.
81. Bavly, *Dreams and Missed Opportunities*, p. 37.
82. Cabinet meeting, 18.6.1967 (afternoon session), ISA/8164/7-a, p. 60.
83. Pedatzur, *The Triumph of Embarrassment*, pp. 51–52.
84. Cabinet meeting, 19.6.1967 (morning session), ISA/8164/8-a, p. 56.
85. Cabinet meeting, p. 32.
86. Interview with Victor Shem-Tov (6.9.2006 Jerusalem).
87. Cabinet meeting, 19.6.1967 (afternoon session), ISA/8164/8-a, p. 98.
88. Cabinet meeting, p. 100.
89. Cabinet meeting, 19.6.1967 (morning session), ISA/8164/8-a, p. 100.
90. Cabinet meeting, 19.6.1967 (afternoon session), ISA/8164/8-a, p. 29.
91. Cabinet meeting, 19.6.1967 (morning session), ISA/8164/8-a, p. 54.
92. Bavly, *Dreams and Missed Opportunities*, p. 37.
93. Cabinet meeting, 19.6.1967 (morning session), ISA/8164/8-a, p. 89.
94. Cabinet meeting, pp. 29–33.
95. Cabinet meeting, p. 39.
96. Cabinet meeting, 18.6.1967 (afternoon session), ISA/8164/7-a, pp. 112–113.
97. Cabinet meeting, p. 80.
98. Cabinet meeting, pp. 104–105.
99. Cabinet meeting, 19.6.1967 (morning session), ISA/8164/8-a, p. 14.
100. Cabinet meeting, p. 43.
101. Cabinet meeting, p. 44.
102. Cabinet meeting, pp. 46–47.
103. Cabinet meeting, p. 49.
104. Cabinet meeting, p. 51.
105. Cabinet meeting, p. 23.
106. Cabinet meeting, p. 100.
107. See, for example: Gazit, *Trapped*, p. 137.
108. See: http://www.presidency.ucsb.edu/ws/?pid=28308 (accessed 15.11.2013).
109. Rafael, Gideon. *Destination Peace: Three Decades of Israeli Foreign Policy, a Personal Memoir* (London, Weidenfeld and Nicolson, 1981) p. 163.
110. Eban, Abba. *My Life* (Tel Aviv, Ma'ariv Book Guild, 1978) p. 430.
111. US mission in the UN to the State Department, 22.6.1967, FRUS/Volume XIX, document 314.
112. Shalev, Aryeh. *Israel and Syria: Peace and Security in the Golan* (Tel Aviv, Westview Press, Publication of the Centre for Strategic Studies, 1994) [in Hebrew] p. 60.
113. Shlaim, *The Iron Wall*, p. 254.
114. Bavly, *Dreams and Missed Opportunities*, p. 38.

115. Interview with Yadlin.
116. Rafael, *Destination Peace*, p. 169.
117. Eban, *My Life*, p. 423.
118. Lochery, Neill. *Loaded Dice: The Foreign Office and Israel* (London, Continuum, 2007) pp. 120–121.
119. Cabinet meeting, 25.6.1967, ISA/8164/9-a, pp. 4 and 11.
120. Gazit, *Trapped*, p. 226.
121. Benvenisti, Meron. *Jerusalem: The Torn City* (Jerusalem, Weidenfeld and Nicolson, 1973) [in Hebrew] pp. 55–56.
122. Pedatzur, *The Triumph of Embarrassment*, p. 118.
123. Cabinet meeting, 25.6.1967, ISA/8164/9-a, pp. 20–21.
124. Cabinet meeting, p. 17.
125. Benvenisti, *Jerusalem*, p. 140.
126. Cabinet meeting, 27.6.1967, ISA/8164/9-a, p. 14.
127. US Embassy in Tel Aviv to the State Department, 29.6.1967, FRUS/Volume XIX, Document 338.
128. Rafael, *Destination Peace*, p. 165.
129. Rafael, pp.167–168.
130. Rafael to Goldberg, 31.8.1967, ISA/3978/3-f, p. 5.
131. Shlaim, Avi. *Lion of Jordan: The Life of King Hussein in War and Peace* (London, Allen Lane, Penguin Books, 2007) p. 257.
132. Foreign Ministry Report, 13.7.1967, ISA/7921/2-a.
133. Inter-Departmental Committee's Report, 20.7.1967, ISA/7921/2-a.
134. Committee of the West Bank recommendations, 21.7.1967, ISA/7052/12-a, p. 2.
135. Heads of Services Committee to Eshkol, 27.7.1967, ISA/7052/12-a, p. 3.
136. Heads of Services Committee to Eshkol, Appendix A, p. 2.
137. The Allon Plan, 26.7.1967, YTA/15Allon/6/2.
138. Interview with Yadlin.
139. YAOH, Meeting 3, pp. 14–17.
140. The WZO had been involved in settlement creation in Palestine/Israel from the end of the 19th century. Its settlement department acts alongside and supports – mostly through planning, financing and controlling land – the Israeli governments' housing and land development projects.
141. Pedatzur, *The Triumph of Embarrassment*, p. 148.
142. Weitz, Ra'anan. *An Overview of the History of the Settlement of Israel* (Jerusalem, Bialik Institute, 2003) [in Hebrew] p. 93.
143. Allon Diary, 27.6.1967, YTA/Allon personal notes.
144. The story of the settlement in Eliqa will be discussed in depth in the next chapter.
145. Rafi Secretariat meeting, 3.9.1967, LPA/5-3-1967-24.
146. The Dayan Plan (no date), YTA/15Galili/85/7.
147. Melman,Yossi and Daniel Raviv. *A Hostile Partnership: The Secret Relationship between Israel and Jordan* (Tel Aviv, Yedioth Ahronoth, 1987) [in Hebrew] p. 71.
148. Pedatzur, *The Triumph of Embarrassment*, p. 149.
149. Shem-Tov, Victor. *One of Them* (Kibbutz Dalia, Maarachot, 1997) [in Hebrew] pp. 82–83. Interview with Shem-Tov.
150. Dayan at the Knesset Foreign Affairs and Defence Committee (KFDC), 28.6.1967, ISA/8161/7-a, p. 15.

151. Gazit, *The Stick and the Carrot*, pp. 110–119.
152. Dayan, *Story of My Life*, pp. 33–36.
153. Government Regulations in the Held Territories, 23.6.1967, ISA/6304/10-c.
154. Shlomo Gazit: Report on the Held Territories, December 1969, LPA/4-04-1951-48.
155. Dayan meeting with West Bank mayors, 12.10.1967, ISA7921/3-a.
156. Interview with Halperin.
157. Interview with Halperin.
158. Dayan at the KFDC, 25.7.1967, ISA/8161/7-a, p. 21.
159. Interview with Shulamit Aloni (8.11.2007 Kfar Shmaryahu).

2 The 'Wall-to-Wall' Coalition

1. Izhar, *Between Vision and Power*, p. 21.
2. Izhar, pp. 421–422.
3. Cabinet meeting, 18.6.1967 (afternoon session), ISA/8164/7-a, pp. 104–105.
4. IDF's Edicts and Orders in the Golan Heights, order no. 9, 18.7.1967 (IDF).
5. Tzur, *Settlements and the Borders of Israel*, pp. 25–26.
6. Pedatzur, *The Triumph of Embarrassment*, p. 167.
7. YAOH, Meeting 6, p. 11.
8. Admoni, *Decade of Discretion*, p. 22.
9. YAOH, Meeting 6, p. 12.
10. YAOH, Meeting 6, p. 11.
11. Gorenberg, *The Accidental Empire*, p.76.
12. Interview with Nahman Bernstein (6.6.2007 Tel Aviv).
13. Weitz, *History of the Settlement of Israel*, p. 91.
14. Gorenberg, *The Accidental Empire*, p. 97.
15. Admoni, *Decade of Discretion*, p. 25.
16. Government decision, 29.8.1967, ISA/6692/15-c.
17. Nahal (Fighting Pioneer Youth) – army units that combine military service with agricultural settlements.
18. Pedatzur, *The Triumph of Embarrassment*, p. 182.
19. Gorenberg, *The Accidental Empire*, p. 109.
20. Interview with Hillel.
21. *Bamahane* (IDF magazine) 'Interview with Moshe Dayan' 27.5.1968.
22. Pedatzur, *The Triumph of Embarrassment*, p. 177.
23. Gush Etzion proposal, 10.9.1967, YTA/15Allon/6/2/3.
24. Eldar, Akiva and Idith Zertal. *Lords of the Land: The Settlers and the State of Israel 1967–2004* (Or Yehuda, Zmora-Bitan, 2004) [in Hebrew] p. 20.
25. Eshkol meeting with Gush Etzion group, 16.8.1967, ISA/7920/7-a.
26. Pedatzur, *The Triumph of Embarrassment*, p. 191.
27. Meron to Eban, 14.9.1967, ISA/7921/3-a.
28. Eshkol's second meeting with Gush Etzion group, 22.9.1967, ISA/7920/7-a.
29. Admoni, *Decade of Discretion*, p. 53.
30. Isaac, *Israel Divided*, p. 53.
31. Pedatzur, *The Triumph of Embarrassment*, p. 192.
32. Pedatzur, p. 193.
33. Pedatzur, pp. 74–75.

34. YAOH, Meeting 3, p. 23.
35. YAOH, Meeting 4, p. 18.
36. YAOH, Meeting 7, p. 4.
37. Interview with Amit.
38. Government decision no. 866, 1.10.1967, YTA/12-3/94/4.
39. Pedatzur, *The Triumph of Embarrassment*, p. 196.
40. Pedatzur, p. 202.
41. Foreign Ministry cable to embassies, 25.9.1967, ISA/7462/8-a.
42. Herman to Foreign Ministry, 25.9.1967, ISA/7462/8-a.
43. Foreign Ministry to Herman, 26.9.1967, ISA/7462/8-a.
44. Meeting between Eban, Raphael and Goldberg, 20.9.1967, ISA/3976/12-a.
45. Embassy in Washington to Foreign Ministry, 27.9.1967, ISA/7462/8-a.
46. Pedatzur, *The Triumph of Embarrassment*, p. 113.
47. Ben-Meir, *National Security Decision-Making*, p. 25.
48. Meeting between Eshkol, Dayan and IDF generals, 5.12.1967, ISA/7921/3-a, p. 11.
49. Eshkol, Dayan and IDF generals, pp. 13–14.
50. Eshkol, Dayan and IDF generals, p. 17.
51. Eshkol, Dayan and IDF generals, p. 21.
52. Eshkol, Dayan and IDF generals, p. 25.
53. Israel's embassy in Washington report, 21.11.967, ISA/3978/3-f.
54. Bar Zohar, Michael. *Yaacov Hertzog: A Biography* (London, Halban, 2005) p. 317.
55. Bar Zohar, p. 317.
56. Bar Zohar, p. 319.
57. Prime Minister's Office proposal, 5.12.1967, ISA/7921/3-a.
58. Eban to Goldberg, 1.11.1967, ISA/3976/12-a.
59. Eshkol at the KFDC, 17.11.1967, ISA/8161/7-a, p. 19.
60. Eshkol at the KFDC, p. 32.
61. Israeli embassy in London to Eban, 8.11.1967, ISA/3978/3-a.
62. US UN Mission to the State Department, 8.11.1967, FRUS/Volume XIX, Document 512.
63. Eshkol at the KFDC, 17.11.1967, p. 30.
64. Until 1967 France was Israel's main military supplier.
65. Johnson, Rusk and Eshkol meeting, 7.1.1968 (session one), FRUS/Volume XX, Document 39.
66. Eshkol at the KFDC, 17.11.1967, p. 30.
67. Johnson, Rusk and Eshkol meeting, 7.1.1968 (session one), FRUS/Volume XX, Document 39.
68. Quandt, William B. *Peace Process: American Diplomacy and the Arab-Israeli Conflict since 1967* (Harrisonburg, University of California Press, 2001) p. 47.
69. Johnson, Rusk and Eshkol meeting, 7.1.1968 (session two), FRUS/Volume XX, Document 40.
70. Quandt, *Peace Process*, p. 47.
71. Johnson, Rusk and Eshkol meeting, 7.1.1968 (session three), FRUS/Volume XX, Document 41.
72. YAOH, Meeting 3, p. 21.
73. Telegram from the State Department to the embassy in Tel Aviv, 2.3.1968, FRUS/Volume XX, Document 96.

74. Rostow to Johnson, 20.2.1968, FRUS/Volume XX, Document 88.
75. Eshkol, meeting with Hertzog, Eban and Rafael, 3.3.1968, ISA/4780/3-f.
76. Rafi Conference, 12.12.1967, LPA/5-1-1967-17, p. 3.
77. Rafi Conference, p. 8.
78. AMAN and Foreign Ministry meeting, 17.12.1967, ISA/4780/3-f.
79. Deputy Head of AMAN David Carmon at the KFDC, 6.2.1968, ISA/8161/9-a, pp. 13–14.
80. Interview with Amit.
81. Eshkol meeting with Eban and Rabin, 24.5.1968, ISA/7938/11-a.
82. National Security Council (NSC) on the Jarring Mission, 21.2.1968, FRUS/Volume XX, Document 91.
83. Beilin, *The Price of Unity*, p. 41.
84. Medding, *Mapai in Israel*, p. 292.
85. Mapai's Central Committee meeting, 29.10.1967, LPA/2-23-1967-92, p. 48.
86. Interview with Yossi Beilin.
87. Medding, *Mapai in Israel*, p. 294.
88. Mapam's Secretariat meeting, 20.7.1968, YYA/Mapam90/68/8, p. 59.
89. Shapiro, *Politicians as a Hegemonic Class*, p. 111.
90. Medding, *Mapai in Israel*, p. 292.
91. Izhar, *Between Vision and Power*, p. 371.
92. Izhar, p. 417.
93. Shapiro, *Democracy in Israel*, pp. 186–190.
94. Interview with Beilin.
95. Interview with Beilin.
96. Kieval, Gershon. *Party Politics in Israel and the Occupied Territories* (Westport, Greenwood, 1983) p. 24.
97. Yishai, *Land or Peace*, p. 196.
98. Labour Party Secretariat, 2.1.1968, ISA/7550/1-a.
99. LP manifesto, 21.1.1968, LPA/2-021-1977-133.

3 'I don't know, I am looking for someone who does'

1. Yishai, *Land or Peace*, p. 195.
2. Interview with Bernstein.
3. Eshkol at the KFDC, 27.2.1968, ISA/8161/10-a, p. 7.
4. Settlement Committee meeting, 31.12.1967, ISA/6692/15-c.
5. Allon's proposal, 14.1.1968, YTA/15Allon/11/6/2.
6. Elazar at the KFDC, 19.1.1968, ISA/8161/9-a, pp. 4–5.
7. Bar-Lev at the KFDC, 20.2.1968, ISA/8161/9-a, p. 9.
8. Teveth, *The Cursed Blessing*, p. 270.
9. Confidential army interview with Netzer, 9.11.1972, YTA/15Netzer/4/3, p. 5.
10. Netzer, p. 10.
11. Netzer, p. 8.
12. Allon's settlement proposal, 27.2.1968, YTA/15Allon/11/6/2.
13. 'Jordan Valley Development Proposal', 19.3.1968, ISA/6423/1-c.
14. Allon's settlement proposal, 18.2.1968, YTA/15Allon/11/6/2.
15. Allon's settlement proposal, 24.4.1968, YTA/15Allon/11/6/2.
16. Allon's Golan Heights proposal, 29.8.1968, YTA/15Allon/11/6/2.

17. Allon's Druze proposal, 10.10.1967, YTA/15Allon/11/6/2.
18. Eban to Eshkol, 5.9.1968, YTA/15Allon/11/6/2.
19. Meron to Hertzog (no date: relates to previous memo dated 14.3.1968), ISA/3191/8-f.
20. Elazar at the KFDC, 19.1.1968, p. 4.
21. KFDC meeting, 25.6.1968, ISA/8162/1-a, pp. 13–14.
22. Barzilai's personal notes, 1968, YYA/Barzilai 15-95/7/68.
23. Interview with Hillel.
24. Cabinet meeting, 19.6.1967 (morning session), ISA/8164/8-a, p. 56.
25. Cabinet meeting, p. 32.
26. Interview with Shem-Tov; though Shem-Tov found it difficult to explain, in retrospect, the logic of including Gaza.
27. Foreign Ministry Report, 13.7.1967, ISA/7921/2-a, p. 4.
28. The Inter-Departmental Committee's Report, 20.7.1967, ISA/7921/2-a.
29. Heads of Services Committee to Eshkol, 27.7.1967, Appendix-C, ISA/7052/12-a.
30. 'Economic comments to diplomatic considerations', 17.7.1967, ISA/7052/12-a.
31. Meron to Eban, 19.9.1967, ISA/7921/3-a.
32. Eshkol with Dvoretsky and Bechi. 6.12.1967, ISA/7921/3-a.
33. Commander of the Gaza Strip Gur at the KFDC, 19.1.68, ISA/8161/9-a, p. 21.
34. Defence Ministry to Sapir, 8.1.1968, YTA/15Allon/11/6/2.
35. Gur at the KFDC, 19.1.1968, p. 10.
36. Eshkol at the KFDC, 27.2.1968, ISA/8161/10-a, p. 6; Special Task Force preliminary report on immigration from Gaza to Jordan (no date: early February 1968), ISA/7921/4-a; Special Task Force general comments on the emigration of Arabs, 26.3.1968, ISA/7921/4-a.
37. Eshkol with Dvoretsky and Bechi. 6.12.1967, ISA/7921/3-a.
38. Sasson, *Talking Peace*, p. 100.
39. YAOH, Meeting 4, p. 3.
40. Gur at the KFDC, 19.1.1968, p. 11; Weitz to Eshkol, 28.11.1967, ISA/7921/3-a.
41. Foreign Ministry briefing paper, 2.7.167, ISA/7291/2-a.
42. YAOH, Meeting 6, p. 16.
43. Eshkol with Eda Sirani, 13.5.1968, ISA/7921/4-a.
44. Ministerial Committee for the Held Territories (MCHT), 3.7.1968, ISA/7921/5-a, p. 13.
45. Sasson at the KFDC, 9.2.1968, ISA/8161/9-a, p. 19.
46. Eshkol at the KFDC, 27.2.1968, p. 3.
47. Foreign Ministry Assessments, 4.7.1968, ISA/4781/7-f, Appendix 4.
48. Lustick, *Unsettled States: Disputed Lands*, pp. 387–390.
49. Sella and Yishai, *Israel: The Peaceful Belligerent*, p. 167.
50. Harris, *Taking Root*, pp. 135–138.
51. Eldar and Zertal, *Lords of the Land*, p. 30.
52. KFDC meeting, 20.2.1968, ISA/8161/10-a, p. 9.
53. Warhaftig, Zorach. *Fifty Years, from Year to Year* (Jerusalem, Yad Shapira, 1998) p. 299.
54. The mostly ultra-orthodox and non-Zionist Jewish community of Hebron was massacred during inter-ethnic clashes in 1929. The massacre, and the subsequent elimination of the historic Jewish presence in the city, was a traumatic event in the history of Judaism and Zionism during the British Mandate.
55. Hebron Proposal, 13.3.1968, YTA/15Allon/11/6/2.

56. Isaac, *Israel Divided*, pp. 56–57.
57. Eshkol's meeting with the Land of Israel Movement, 12.11.1967, ISA/7920/7-a, p. 24.
58. Friedman, Menachem. 'The State of Israel as a Theological Dilemma'. In: Kimmerling, Baruch. *The Israeli State and Society, Boundaries and Frontiers* (New York, State University of New York Press, 1989) pp. 203–204.
59. According to Judaic and Islamic tradition, the tomb is the burial place of the three patriarchs (Abraham, Isaac and Jacob).
60. Eldar and Zertal, *Lords of the Land*, p. 31.
61. YAOH, Meeting 6, p. 17.
62. Teveth, *The Cursed Blessing*, p. 276.
63. Ministerial meeting, 21.5.1968, ISA/7921/4-a, p. 1.
64. Al-Ja'bari to Eshkol, 21.4.1968, YTA/15Allon/11/6/2.
65. Report on 'Possible Settlement Opportunities in the Hebron Area', 25.9.1968, ISA/7920/7-a.
66. Meir at the KFDC, 27.5.1969, ISA/8162/5-a, p. 1.
67. Report by Gazit, 4.1.1972, ISA/6646/2-c.
68. Allon's proposals, dated 29.1.1969 and 30.4.1969, YTA/15Allon/11/6/2.
69. Sasson letter of appointment, 12.11.1967, ISA/7291/3-a.
70. 'The Diplomatic Effort among Palestinians' (no date: June 1968), ISA/7921/5-a.
71. Sasson's meeting with Eshkol, 9.6.1968, ISA/7052/12-a.
72. Prime Minister's Guidelines, 9.4.1968, ISA/7052/12-a.
73. Sasson to Eshkol, 22.1.1968, ISA/7921/4-a.
74. At the time the PLO was an umbrella organisation that encompassed a variety of Palestinian groups committed to the liberation and independence of historical Palestine (the Gaza Strip, the West Bank and Israel).
75. Briefing paper by Sasson, 28.1.1968, ISA/7921/4-a.
76. Sasson at the KFDC, 9.2.1968, ISA/8161/9-a, pp. 18–19.
77. Briefing paper by Sasson, 28.1.1968, ISA/7921/4-a, p. 5.
78. Sasson to Eshkol, 6.4.1968, ISA/7921/12-a.
79. Sasson on Shaka'a's meeting with Eshkol, 31.3.1968, ISA/7045/12-a.
80. Sasson to Eshkol, 2.4.1968, ISA/7045/12-a.
81. Sasson's meeting with Shaka'a, 18.3.1968, ISA/7045/12-a.
82. Sasson's meeting with Shaka'a, 31.3.1968, ISA/7045/12-a.
83. Sasson's meeting with Shaka'a, 31.3.1968.
84. Sasson's meeting with Nashashibi, 15.9.168, ISA/7045/12-a.
85. 'The Diplomatic Effort among Palestinians', ISA/7921/5-a, p. 2
86. Sasson meeting with Dayan, 6.4.1968, ISA/7045/12-a.
87. In August 1968 the PLO, in its amended charter, rejected Israel's right to exist and claimed that the armed struggle was the only way to liberate Palestine (the West Bank, the Gaza Strip and Israel).
88. Sahliyeh, Emile. *In Search of Leadership: West Bank Politics Since 1967* (Washington, DC, Brookings Institution, 1988), p. 29; Sasson's meeting with Janho, 14–15.9.1968, ISA/7045/12-a (interestingly, Janho was assassinated in 1978 by the PLO for his close association with Israel); Sasson to Eshkol, 25.11.1968, ISA/7045/12-a.
89. Sasson's meeting with Shehadeh, 8.12.1968, ISA/7045/12-a.
90. Dayan with Can'an and Shehadeh, 14.4.1968, ISA/7052/12-a.

91. Dayan with Can'an and Shehadeh.
92. Sasson to Eban, 23.4.1968, ISA/7052/12-a.
93. Prime Minister's Report and Guidelines, ISA/7052/12-a, p. 2.
94. Special Steering Committee (SSC) meeting, 21.5.1968, ISA/7921/4-a, p. 1
95. SSC meeting, p. 2.
96. Sasson on the views of the Arab dignitaries of Jerusalem, Judea and Samaria, 30.1.1968, ISA/7052/12-a, p. 2.
97. 'The Diplomatic Effort among Palestinians', ISA/7921/5-a.
98. Sasson's meeting with Shehadeh, 17.6.1968, ISA/7045/12-a.
99. SSC meeting, 3.7.1968, ISA/7052/12-a.
100. SSC meeting.
101. SSC meeting.
102. Sasson's meeting with al-Ja'bari, 28.6.1968, ISA/7045/12-a.
103. Sasson's meeting with al-Ja'bari. This meeting followed a discussion between the Mayor of Bethlehem Elias Bandak and Sasson, in which Bandak agreed, in principle, to a self-rule plan. See: Sasson's meeting with Bandak, 7.7.1968, ISA/7045/12-a. Beit Jala was also expected to follow, see: Sasson to Eshkol, 26.7.1968, ISA/7045/12-a.
104. Sasson's meeting with Can'an and Shaka'a , 7.8.1968; ISA/7045/12-a; Sasson's meeting with Al-Masri, 11.8.1968, ISA/7045/12-a.
105. SSC meeting, 23.7.1968, ISA/7921/5-a, p. 3.
106. Sasson interim report, 1.8.1968, ISA/7052/12-a.
107. For example, see: Al-Ja'bari's meeting with Eshkol, 12.8.1968, ISA/7045/12-a; Al-Ja'bari's meeting with Meir, 26.8.1969, 7045/12-a.
108. SSC meeting, 17.7.1968, ISA/7052/12-a.
109. Sasson's meeting with al-Ja'bari, 7.7.1968, ISA/7045/12-a.
110. SSC meeting, 17.7.1968, ISA/7052/12-a.
111. Sasson to Eshkol, 13.8.1968, ISA/7052/12-a.
112. Eshkol at the KFDC, 25.6.1968, ISA/8162/1-a, pp. 8–9.
113. SSC meeting, 21.5.1968, ISA/7921/4-a, p. 8.
114. Informal ministerial meeting, 21.5.1968, ISA/7921/4-a, p. 9.
115. As a result of the party holding a majority of seats in the Knesset, talks at its Political Committee were as, if not more, important than cabinet discussions.
116. Ma'arach's Political Committee (MPC) meeting, 3.6.1968, ISA/7921/13-a, pp. 1–2
117. MPC meeting, p. 4.
118. MPC meeting, p. 5.
119. Israel's embassy in Washington to Foreign Ministry, 18.3.1968, ISA/4780/3-f, pp. 1–3.
120. MPC meeting, p. 7.
121. MPC meeting, p. 17.
122. MPC meeting, p. 19.
123. MPC meeting, p. 30.
124. MPC meeting, pp. 33–34.
125. MPC meeting, p. 66.
126. SSC meeting, 3.7.1968, ISA/7921/4-a, pp. 28–29.
127. MPC meeting, 20.9.1968, ISA7921/13-a, p. 14.
128. MPC meeting, pp. 17–18.
129. MPC meeting, p. 27.

130. MPC meeting, pp. 30–31.
131. Eban's meeting with Hussein (no date), ISA/7043/15-a, p. 2.
132. YAOH, Meeting 6, p. 3.
133. Eban's meeting with Hussein, pp. 5–6.
134. MPC meeting, 27.12.1978, ISA/7821/13-a, pp. 13–14.
135. YAOH, Meeting 8, p. 3.
136. YAOH, Meeting 8, pp. 5–6.
137. Interview with Amit.
138. Bar Zohar, *Yaacov Hertzog*, pp. 327–328.
139. Nisan, *Israel and the Territories*, p. 36.
140. Teveth, *The Cursed Blessing*, p. 337.
141. Nisan, *Israel and the Territories*, pp. 34–35.
142. Committee for the Development of the Held Territories (no date) probably late 1967, ISA/7552/10-a, pp. 12–13.
143. Teveth, *The Cursed Blessing*, p. 343.
144. Eshkol to Dayan, 19.11.1968, YTA/15Galili/91/8/1.
145. Kieval, *Party Politics in Israel*, p. 27.
146. 'Israel's Economic Policy in the Territories' (no date), LPA/2-932-1969-462, p. 5.
147. Interview with Halperin.
148. Sandler, Shmuel and Hillel Frisch. 'The Political Economy of the Administrated Territories'. In: Elazar, Daniel J. *Judea, Samaria and Gaza: Views on the Present and Future* (Washington, American Enterprise Institute For Public Policy Research, 1982) p. 141.
149. Interview with Halperin.
150. Dayan at the KFDC, 24.12.1968, ISA/8162/3-a, p. 12.
151. Nisan, *Israel and the Territories*, p. 93.
152. 'Economic Activity in the West Bank and the Gaza Strip', 21.5.1968, ISA/3191/8-f.
153. Pedatzur, *The Triumph of Embarrassment*, p. 155.
154. Teveth, *The Cursed Blessing*, p. 338.

4 The Best Man in the Government

1. Prime Minister Levi Eshkol passed away on 26 February 1969.
2. Polls conducted by Israeli newspapers showed an overwhelming public support for Dayan's nomination.
3. Interview with Halperin.
4. Beilin, *The Price of Unity*, p. 52.
5. Interview with Halperin.
6. Spyer, A.J. *The Decline of Statism: The Changing Political Culture of the Israeli Labour Party and the Party's Policy Proposals Regarding the West Bank, 1967–1999* (PhD, UCL, 2003) p. 138.
7. Gorenberg, *The Accidental Empire*, p. 271.
8. Intelligence Report, 7.5.1968, ISA/4221/4-a.
9. Shimshoni, Jonathan. *Israel and Conventional Deterrence: Border Warfare from 1953 to 1970* (London, Cornell University Press, 1988) p. 143.
10. Korn, *Stalemate*, p. 109.

11. Quandt, *Peace Process*, p. 63.
12. Quandt, *Peace Process*, pp. 63–64.
13. Goldstein, *Rabin – Biography* (Tel Aviv, Schocken, 2006) [in Hebrew] p. 216.
14. Eban's meeting with Rogers, 13.3.1969, ISA/4780/2-f, pp. 4–5.
15. Meir's meeting with Barbour, 19.3.1969, ISA/4780/2-f.
16. Meir at the KFDC, 31.3.169, ISA/8162/4-a, pp. 3–4.
17. Meir to Eban, 18.3.1969, ISA/4780/2-f.
18. Torgovnik, Efraim. 'Party Factions and Election Issues'. In: Arian, Asher (ed.). *The Elections in Israel 1969* (Jerusalem, Jerusalem Academic Press, 1972) p. 21.
19. Mapam, though still an independent political party, joined the Labour Party in the parliamentary block known as the Alignment (Ma'arach). As part of the Alignment, it participated in the main political discussions.
20. A movement to install Dayan as prime minister collected more than 100,000 signatures.
21. Kieval, *Party Politics in Israel*, p. 29.
22. Beilin, *The Price of Unity*, pp. 54–56.
23. Izhar, *Between Vision and Power*, pp. 442–444.
24. LP's Electoral Committee meeting (no date), LPA/2-007-1969-244, pp. 2–3.
25. LP's Electoral Committee meeting.
26. Kieval, *Party Politics in Israel*, p. 31.
27. Allon's diary, 27.7.1969, YTA/15Allon.
28. MCHT decision no. 28, 9.7.1969, YTA/15Galili/64/2.
29. Head of IDF's Gaza and Sinai administration to Interior Ministry, 20.7.1969, YTA/15Galili/64/2.
30. Eban's corrections of Dayan's text, 13.8.1969, YTA/15Galili/64/2.
31. LP Convention, 4.8.1969, LPA/2-021-1969-95, p. 27.
32. LP Convention, p. 57.
33. LP Convention, pp. 57–58.
34. LP Convention, pp. 57–58.
35. LP Convention, 4.8.1969 (third session), LPA/2-021-1969-95, p. 37.
36. LP Convention, pp. 40–41.
37. LP Convention, pp. 40–41.
38. Ernest Stock, 'Foreign Policy Issues'. In: Arian (ed.) *The Elections in Israel 1969*, p. 44.
39. Stock, 'Foreign Policy Issues'.
40. Interview with Beilin.
41. Allon's diary, 27.7.1969, YTA/15Allon.
42. Interview with Halperin.
43. Hand-written note from Galili to Barkatt (no date), LPA/2-232-1969-374.
44. Kieval, *Party Politics in Israel*, pp. 32–33.
45. Torgovnik, 'Party Factions', p. 25.
46. LP Convention, 5.8.1969, LPA/2-021-1969-95, p. 23.
47. The Oral Law, LPA/2-23-1969-98.
48. Galili to Meir, 7.8.1969, LPA/2-932-1969-462.
49. YAOH, Meeting 9, pp. 8–11.
50. YAOH, Meeting 9, p. 12.
51. Beilin, *The Price of Unity*, p. 57.
52. LP Convention, 11.9.1969, LPA/2-23-1969-98, pp. 6–7.
53. LP Convention, p. 9.

54. LP Convention, p. 10.
55. LP Convention, p. 10.
56. LP Convention, pp. 6–7.
57. Beilin, *The Price of Unity*, p. 56.
58. LP Convention, 11.9.1969, LPA/2-23-1969-98, p. 44.
59. LP Convention, 11.9.1969, LPA/2-23-1969-98, p. 42.
60. Interview with Beilin.
61. LP Convention, 11.9.1969, ISA/7042/4-a, p. 50.
62. Mapam Secretariat meeting, 11.9.1969, YYA/Mapam/90/68/9, p. 16.
63. Stock, 'Foreign Policy Issues', p. 41.
64. Gahal Political Committee meeting, 18.7.1969 and 30.7.1969, ZA/28/2/2e.
65. Torgovnik, 'Party Factions', p. 31.
66. Goldstein, *Rabin*, p. 219.
67. Goldstein, *Rabin*, p. 219.
68. Quandt, *Peace Process*, p. 66.
69. Israel's assessment of joint US–USSR paper, Dec. 1969, ISA/7038/14-a.
70. Statement by Secretary of State Rogers, 9 December 1969, XII, Document 9, Israel's Ministry of Foreign Affairs.
71. Margalit, Dan. *Dispatch from the White House* (Tel Aviv, Otpaz, 1971) [in Hebrew] p. 15.
72. Margalit, *Dispatch from the White House*, p. 25.
73. Brecher, *Decisions in Israel's Foreign Policy* (London, Oxford University Press) p. 484.
74. Eban's meeting with Rogers, 145.3.1969, ISA/4780/2-f, p. 1.
75. The Yost Document, 18.12.1969, ISA/7038/14-a.
76. Special committee report, 13.2.1969, ISA/4781/7-f.
77. Israel's Cabinet Statement, 2 2December 1969, XII, Document 10, Israel's Ministry of Foreign Affairs.
78. Quandt, *Peace Process*, p. 68.
79. Goldstein, *Rabin*, p. 219.
80. Shem-Tov Diary notes, 1970–1974, YYA/Victor Shem-Tov/87-95/1/2.
81. Hand-written note by Galili relating to a conversation with Sapir (no date), ISA/7038/14-a.
82. Sasson to Eban, 23.1.1970, ISA/7052/12-a.
83. Rabin's meeting with Rogers and Sisco, ISA/7438/5-a, p. 4.
84. Rabin's meeting with Rogers and Sisco, p. 5.
85. Telegram from Sisco to Nixon, 14.7.1969, FRUS/Volume XII, Document 67.
86. Goldstein, *Rabin*, p. 220.
87. Margalit, *Dispatch from the White House*, pp. 49–50.
88. Beilin, *The Price of Unity*, pp. 85–86.
89. Shimshoni, *Israel and Conventional Deterrence*, pp. 161–162.
90. Yaacobi, Gad. *On The Razor's Edge* (Tel Aviv, Edanim Publishers, 1989) [in Hebrew] p. 19.
91. Gazit, *The Peace Process (1969–1973)* (Tel Aviv, Yad Tabenkin, 1989) p. 59.
92. Gazit, *The Peace Process*, p. 58.
93. Brecher, *Decisions in Israel's Foreign Policy*, p. 491.
94. Gazit, *The Peace Process*, pp. 62–63.
95. Margalit, *Dispatch from the White House*, p. 157.
96. Rabin to Foreign Ministry, 27.7.1970, ISA/7021/3-a.

97. Nixon to Meir, 27.7.1970, ISA/7021/3-a.
98. Brecher, *Decisions in Israel's Foreign Policy*, p. 494.
99. Brecher, *Decisions in Israel's Foreign Policy*, p. 494.
100. Gahal MK meeting, 30.7.1970 and 4.8.1970, ZA/12/2/2e.
101. Government decision no. 812, 31.7.1970, ISA7336/7-a.
102. Rabin's meeting with Sisco, July 1970, ISA/7021/3-a.
103. Israel's response to the US, 4.8.1970, ISA/7021/4-a.

5 Golda's Kitchenette

1. Yaacobi, *On the Razor's Edge*, p. 37.
2. Allon on the peace plan, 15.9.1970, YTA/15Allon/11/6/2, pp. 1–3.
3. Shalev, *Israel and Syria*, pp. 55–57.
4. Israel's peace plan, 15.9.1970, YTA/15Allon/11/6/2.
5. Mordechai Gazit to Rabin, 31.10.1971, ISA/7021/3-a.
6. Allon on the peace plan, 15.9.1970, YTA/15Allon/11/6/2, p. 3.
7. Shalev, *Israel and Syria*, pp. 57–58.
8. Jordan had, and still has, a large Palestinian population, many of whom were refugees from the 1948 war. Fatah and the PLO had been active in Palestinian life in Jordan from the early 1960s.
9. Shlaim, *Lion of Jordan*, p. 323.
10. Lukacs, *Israel, Jordan and the Peace Process* (Syracuse, Syracuse University Press, 1997) p. 107.
11. YAOH, Meeting 5, pp. 14–16.
12. Shlaim, *Lion of Jordan*, p. 335.
13. Self-Rule proposal, 23.9.1970, ISA/7026/9-a, pp. 1–4.
14. YAOH, Meeting 5, pp. 17–18.
15. YAOH, p. 20.
16. Shlaim, *Lion of Jordan*, p. 337.
17. The term used to describe Meir's preferred decision-making unit, which used to meet in her kitchen before important cabinet meetings.
18. YAOH, Meeting 5, p. 18.
19. YAOH, p. 19.
20. Meir's meeting with Hussein, 26.1.1974, ISA/7043/26-a.
21. Interview with Shem-Tov.
22. Interview with Shem-Tov.
23. Yaacobi, *On the Razor's Edge*, p. 61.
24. Yaacobi, *On the Razor's Edge*, pp. 66–67.
25. Interview with Hillel and Amit.
26. Gazit on Israel's diplomatic options, 1.1.1968, ISA/4780/3-f, pp. 1–6.
27. Yaacobi, *On the Razor's Edge*, p. 81.
28. The Jarring Document, 8.2.1970, ISA/7021/4-a.
29. LP ministers' meeting, 21.2.1971, ISA/7021/4-a, p. 1.
30. LP ministers' meeting, p. 4.
31. Egypt's response to Jarring, 17.2.1971, ISA/7021/4-a.
32. See, for example, 'Oil Extraction in Sinai', 13.2.1969, ISA/3191/9-f.
33. Interview with Netzer, pp. 11–12.
34. Inter-Ministerial Committee for the Development of the Shlomo Region, 7.9.1969, ISA/3191/9-f.

35. MSC meeting, 24.10.1972, ISA/5208/1-f.
36. Weitz's diary, 1969, YTA/15Weitz/4/28, pp. 173–174.
37. MSC meeting, 24.10.1972, ISA/5208/1-f.
38. In early 1970, Galili took over from Allon as Israel's settlement Tsar and the head of the MSC. Under Galili, the process of creating facts on the ground was performed in a more 'organised and transparent manner'.
39. MSC meeting, 31.12.1972, ISA/5208/1-f.
40. MSC meeting, 31.1.1972, ISA/5208/1-f.
41. Interview with Netzer, pp. 22–23.
42. Israel's letter to Jarring, 21.2.1971, ISA/7021/4-a.
43. Foreign Ministry to Washington embassy, Feb. 1971, ISA/7021/4-a.
44. Government decision no. 368, ISA/7021/4-a.
45. Rabin's meeting with Sisco, 24.2.1971, ISA/7021/4-a.
46. Meir at the Knesset (16.3.1971), 23.11.1971, ISA/7336/7-a.
47. Rafael, *Destination Peace*, p. 264.
48. Galili personal note, 18.6.1971, YTA/15Galili.
49. Interview with Aloni.
50. Yaacobi, *On the Razor's Edge*, pp. 127–128.
51. Meir at the LP Convention, 1971, LPA/2-021-1971-106, pp. 3 and 6.
52. LP Convention, p. 7.
53. LP Convention, pp. 9–10.
54. LP Convention, pp. 14–16.
55. Dayan at the LP Convention, 1971, LPA/2-021-1971-106, p. 2.
56. LP Convention, p. 4.
57. LP Convention, pp. 6–7.
58. LP Convention, p. 19.
59. Galili at the LP Convention, 1971, LPA/2-021-1971-106, p. 4.
60. LP Convention, p. 5.
61. LP Convention, pp. 10–11.
62. Meir's meeting with Sisco, 2.8.1971, ISA/7037/16-a, p. 7.
63. Meir's meeting with Sisco, pp. 10–12.
64. Meir's meeting with Sisco.
65. Eban's meeting with Primakov, 29.8.1971, ISA/7037/17-a, p. 21.
66. Eban's meeting with Primakov, pp. 22–23.
67. Eban's meeting with Primakov, pp. 23–24.
68. Eban's meeting with Primakov, p. 25.
69. Meir's meeting with Primakov, 30.8.1971, ISA/7037/17-a, pp. 1–2.
70. Dayan's meeting with Primakov, 31.8.1971, ISA/7037/17-a, p. 6.
71. Mapam's Youth Movement.
72. Hashomer Hatz'air's report, 15.3.1972, YYA/Mapam/90/68.
73. Hashomer Hatz'air's report, pp. 3–5.
74. Mapam Central Committee (MCC) meeting, 15.3.1972, YYA/Mapam/90/68, p. 18.
75. MCC meeting, p. 22.
76. Interview with Hillel.
77. Allon's proposal, 10.12.1968, YTA/15Allon/11/6/2.
78. Settlement Department proposal (no date), ISA/7920/7-a.
79. Pedatzur, *The Triumph of Embarrassment*, p. 247.
80. The exact ministerial make-up of the meeting is not available.

81. Pedatzur, *The Triumph of Embarrassment*, p. 249.
82. Interview with Hillel.
83. Gur at the KFDC, 13.2.1969, ISA/8162/4-a, pp. 5–9.
84. Demant, Peter Robert. *Ploughshares into Swords: Israeli Settlement Policy in the Occupied Territories, 1967–1977* (PhD, University of Amsterdam, 1988) p. 231.
85. Interview with Hillel.
86. Galili's Gaza Strip proposal, 8.9.1970, YTA/15Galili/40/1/30.
87. Gorenberg, *The Accidental Empire*, p. 213.
88. Galili on Israeli-Jordanian relations, 9.8.1973, YTA/15Galili.
89. Interview with Yadlin.
90. Eldar and Zertal, *Lords of the Land*, p. 454.
91. Eldar and Zertal, p. 455.
92. Interview with Bernstein.
93. Dayan at the KFDC, 27.3.1973, ISA/8163/4-a, pp. 8–10.
94. Gordon, Neve. *Israel's Occupation* (Los Angeles, University of California Press, 2008) pp. 62–68.
95. Gazit, *The Stick and the Carrot*, p. 74.
96. Benziman, Uzi. *Sharon: An Israeli Caesar* (London, Robson Books, 1987) p. 119.
97. Galili to Meir, 22.10.1972, ISA/6692/15-c.
98. Interview with Halperin.
99. Shem-Tov personal notes, 1970–1974, YYA/Victor Shem-Tov/87-95/1/2.
100. Shem-Tov personal notes, 1970–1974.
101. Bergman, Arie. *Economic Growth in the Administered Areas 1968–1973* (Jerusalem, Bank of Israel Research Department, 1974) pp. 4–13.
102. Levi, Sasson. 'Local Government in the Administered Territories' in Elazar, *Judea, Samaria and Gaza*, pp. 116–119.
103. Nisan, *Israel and the Territories*, pp. 122–123.
104. Lukacs, *Israel, Jordan and the Peace Process*, p. 117.
105. Shlaim, *Lion of Jordan*, pp. 343–344
106. Cohen, Yeruham. *Allon's Plan* (Tel Aviv, Hakibbutz Hameuchad, 1972) [in Hebrew] p. 155.
107. *Ma'ariv*, interview with Allon, 24.3.1972.
108. Summary of Israeli-Jordanian negotiations: West Bank, 1973, ISA/7034/15-a, p. 3.
109. Israeli-Jordanian negotiations: West Bank, pp. 1 and 3.
110. Israeli-Jordanian negotiations: Jerusalem, 1973, ISA/7034/15-a, p. 1.
111. Israeli-Jordanian negotiations: the Jordanian position, 1973, ISA/7034/15-a, pp. 3–4.
112. Dinitz to Rabin regarding Meir's meeting with Hussein, March 1972, ISA/7042/1-a, pp. 1–2
113. Israeli-Jordanian negotiations: Major Points of Discussion, 1973, ISA/7034/15-a, p. 2.
114. Dinitz to Rabin, March 1972, ISA/7042/1-a, p. 3.
115. Ministerial consultation at Meir's house, 18.6.1972, ISA/7038/14-a, p. 2.
116. Ministerial consultation, p. 3.
117. Shlaim, *Lion of Jordan*, p. 350.
118. Summary of Israeli-Jordanian negotiations: West Bank, p. 1.

119. *Al-Hamishmar*, front page, 30.7.1972.
120. *Yedioth Aharonot*, front page, 23.8.1972.
121. Israeli-Jordanian negotiations: the Jordanian position, p. 3.
122. *Ha'aretz*, front page, 24.8.1972.
123. In the aftermath of the Yom Kippur War (1973) Hussein made similar offers.
124. *Ha'aretz*, Editorial, 25.8.1972.
125. Israeli-Jordanian negotiations: the Jordanian position, p. 6.

6 The Grand Debate

1. Interview with Yadlin.
2. Kieval, *Party Politics in Israel*, p. 73.
3. Yishai, *Land or Peace*, p. 91.
4. LP meeting, 21.9.1972, LPA/2-024-1972-100, pp. 48–50
5. LP meeting, 1.2.1973, LPA/2-024-1973-101, p. 40.
6. LP meeting, p. 41.
7. Ben-Aharon's meeting with *Jerusalem Post* staff, 15.11.1972, YTA/15Ben-Aharon/8/3/38.
8. Ben-Aharon's personal notes, 11.2.1973, YTA/15Ben-Aharon/8/4/3.
9. LP meeting, p. 7.
10. LP meeting, 9.11.1972, LPA/2-024-1972-100, p. 22.
11. LP meeting, p. 40.
12. LP meeting, p. 41.
13. LP meeting, p. 32.
14. LP meeting, p. 36.
15. LP meeting, p. 42.
16. LP meeting, p. 3.
17. LP meeting, p. 6.
18. LP meeting, p. 3.
19. LP meeting, p. 7.
20. LP meeting, p. 12.
21. LP meeting, p. 11.
22. LP meeting, p. 17.
23. LP meeting, 23.11.1972, LPA/2-024-1972-10, p. 42.
24. LP meeting, pp. 49–50.
25. LP meeting, p. 57.
26. LP meeting, 12.4.1973, LPA/2-024-1973-101, p. 18.
27. LP meeting, p. 22.
28. LP meeting, pp. 24–26.
29. LP meeting, p. 30.
30. LP meeting, p. 39.
31. Gazit at the KFDC, 27.2.1973, ISA/8163/3-a, p. 14.
32. Gazit, *Trapped*, p. 288.
33. LP meeting, 12.4.1973, LPA/2-024-1973-101, pp. 14–15.
34. LP meeting, p. 3.
35. LP meeting, pp. 9–11.
36. LP meeting, p. 13.
37. LP meeting, pp. 9–10.

38. LP meeting, p. 11.
39. LP meeting, p. 42.
40. LP meeting, p. 47.
41. LP meeting, pp. 48–50.
42. LP meeting, p. 51.
43. LP meeting, p. 58.
44. Gazit, *Trapped*, p. 228.
45. Harris, *Taking Root*, p. 56.
46. Gazit, *Trapped*, pp. 228–229.
47. LP press office, 14.4.1973, LPA/2-914-1970-272.
48. Yishai, *Land or Peace*, p. 91.
49. Galili to Allon (about the Galili Document), 14.8.1973, YTA/12-3/94/2.
50. Harris, *Taking Root*, p. 57.
51. LP Secretariat meeting, 3.9.1973, LPA/2-024-1973-101, p. 2.
52. LP Secretariat meeting, pp. 8–9.
53. LP Secretariat meeting, pp. 14–16.
54. LP Secretariat meeting, p. 22.
55. LP Secretariat meeting, p. 36.
56. Mapam's Political Committee decision (no date), YYA/Mapam/4/331/90.
57. Kieval, *Party Politics in Israel*, p. 77.
58. Yishai, *Land or Peace*, p. 92.
59. The Galili Document, LPA/2-024-1973-101.
60. Goldstein, *Rabin*, p. 237.
61. Perlmutter, Amos. *Politics and the Military in Israel 1967–1977* (London, Frank Cass, 1978) pp. 65–66.
62. Rabinovich, Abraham. *The Yom Kippur War* (New York, Schocken Books, 2004) p. 15.
63. Eban at the KFDC, 3.4.1973, ISA/8163/4-a/KFDC, pp. 3–5.
64. Interview with Beilin.
65. Goldstein, *Rabin*, p. 243.
66. A series of Israeli fortifications along the Suez Canal that were meant to slow down any Egyptian crossing attempt.
67. Golan, Matti. *The Secret Conversations of Henry Kissinger: Step-by-Step Diplomacy in the Middle East* (New York, Bantam Books, 1976) p. 146.
68. See, for example: Meir's meeting with Barbour, 13.3.1972, ISA/7042/3-a, p. 3.
69. Israel's 'Security Assessments', 4.7.1968, ISA/4781/7-f.
70. Rabinovich, *The Yom Kippur War*, p. 304.
71. Rabinovich, p. 491.
72. Safran, *Israel: The Embattled Ally*, p. 316.
73. Quandt, *Peace Process*, p. 131.
74. Lochery, *The Israeli Labour Party*, p. 17.
75. Harris, *Taking Root*, p. 125.
76. Rabinovich, *The Yom Kippur War*, p. 501.
77. Interview with Yadlin.
78. Kieval, *Party Politics in Israel*, pp. 95–96.
79. Aronoff, *Power and Ritual*, pp. 144–145.
80. LP Central Committee meeting, 5.12.1973 (morning session), LPA/2-15-1973-92, pp. 16–17.
81. LP Central Committee meeting, p. 24.

82. Harris, *Taking Root*, p. 126.
83. Kieval, *Party Politics in Israel*, p. 98.
84. Interview with Yadlin.
85. LP Electoral Platform, 20.12.1973, LPA/2-023-1973-108.
86. LP Central Committee meeting, 5.12.1973 (evening session), LPA/2-15-1973-92, p. 121.
87. Interview with Yadlin.
88. LP Central Committee meeting, 5.12.1973 (evening session), p. 122.
89. Aronoff, *Power and Ritual*, p. 151.
90. Mendolow, Jonathan. *Ideology, Party Change, and Electoral Campaigns in Israel, 1965–2001* (Albany, State University of New York Press, 2003) p. 82.
91. Nachmias, David. 'Coalition Myth and Reality'. In: Arian (ed.) *The Elections in Israel 1973*, p. 250.
92. NRP–Labour Coalition agreement, 8.3.1974, ISA/7025/18-a.
93. Shlaim, *Lion of Jordan*, p. 373.
94. Meir's meeting with Hussein, 26.1.1974, ISA/7043/26-a, pp. 12–13.
95. Meir's meeting with Hussein, p. 19.
96. Meir's meeting with Hussein, p. 21.
97. Meir's meeting with Hussein, pp. 27–28.
98. Meir's meeting with Hussein, p. 31.
99. Meir's meeting with Hussein, pp. 42–44.
100. Meir's meeting with Hussein, p. 59.
101. Meir's meeting with Hussein, p. 60.
102. Meir's meeting with Hussein, p. 66.
103. Meir's meeting with Hussein, pp. 70–71.
104. Meir's meeting with Hussein, p. 72.
105. Meir's meeting with Hussein, pp. 76–77.
106. Meir's meeting with Hussein, p. 79.
107. Meir at the KFDC, 25.2.1973, ISA/8163/3-a/KFDC Meeting, p. 17.
108. Rabinovich, *The Yom Kippur War*, p. 502.
109. Rabinovich, p. 502.
110. Gorenberg, *The Accidental Empire*, p. 270.

7 Hand Picked

1. Baram, Moshe. *Not in a Furrow* (Tel Aviv, Am Oved, 1981) [in Hebrew] pp. 217–220.
2. YAOH, Meeting 10, p. 5.
3. Bar Zohar, Michael. *Phoenix: Shimon Peres – A Political Biography* (Tel Aviv, Yedioth Ahronoth Books, 2006) pp. 416–418.
4. Rabin, *The Rabin Memoirs*, p. 257.
5. Interview with Hillel.
6. Rabin, *The Rabin Memoirs*, p. 189.
7. YAOH, Meeting 10, p. 12.
8. Roberts, *Party and Policy in Israel*, p. 37.
9. Kieval, *Party Politics in Israel*, p. 106.
10. Interview with Yadlin.
11. Israel–Syria 'Separation-of-forces agreement' (no date), ISA/7033/11-a.

12. Golan, *The Secret Conversations of Henry Kissinger*, p. 179.
13. Israeli-US memorandum of understanding, June 1974, ISA/7033/11-a.
14. Israel's negotiating team meeting with Kissinger, 29.5.1974, ISA/7033/11-a.
15. Allon's personal note (no date), YTA/15Allon/Notes.
16. Interview with Yadlin.
17. Touval, Saadia. *The Peace Brokers: Mediators in the Arab-Israeli Conflict, 1948–1979* (New Jersey, Princeton University Press, 1982) p. 259.
18. Israel's Foreign Ministry dossier, 26.8.1974, YTA/15Galili/32/4/5.
19. Interview with Hillel.
20. Zeira, Avi. 'The Settlement in the Golan and the Struggle to Maintain It'. In: Maoz, Moshe (ed.) *The Golan: Between War and Peace* (OrYehuda, Hed Arzi, 1999) [in Hebrew] pp. 101–102.
21. Interview with Hillel.
22. Settlement Department's 'Regional plan for the Golan Heights', Jan. 1969, YTA/15Galili/72/1/2.
23. Harris, *Taking Root*, pp. 67–77.
24. Merom Golan Secretariat to the government, 12.3.1970, ISA/6503/32-c.
25. MKs' letter to the Knesset chairman (regarding a visit to Ramat-Magshimim), 18.8.1970, ISA/6504/31-c.
26. Settlements Department's 'Development plan for the Golan heights 1973–1977', July 1973, YTA/15Galili/77/1/11.
27. Interview with Hillel; interview with Yadlin.
28. Harris, *Taking Root*, p. 71.
29. Settlement Department's 'Development plan for the Golan heights 1975', YTA/15Galili/77/4/13.
30. Galili personal note, 11.7.1974, YTA/15Galili/Notes.
31. Interview with Hillel.
32. Interview with Aloni; interview with Yadlin.
33. YAOH, Meeting 4, p. 18.
34. Interview with Hillel.
35. The government's principles, 3.6.1974, LPA/2-021-1977-133.
36. Galili to Rabin, 27.2.1975, YYA/Victor Shem-Tov 87-95/1/2.
37. Israel's Foreign Ministry dossier, 26.8.1974, YTA/15Galili/32/4/5.
38. Interview with Yadlin; interview with Shem-Tov.
39. YAOH, Meeting 5, p. 11.
40. Lukacs, *Israel, Jordan and the Peace Process*, p. 133.
41. Kissinger, Henry. *Days of Upheaval* (Boston, Little, Brown and Company, 1982) p. 1139.
42. Zak, Moshe. *Hussein makes Peace* (Jerusalem, Bar-Ilan University, 1996) [in Hebrew] p. 164.
43. Shlaim, *Lion of Jordan*, p. 382.
44. YAOH, Meeting 8, p. 16.
45. Interview with Aloni.
46. Interview with Hillel; interview with Yadlin.
47. Interview with Aloni; interview with Shem-Tov; interview with Yadlin.
48. Interview with Aloni.
49. Haika Grossman's personal notes (no date, prior to the Rabat Summit), YYA/Haika Grossman 69-95/30/4.
50. Shlaim, *Lion of Jordan*, p. 384–385.

51. YAOH, Meeting 8, p. 17.
52. Interview with Aloni.
53. MCC meeting, 15.7.1974, YYA/Mapam Protocols 79-90/7/79/9, p. 146.
54. MCC meeting, pp. 168–169.
55. MK Meir Talmi regarding coalition agreements, 10.11.1975, YYA/Mapam90/36/2.
56. MCC meeting, 21.8.1974, YYA/Mapam Protocols 79-90/7/79/9, pp. 172–173.
57. Interview with Yadlin.
58. Smooha, Sammy. *Israel: Pluralism and Conflict* (London, Routledge and Kegan Paul, 1978) pp. 236–237.
59. Yishai, Yael. 'Factionalism in the National Religious Party: The Quiet Revolution'. In: Arian (ed.) *The Elections in Israel 1977*, p. 58.
60. Yishai, 'Factionalism in the National Religious Party', p. 58.
61. Torgovnik, 'Party Factions and Election Issues', p. 26.
62. Stock, 'Foreign Policy Issues', p. 48.
63. Azrieli, Yehuda. *The Generation of the Knitted Skullcap* (Israel, Avivim, 1990) [in Hebrew] pp. 36–37.
64. Stock, 'Foreign Policy Issues', p. 47.
65. Roberts, *Party and Policy in Israel*, p. 68.
66. Azrieli, *The Generation of the Knitted Skullcap*, pp. 37–38.
67. Eldar and Zertal, *Lords of the Land*, p. 273.
68. Shprinzak, Ehud. *The Ascendance of Israel's Radical Right* (New York, Oxford University Press, 1991) p. 45.
69. Shprinzak, p. 44.
70. Yishai, *Land or Peace*, p. 131.
71. Segal, Haggai. *Dear Brother* (Jerusalem, Keter Publishing House, 1987) [in Hebrew] pp. 26–27.
72. Seliktar, *New Zionism*, pp. 158–159.
73. Yishai, *Land or Peace*, pp. 127–128.
74. Shprinzak, Ehud, *Everyman Whatsoever Is Right in His Own Eyes: Illegalism in Israeli Society* (Tel Aviv, Sifriat Poalim, 1986) [in Hebrew] pp. 126–128.
75. Interview with Aloni.
76. Shafat, Gershon. *Gush Emunim: The Story Behind the Scenes* (Beit-El Library, 1995) [in Hebrew] pp. 74–77.
77. Shprinzak, *Everyman Whatsoever*, pp. 124–126.
78. Yishai, *Land or Peace*, p. 131.
79. Allon's proposal, 10.12.1968, YTA/15Allon/11/6/2.
80. Allon's proposal, 29.1.1969, YTA/15Allon/11/6/2.
81. Ad hoc committee meeting (no date), YTA/15Galili/143/7/16.
82. Galili summary of government decision, 9.8.1973, YTA/15Galili/39/1/16.
83. YAOH, Meeting 9, p. 16.
84. YAOH, p. 17.
85. Admoni, *Decade of Discretion*, p. 102.
86. Benvenisti, Meron. *The West Bank Handbook* (Jerusalem, Kana, 1987) [in Hebrew] p. 148.
87. Galili to Rabin, 20.10.1974, YTA/15Galili/4/10/3.
88. Demant, *Ploughshares into Swords*, pp. 358–359.
89. Demant, p. 358.
90. Interview with Hillel.

91. Galili to Rabin, 15.12.1974, ISA/7032/14-a.
92. Galili to Rabin, 9.12.1974, ISA/7032/14-a.
93. Galili to Rabin, 7.1.1974, YTA/15Galili/4/10/13.
94. Galili to Rabin, 7.1.1975, ISA/7032/14-a.
95. Galili to Rabin, 24.1.1975, YTA/Galili/4/10/16.
96. Ma'ale Adumim Committee (MAC) meeting, 8.1.1975, ISA/7032/14-a, p. 7.
97. Galili to Rabin, 24.1.1975, ISA/7032/14-a.
98. MAC meeting, p. 11.
99. MAC meeting, 10.1.1975, ISA/7032/14-a, p. 3.
100. MAC decisions, 19.2.1975, ISA/7032/14-a.
101. Galili to Rabinowitz, 12.1.1975, YTA/15Galili/4/10/14
102. Galili to Rabin, 26.1.1975, ISA/7032/14.
103. Galili to the Knesset's Finance Committee, 26.1.1975, YTA/15Galili/2/2/37.
104. Galili to Rabin, 26.1.1975, ISA/7032/14-a.
105. Demant, *Ploughshares into Swords*, p. 358.
106. Rabin's meeting with Peres, Galili and Hillel, 26.1.1975, ISA/7020/6-a.
107. MAC meeting, 10.1.1975.
108. Netzer, Moshe. *Life Story* (Ministry of Defence, 2002) [in Hebrew] p. 290.
109. Netzer, *Life Story*, p. 290.
110. Galili to the Defence Ministry, 29.4.1975, YTA/15Galili/46/2/2/52.
111. Interview with Yadlin.
112. Gorenberg, *The Accidental Empire*, p. 317.
113. Interview with Hillel.
114. Netzer, *Life Story*, pp. 290–292.
115. Bar Zohar, *Phoenix*, p. 429.
116. Interview with Hillel.
117. US embassy in Tel Aviv to the State Department, 20.6.1975, NARA/
     D750215-0635.

8 Submission to Gush Emunim

1. Interview with Yadlin.
2. Galili's memo, 26.8.1974, YTA/15Galili/32/4/5.
3. Government decision, 10.11.1974, ISA/7044/17-a.
4. Kieval, *Party Politics in Israel*, pp. 113–114.
5. Attorney-General dossier, 7.10.1974, ISA/7044/17-a.
6. Foreign Policy paper (no date), ISA/7044/17-a.
7. Rabin, *The Rabin Memoirs*, p. 278.
8. Kissinger, Henry. *Days of Renewal* (New York, Simon and Schuster, 1999) p. 458.
9. Kieval, *Party Politics in Israel*, p. 116.
10. Quandt, *Peace Process*, pp. 168–170.
11. Maoz, Zeev. *Defending the Holy Land: A Critical Analysis of Israel's Security and Foreign Policy* (Ann Arbor, University of Michigan Press, 2006) p. 420.
12. Interview with Hillel.
13. Interview with Hillel.
14. Interview with Hillel.
15. Government memo, 18.10.1976, ISA/6692/15-c.

16. Interview with Hillel.
17. Seliktar, *New Zionism*, p. 162.
18. Foreign policy paper (no date), ISA/7044/17-a
19. LP Political Committee, 14.1.1977, LPA/2-021-1977-133, pp. 8–9.
20. YAOH, Meeting 18, pp. 30–31.
21. YAOH, pp. 27–29.
22. Interview with Yadlin.
23. YAOH, Meeting 18, pp. 27–29.
24. Kissinger, *Days of Upheaval*, p. 1051–1056.
25. Beker, Avi. *The United Nations and Israel: From Recognition to Reprehension* (Toronto, Lexington Books, 1988) p. 84.
26. Netzer, *Life Story*, p. 293.
27. Shafat, *Gush Emunim*, pp. 131–132.
28. Demant, *Ploughshares into Swords*, p. 378.
29. MPC meeting, 3.12.1975, YYA/(2)155.90/899.
30. Eldar and Zertal, *Lords of the Land*, pp. 72–73.
31. Netzer, *Life Story*, p. 293.
32. Interview with Hillel.
33. Demant, *Ploughshares into Swords*, pp. 388–389.
34. Interview with Shem-Tov.
35. Interview with Hillel.
36. Bar Zohar, *Phoenix*, pp. 431–432.
37. MPC meeting, 10.12.1975, YYA/(2)155.90/899, p. 50.
38. Interview with Yadlin; interview with Hillel.
39. Defence Ministry to Rabin, 27.4.1976, ISA/7037/11-a.
40. Rabin to Peres, 1.6.1976, ISA/7037/11-a.
41. Galili to Rabin, 1.6.1976, YTA/15Galili/4/10/47.
42. Defence Ministry to Rabin (no date), ISA/7037/11-a.
43. Galili to Rabin, 15.6.1976, YTA/15Galili/4/10/49.
44. Galili to Rabin, 13.6.1976, YTA/15Galili/4/10/48.
45. Admoni to Galili, 1.7.1976, YTA/15Galili/4/10/52.
46. Shem-Tov to the Government's Secretary, 26.7.1976, ISA/7037/11-a.
47. Netzer to Shem-Tov, 27.7.1976, ISA/7037/11-a.
48. Kol to Rabin, 9.8.1976, ISA/7037/11-a.
49. Barak to Rabin, 31.8.1976, ISA/7037/11-a.
50. Interview with Hillel.
51. Interview with Yadlin.
52. Golan, Matti. *The Road to Peace: A Biography of Shimon Peres* (New York, Warner Books, 1989) pp. 133–136.
53. Rabin, *The Rabin Memoirs*, p. 281.
54. Bar Zohar, *Phoenix*, p. 432.
55. Interview with Hillel, interview with Yadlin.
56. Bar Zohar, *Phoenix*, pp. 432–433.
57. Demant, *Ploughshares into Swords*, pp. 382–383.
58. Interview with Shem-Tov.
59. Interview with Hillel.
60. Interview with Netzer, p. 9.
61. Harris, *Taking Root*, p. 113.
62. LP Political Committee meeting, 21.1.1977, LPA/2-021-1977-133, p. 10.

63. Galili to Rabin, 27.6.1976, YTA15Galili/4/10/51.
64. Alpher, Joseph. *And the Wolf Shall Dwell with the Wolf: The Settlers and the Palestinians* (Tel Aviv, Hakibbutz Hameuchad, 2001) [in Hebrew] p. 23.
65. Interview with Hillel.
66. Admoni, *Decade of Discretion*, p. 178.
67. Demant, *Ploughshares into Swords*, pp. 494–495.
68. Galili to Mescha group, 19.10.1975, YTA/15Galili/2/2/114.
69. Galili to Rabin, 11.7.1976, YTA/15Galili/4/10/53.
70. Galili's meeting with Hammer, 1.3.1977, YTA/ 15Galili/4/10/66.
71. Galili to Rabin, 22.12.1976, YTA/15Galili/4/10/58.
72. Interview with Aloni.
73. US embassy in Tel Aviv to the State Department, 20.11.1975, NARA/ D570405-0029.
74. Little, Douglas. *American Orientalism: The United States and the Middle East since 1945* (London, I.B.Tauris, 2003) p. 288.
75. Allon's self-rule proposal, 26.10.1975, YTA/15Allon/11/6/2.
76. Government Secretary to ministers, 15.4.1975, ISA/7022/3-a.
77. Little, *American Orientalism*, p. 288.
78. Foreign Ministry's analysis of the Saunders Report, 16.11.1976, ISA/7027/7-a.
79. Gazit, *Trapped*, p. 190.
80. Gazit, p. 82.
81. Lukacs, *Israel, Jordan and the Peace Process*, p. 143.
82. Bar Zohar, *Phoenix*, p. 433.
83. Gazit, *Trapped*, p. 81.
84. Government decision, 7.11.1976, YYA/Victor Shem-Tov 87-95/1/2.
85. Shem-Tov to Galili, 8.9.1979, YYA/Victor Shem-Tov 87-95/1/2.
86. Gazit, *Trapped*, pp. 85–86.
87. LP Political Committee, 21.1.1977, LPA/2-021-1977-133, p. 18.
88. LP Political Committee, 31.12.1976, p. 11.
89. LP Political Committee, pp. 2–3.
90. LP Conference, 24.2.1977, LPA/2-021-1977-133, p. 68.
91. LP Political Committee, 14.1.1977, LPA/2-021-1977-133, pp. 22–23.
92. LP Political Committee, 21.1.1977, LPA/2-021-1977-133, p. 18.
93. LP Political Committee, 31.12.1976, LPA/2-021-1977-133, p. 24.
94. LP Political Committee, p. 15.
95. LP Political Committee, p. 5.
96. Interview with Yadlin.
97. LP Political Committee, 7.1.1977, LPA/2-021-1977-133, p. 20.
98. LP Political Committee, 14.1.1977, LPA/2-021-1977-133, p. 17.
99. LP Political Committee, 31.12.1976, LPA/2-021-1977-133, p. 4.
100. Hakibbutz Hameuchad Central Committee's resolution, 6.1.1977, LPA/ 2-021-1977-133.
101. Alternative peace plan, 27.10.1977, LPA/2-021-1977-133.
102. LP Political Committee, 7.1.1977, LPA/2-021-1977-133, p. 4.
103. LP Political Committee, p. 9.
104. LP Political Committee, p. 22.
105. Paper explaining the Functional Solution (no date), LPA/2-021-1976-232.
106. LP Political Committee, 31.12.1976, LPA/2-021-1977-133, p. 14.
107. LP Political Committee, 14.1.1977, LPA/2-021-1977-133, p. 8.

108. LP Political Committee, p. 15.
109. LP Political Committee, p. 14.
110. LP Political Committee, p. 10.
111. LP Political Committee, 21.1.1977, LPA/2-021-1977-133, p. 12.
112. LP Political Committee, p. 4.
113. LP Political Committee, p. 9.
114. LP Political Committee, 7.1.1977, LPA/2-021-1977-133, pp. 17–20.
115. LP Political Committee, 31.12.1976, LPA/2-021-1977-133, p. 5.
116. LP Political Committee, 21.1.1977, LPA/2-021-1977-133, p. 23.
117. LP's electoral platform, 6.2.1977, YTA/15Galili/60/3/2.
118. Lochery, *The Israeli Labour Party*, pp. 60–61.

Epilogue

1. In March 1979, Likud Prime Minister Menahem Begin negotiated with Egypt for an Israeli withdrawal from the entirety of the Sinai Peninsula, including the Rafah plains, in exchange for a comprehensive peace agreement. As a result of the increasingly genocidal war in Syria, it is unlikely that there will be negotiations over the Golan Heights any time soon; in fact, one could go further and suggest that in the near future, Israel's annexation of the Golan Heights might even be internationally recognised.

Bibliography

Interviews

Aloni, Shulamit: former minister without portfolio in 1974 during the first Rabin government (8.11.2007 Kfar Shmaryahu).

Amit, Meir: head of the Mossad until 1968 (14.06.2007 Correspondence).

Beilin, Yossi: author of *The Price of Unity* and former Israeli deputy foreign minister (5.06.2007 Tel Aviv).

Bernstein, Nahman: treasurer of the Jewish Agency's Settlement Department throughout the period researched (6.06.2007 Tel Aviv).

Halperin, Danny: personal assistant to Pinhas Sapir and a member of the Director's-General Committee until 1974 (6.09.2006 Jerusalem).

Hillel, Shlomo: deputy director-general of the Foreign Ministry until 1969 and police minister from 1969 to 1977 (23.9.2007 Ra'anana).

Shem-Tov, Victor: minister without portfolio from 1969 to 1970 and health minister from 1970 to 1977 (5.09.2006 Jerusalem).

Yadlin, Aharon: Labour Party secretary-general, and education minister from 1974 to 1977 (29.09.2007 Kibbutz Hatzerim).

Archives

Ahdut-Ha'avoda Archives (YTA) [Yad Tabenkin]
Foreign Relations of the United States Series (FRUS)
Israel's State Archives (ISA)
Labour Party Archives (LPA)
Likud Party Archives (ZA) [Zabotinsky Institute]
Mapam Party Archives (YYA) [Yad Ya'ari]
US National Archives and Online Archival Database (NARA)
Yigal Allon Oral History (YAOH)

Israeli newspapers

Al Hamishmar
Davar
Ha'aretz
Ma'ariv
Yedioth Ahronoth

Secondary sources

Admoni, Yehiel. *Decade of Discretion: Settlement Policy in the Territories 1967–1977* (Tel Aviv, Yad Tabenkin, 1992) [in Hebrew]

Alpher, Joseph. *And the Wolf Shall Dwell with the Wolf: The Settlers and the Palestinians* (Tel Aviv, Hakibbutz Hameuchad, 2001) [in Hebrew]

Amit, Meir. *Head On...* (Or Yehuda, Hed Artzi, 1999) [in Hebrew]

Arian, Asher (ed.). *The Elections in Israel 1969* (Jerusalem, Jerusalem Academic Press, 1972)

Arian, Asher (ed.). *The Elections in Israel 1973* (Jerusalem, Jerusalem Academic Press, 1975)

Arian, Asher (ed.). *The Elections in Israel 1977* (Jerusalem, Jerusalem Academic Press, 1980)

Aronoff, J. Myron. *Israeli Visions and Divisions Cultural Change and Political Conflict* (New Brunswick, Transaction Publishers, 1989)

Aronoff, J. Myron. *Power and Ritual in the Israel Labour Party: A Study in Political Anthropology* (New York, M.E. Sharpe, 1993)

Aronson, Geoffrey. *Israel, Palestinians and the Intifada: Creating Facts on the West Bank* (London, Kegan Paul International, 1990)

Azrieli, Yehuda. *The Generation of the Knitted Skullcaps* (Israel, Avivim, 1990) [in Hebrew]

Bacharach, Peter and Morton Baratz (1963) 'Decisions and Nondecisions: An Analytical Framework' *American Political Science Review* 57(3) pp. 632–642

Bamahane (IDF magazine) (1968) 'Interview with Moshe Dayan' 27 May.

Baram, Moshe. *Not in a Furrow* (Tel Aviv, Am Oved, 1981) [in Hebrew]

Bartov, Hanoch. *Daddo 48 years and 20 More Days* (Or Yehuda, Dvir, 2002) [in Hebrew]

Bar Zohar, Michael. *Phoenix: Shimon Peres – A Political Biography* (Tel Aviv, Miskal – Yedioth Ahronoth Books and Chemed Books, 2006)

Bar Zohar, Michael. *Yaacov Hertzog: A Biography* (London, Halban, 2005)

Bavly, Dan. *Dreams and Missed Opportunities 1967–1973* (Jerusalem, Carmel, 2002) [in Hebrew]

Beilin, Yossi. *The Price of Unity The History of the Labour Party to the Yom Kippur War* (Tel Aviv, Revivim, 1985) [in Hebrew]

Beker, Avi. *The United Nations and Israel: From Recognition to Reprehension* (Toronto, Lexington Books, 1988)

Ben-Meir, Yehuda. *National Security Decision-Making: The Israeli Case* (Tel Aviv, Hakibbutz Hameuchad, 1987) [in Hebrew]

Ben-Meir, Yehuda. *Civil–Military Relations: The Israeli Case* (New York, Columbia University Press, 1995)

Benvenisti, Meron. *Jerusalem, the Torn City* (Jerusalem, Weidenfeld and Nicolson, 1973) [in Hebrew]

Benvenisti, Meron. *The West Bank Handbook* (Jerusalem, Kana, 1987) [in Hebrew]

Benziman, Uzi. *Jerusalem: City without a Wall* (Jerusalem, Schocken, 1973) [in Hebrew]

Benziman, Uzi. *Sharon: An Israeli Caesar* (London, Robson Books, 1987)

Bergman, Arie. *Economic Growth in the Administered Areas 1968–1973* (Jerusalem, Bank of Israel Research Department, 1974)

Bergman, Arie. *Economic Growth in the Administered Areas 1974–1975* (Jerusalem, Bank of Israel Research Department, 1976)

Bier, Aharon. *Outposts and Settlements: The Golan Heights, the Jordan Valley, Samaria, Judea, the Gaza Strip and the Sinai Peninsula* (Jerusalem, Hemed Press, 1976) [in Hebrew]

Bleaney, Heather and Richard Lawless. *The First Day of the Six Day War* (London, Dryad Press, 1990).

Bowen, Jeremy. *Six Days: How the 1967 War Shaped the Middle East* (London, Simon and Schuster, 2003)

Brecher, Michael. *The Foreign Policy System of Israel: Settings, Images, Process* (New Haven, CT, Yale University Press, 1973)

Brecher, Michael. *Decisions in Israel's Foreign Policy* (London, Oxford University Press, 1974)

Brownstein, Lewis (1977) 'Decision Making in Israeli Foreign Policy: An Unplanned Process' *Political Science Quarterly* 92(2) pp. 259–279

Cohen, Avner. *Israel and the Bomb* (New York, Columbia University Press, 1999)

Cohen, Yeruham. *The Allon Plan* (Tel Aviv, Hakibbutz Hameuchad, 1972) [in Hebrew]

Dayan, Moshe. *Story of My Life* (London, Weidenfeld and Nicolson, 1976)

Demant, Peter Robert. *Ploughshares into Swords, Israeli Settlement Policy in the Occupied Territories, 1967–1977* (PhD, University of Amsterdam, 1988)

Eban, Abba. *My Life* (Tel Aviv, Ma'ariv Book Guild, 1978)

Efrat, Elisha. *Geography and Politics in Israel since 1967* (London, Frank Cass, 1988)

Efrat, Elisha. *Geography of Occupation: Judea, Samaria and the Gaza Strip* (Jerusalem, Carmel, 2002)

Elazar, Daniel J. (ed.). *Judea, Samaria and Gaza: Views on the Present and Future* (Washington DC, American Enterprise Institute For Public Policy Research, 1982)

Eldar, Akiva and Zertal, Idith. *Lords of the Land: The Settlers and the State of Israel 1967–2004* (Or Yehuda, Kinneret, Zmora-Bitan, Dvir Publishing House, 2004) [in Hebrew]

Farsakh, Leila. *Palestinian Labour Migration to Israel: Labour, Land and Occupation* (Abingdon, Routledge, 2005)

Feige, Michael. *Settling in the Hearts: Jewish Fundamentalism in the Occupied Territories* (Detroit, Wayne State University Press, 2009)

Freilich, D. Charles (2006) 'National Security Decision-Making in Israel: Processes, Pathologies, and Strengths' *Middle East Journal* 60(4) pp. 635–663

Freilich, D. Charles. *Zion's Dilemmas: How Israel makes National Security Policy* (New York, Cornell University Press, 2012)

Garfinkle, Adam. *Israel and Jordan in the Shadow of War: Functional Ties and Futile Diplomacy in a Small Place* (London, Macmillan, 1992)

Gat, Moshe. *In Search of a Peace Settlement: Egypt and Israel Between the Wars 1967–1973* (Basingstoke, Palgrave Macmillan, 2012)

Gazit, Mordechai. *The Peace Process (1969–1973)* (Tel Aviv, Yad Tabenkin, 1984) [in Hebrew]

Gazit, Mordechai. *Israeli Diplomacy and the Quest for Peace* (London, Frank Cass, 2002)

Gazit, Shlomo. *The Stick and the Carrot* (Tel Aviv, Zmora-Bitan, 1985) [in Hebrew]

Gazit, Shlomo. *Trapped* (Tel Aviv, Zmora-Bitan, 1999) [in Hebrew]

Gharaibeh, Fawzi. *The Economics of the West Bank and Gaza Strip* (Boulder, Westview Special Studies on the Middle East, 1985)

Gluska, Ami. *Eshkol, Give the Order! Israeli Army Command and Political Leadership on the Road to the Six Day War 1963–1967* (Tel Aviv, Ma'arachot, Ministry of Defence Books, 2004) [in Hebrew]

Golan, Matti. *The Secret Conversations of Henry Kissinger: Step-by-step Diplomacy in the Middle East* (New York, Bantam Books, 1976)

Golan, Matti. *The Road to Peace: A Biography of Shimon Peres* (New York, Warner Books, 1989)

Goldstein, Yossi. *Eshkol – Biography* (Jerusalem, Keter Publishers, 2003) [in Hebrew]

Goldstein, Yossi. *Rabin – Biography* (Tel Aviv, Schocken, 2006) [in Hebrew]

Gordon, Neve. *Israel's Occupation* (Los Angeles, University of California Press, 2008)

Gorenberg, Gershom. *The Accidental Empire: Israel and the Birth of the Settlements, 1967–1977* (New York, Times Books, 2006)

Green, Stephen. *Living by the Sword: America and Israel in the Middle East 1968–87* (Brattleboro, Amana Books, 1988)

Gresh, Allen. *The PLO: The Struggle Within, Towards an Independent Palestinian State* (London: Zed Books, 1985)

Haber, Eitan. *Today War will Break Out: The Reminiscences of Brig. Gen. Israel Lior* (Jerusalem, Edanim Publishers, 1987) [in Hebrew]

Hagan, Joe D. 'Domestic Political Explanations in the Analysis of Foreign Policy'. In: Neack, Laura, Hey, Jeanne and Haney, Patrick J. (eds) *Foreign Policy Analysis: Continuity and Change in its Second Generation* (Upper Saddle River, Prentice Hall, 1995)

Halfom, Moshe. *From War to Peace: The Peace Course between Egypt and Israel 1970–1979* (Tel Aviv, Hakibbutz Hameuchad, 2002) [in Hebrew]

Harnoy, Meir. *The Settlers* (Or Yehuda, Ma'ariv Book Guild, 1999) [in Hebrew]

Harkabi, Yoshafat. *Fateful Decision* (Tel Aviv, Am Oved, 1986) [in Hebrew]

Harris, W.W. *Taking Root: Israeli Settlements in the West Bank, the Golan Heights and the Gaza Strip 1967–1980* (New York, Research Studies Press, 1980)

Herzog, Haim. *Living History* (Tel Aviv, Miskal-Yedioth Ahronoth Books, 1997) [in Hebrew]

Heywood, Andrew. *Politics* (New York, Palgrave Foundations, 2002)

Hill, Christopher. *The Changing Politics of Foreign Policy* (Basingstoke, Palgrave Macmillan, 2003)

Huberman, Haggai. *Against All the Odds: 40 Years of Settlement in Judea and Samaria, Binyamin and the Valley* (Jerusalem, Sifriyat Netsarim, 2008) [in Hebrew]

Inbar, Efraim. *War and Peace in Israeli Politics: Labour Party Position on National Security* (London, Lynne Rienner Publishers, 1991)

Inbar, Efraim. *Rabin and Israel's National Security* (Washington, Woodrow Wilson Center Press and Johns Hopkins University Press, 1999)

Isaac, Rael Jean. *Israel Divided: Ideological Politics in the Jewish State* (Baltimore, Johns Hopkins University Press, 1976)

Isaac, Rael Jean. *Party and Politics in Israel* (New York, Longman, 1981)

Israeli, Raphael (ed.). *Ten Years of Israeli Rule in Judea and Samaria* (Jerusalem, The Magnes Press, The Hebrew University, 1980) [in Hebrew]

Izhar, Uri. *Between Vision and Power: The History of Ahdut-Ha'avoda-Poalei-Zion Party* (Tel Aviv, Yad Tabenkin, 2002) [in Hebrew]

Karbo, Juliet. *Coalition Politics and Cabinet Decision Making: A Comparative Analysis of Foreign Policy Choices* (Ann Arbor, University of Michigan Press, 2012)

Kieval, Gershon. *Party Politics in Israel and the Occupied Territories* (Westport, Greenwood, 1983)

Kimche, David. *After Nasser, Arafat and Saddam Hussein: The Last Option, the Quest for Peace in the Middle East* (London, Weidenfeld and Nicolson, 1991)

Kimche, David and Bavly, Dan. *The Sandstorm: The Arab-Israeli War of June 1967, Prelude and Aftermath* (London, Secker and Warburg, 1968)

Kimmerling, Baruch. *Zionism and Territory: The Socio-Territorial Dimensions of Zionist Politics* (Institute of International Studies, University of California Berkeley, 1983)

Kimmerling, Baruch (ed.). *The Israeli State and Society, Boundaries and Frontiers* (New York, State University of New York Press, 1989)

Kissinger, Henry. *Days of Upheaval* (Boston, Little, Brown and Co., 1982)

Kissinger, Henry. *Days of Renewal* (New York, Simon and Schuster, 1999)

Klieman, Aaron S. *Israel and the World after 40 Years* (New York, Brassey's)

Kliot, Nurit and Shemuel Albeck. *Sinai: Anatomy of Settlement Evacuation* (Tel Aviv, Ministry of Defence, Israel, 1995) [in Hebrew]

Korn, Dani and Boaz Shapira. *Coalition Politics in Israel* (Tel Aviv, Zmora-Bitan, 1987) [in Hebrew]

Korn, A. David. *Stalemate: The War of Attrition and Great Power Diplomacy in the Middle East, 1967–1970* (Boulder, Westview Press, 1992)

Lifshitz, Yaacov. *Economic Development in the Administered Areas 1967–1969* (Tel Aviv, Maarachot Ministry of Defence)

Little, Douglas. *American Orientalism: The United States and the Middle East since 1945* (London, I.B.Tauris, 2003)

Litvak, Meir. 'Inside Versus Outside: The Challenge of the Local Leadership 1967–1994', in Avraham Sela and Moshe Maoz (eds) *The PLO and Israel: From Armed Conflict to Political Solution 1964–1994* (London, Palgrave Macmillan, 1997)

Lochery, Neill. *The Israeli Labour Party: In the Shadow of the Likud* (Reading, Ithaca Press, 1997)

Lochery, Neill. *Loaded Dice: The Foreign Office and Israel* (London, Continuum, 2007)

Lukacs, Yehuda. *Israel, Jordan and the Peace Process* (Syracuse, Syracuse University Press, 1997)

Lustick, Ian. *Unsettled States: Disputed Lands* (New York, Cornell University Press, 1993)

Maoz, Moshe. *Palestinian Leadership of the West Bank: The Changing Role of the Mayors under Jordan and Israel* (London, Frank Cass, 1984)

Maoz, Moshe. *Syria and Israel: From War to Peace-making* (Oxford, Oxford University Press, 1995)

Maoz, Moshe (ed.). *The Golan: Between War and Peace* (Or Yehuda, Hed Arzi, 1999) [in Hebrew]

Maoz, Zeev. *Defending the Holy Land: A Critical Analysis of Israel's Security and Foreign Policy* (Ann Arbor, University of Michigan Press, 2006)

Margalit, Dan. *Dispatch from the White House* (Tel Aviv, Otpaz, 1971) [in Hebrew]

Medding, Y. Peter. *Mapai in Israel: Political Organisation and Government in a New Society* (London, Cambridge University Press, 1972)

Medding, Y. Peter. *The Founding of Israeli Democracy 1948–1967* (New York, Oxford University Press, 1990)

Medzini, Meron. *Golda: A Political Biography* (Tel Aviv, Yedioth Ahronoth Books, 2008)

Meir, Golda. *My Life* (London, Weidenfeld and Nicolson, 1975)

Melman, Yossi and Daniel Raviv. *A Hostile Partnership: The Secret Relationship between Israel and Jordan* (Tel Aviv, Mitam-Yedioth Ahronoth, 1987) [in Hebrew]

Melman, Yossi and Daniel Raviv. *Behind the Uprising: Israelis, Jordanians and Palestinians* (Westport, Greenwood Press, 1989)

Mendolow, Jonathan. *Ideology, Party Change, and Electoral Campaigns in Israel, 1965–2001* (Albany, State University of New York Press, 2003)

Metzger, Jan et al. *This Land is Our Land: The West Bank under Israeli Occupation* (London, Zed Press, 1983)

Mishal, Shaul. *The PLO under 'Arafat: Between Gun and Olive Branch* (New Haven, Yale University Press, 1986)

Morris, Benny. *Righteous Victims: A History of the Zionist–Arab conflict 1881–2001* (Tel Aviv, Am Oved Publishers, 2003) [in Hebrew]

Nadel, Chaim. *Between the Two Wars: The Security and Military Activities to Achieve Readiness and Alert in the I.D.F from the End of the Six Day War to the Yom Kippur War* (Tel Aviv, Maarachot, 2006) [in Hebrew]

Naor, Arye. *Greater Israel: Theology and Politics* (Haifa, Haifa University Press and Zmora Bitan, 2001) [in Hebrew]

Netzer, Moshe. *Life Story* (Ministry of Defence, 2002) [in Hebrew]

Nisan, Mordechai. *Israel and the Territories: A Study in Control 1967–1977* (Ramat Gan, Turtledove, 1978)

Oren, Michael B. *Six Days of War: June 1967 and the Making of the Modern Middle East* (New York, Oxford University Press, 2002)

Pedatzur, Reuven. *The Triumph of Embarrassment: Israel and the Territories after the Six Day War* (Tel Aviv, Yad Tabenkin, 1996) [in Hebrew]

Perlmutter, Amos. *Military and Politics in Israel: Nation-Building and Role Expansion* (London, Frank Cass, 1969)

Perlmutter, Amos. *Politics and the Military in Israel 1967–1977* (London, Frank Cass, 1978)

Quandt, William B. *Peace Process: American Diplomacy and the Arab-Israeli Conflict Since 1967* (Harrisonburg, Brookings Institution Press and the University of California Press, 2001)

Rabin, Yitzhak. *The Rabin Memoirs* (London, Weidenfeld and Nicolson, 1979)

Rabinovich, Abraham. *The Yom Kippur War* (New York, Schocken Books, 2004)

Rafael, Gideon. *Destination Peace: Three Decades of Israeli Foreign Policy* (New York, Stein and Day, 1981)

Raviv, Moshe. *Israel at Fifty: Five Decades of the Struggle for Peace* (London, Weidenfeld and Nicolson, 1998)

Reich, Bernard. *Quest for Peace: United States–Israel Relations and the Arab Israeli Conflict* (New Brunswick, Transaction Books, 1977)

Rekhess, Elie and Asher Susser. 'Political Factors and Trends in the Israeli-Administered Territories' in Rabinovich, Itamar and Shaked, Haim (eds) *From June to October: The Middle East Between 1967 and 1973* (New Brunswick: Transaction, 1978), pp. 269–276

Roberts, Samuel J. *Survival or Hegemony? The Foundations of Israeli Foreign Policy* (Baltimore, Johns Hopkins University Press, 1973)

Roberts, Samuel J. *Party and Policy in Israel: The Battle Between Hawks and Doves* (London, Westview Press, 1990)

Rozental, Iamima (ed.). *Levi Eshkol: The Third Prime Minister 1895–1969* (Jerusalem, State of Israel National Archive, 2002) [in Hebrew]

Rozental, Iamima (ed.). *Itzhak Rabin: Prime Minister of Israel 1977–74/1995–92. Part One 1922–1967* (Jerusalem, State of Israel National Archive, 2005) [in Hebrew]

Safran, Nadav. *Israel: The Embattled Ally* (Cambridge, The Belknap Press of Harvard University Press, 1981)

Sahliyeh, Emile. *In Search of Leadership: West Bank Politics since 1967* (Washington DC, Brookings Institution, 1988)

Sayigh, Yezid. *Armed Struggle and the Search for State: The Palestinian National Movement 1949–1993* (Oxford, Oxford University Press, 2004)

Sandler, Shmuel. *The State of Israel, the Land of Israel: The Statist and Ethnonational Dimensions of Foreign Policy* (Westport, Greenwood Press, 1993)

Sasson, Moshe. *Talking Peace* (Or Yehuda, Ma'ariv Book Guild, 2004) [in Hebrew]

Schiff, Zeev. *October Earthquake: Yom Kippur 1973* (Tel Aviv, University Publishing Projects Ltd, 1974)

Schiftan, Dan. *A Jordanian Option: The Yishuv and the State of Israel vis-à-vis the Hashemite Regime and the Palestinian National Movement* (Tel Aviv, Yad Tabenkin, 1986) [in Hebrew]

Segal, Haggai. *Dear Brother* (Jerusalem, Keter Publishing House, 1987) [in Hebrew]

Segev, Tom. *Israel in 1967* (Jerusalem, Keter Books, 2005) [in Hebrew]

Seliktar, Ofira. *New Zionism and the Foreign Policy System of Israel* (London, Croom Helm, 1986)

Sella, Amnon and Yael Yishai. *Israel: The Peaceful Belligerent, 1967–1979* (London, Macmillan in association with St Anthony's College Oxford, 1986)

Shafat, Gershon. *Gush-Emunim: The Story behind the Scenes* (Beit-El Library, 1995) [in Hebrew]

Shalev, Aryeh. *The West Bank Line of Defence* (New York, Praeger, The Centre for Strategic Studies Jaffe Tel-Aviv University, 1985)

Shalev, Aryeh. *Israel and Syria: Peace and Security on the Golan* (Westview Press, Publication of the Jaffe Center for Strategic Studies, Tel Aviv, 1994) [in Hebrew]

Shapiro, Yonathan. *Democracy in Israel* (Ramat Gan, Massada, 1977) [in Hebrew]

Shapiro, Yonathan. *Politicians as a Hegemonic Class: The Case of Israel* (Tel Aviv, Sifriat Hapoalim, 1996) [in Hebrew]

Shapiro, Yonathan. *The Road to Power: Herut Party in Israel* (Albany, State University of New York Press, 1991) [in Hebrew]

Sharkansky, Ira and Asher Friedberg (2002) 'Towards a Typology of Non-Decisions: Three Israeli Cases' *International Journal of Organization Theory and Behaviour* 5(1) pp. 145–159

Sharon, Ariel, with Chanoff, David. *Warrior: An Autobiography* (New York, Simon and Schuster, 1989)

Shemesh, Moshe. *The Palestinian Entity 1959–1974: Arab Politics and the PLO* (Abingdon, Frank Cass, 1996)

Shemesh, Moshe (2010) 'On Two Parallel Tracks – The Secret Jordanian-Israeli Talks' *Israel Studies* 15(3) pp. 87–120

Shem-Tov, Victor. *One of Them* (Kibbutz Dalia, Maarachot, 1997) [in Hebrew]

Shimshoni, Daniel. *Israeli Democracy: The Middle of the Journey* (New York, Free Press, 1992)

Shimshoni, Jonathan. *Israel and Conventional Deterrence: Border Warfare from 1953 to 1970* (London, Cornell University Press, 1988)

Shindler, Colin. *The Land Beyond Promise: Israel, Likud and the Zionist Dream* (London, I.B.Tauris, 2002)

Shlaim, Avi. *The Iron Wall: Israel and the Arab World* (London, Penguin Books, 2000)

Shlaim, Avi. *Lion of Jordan: The Life of King Hussein in War and Peace* (London, Allen Lane, Penguin Books, 2007)

Shprinzak, Ehud. *Everyman Whatsoever is Right in his own Eyes: Illegalism in Israeli Society* (Tel Aviv, Sifriat Poalim, 1986) [in Hebrew]

Shprinzak, Ehud. *The Ascendance of Israel's Radical Right* (New York, Oxford University Press, 1991)

Shuaibi, Issa (1980) 'The Development of Palestinian Entity-Consciousness: Part II' *Journal of Palestine Studies* 9(2) pp. 58–66.

Shvut, Avraham (ed.). *Ascent to the Mountains: Renewal of Jewish Settlements in Judea and Samaria* (Jerusalem, Sifriat Beit-El, 2002) [in Hebrew]

Smooha, Sammy. *Israel: Pluralism and Conflict* (London, Routledge and Kegan Paul, 1978)

Spyer, A.J. *The Decline of Statism: The Changing Political Culture of the Israeli Labour Party and the Party's Policy Proposals Regarding the West Bank, 1967–1999* (PhD, UCL, 2003)

Sutton, Rafi. *Lost Opportunities* (Or Yehuda, Ma'ariv Book Guild, 1999) [in Hebrew]

Teveth, Shabtai. *The Cursed Blessing: The Story of Israel's Occupation of the West Bank* (London, Weidenfeld and Nicolson, 1970) [in Hebrew]

Teveth, Shabtai. *Moshe Dayan: The Soldier, the Man, the Legend* (London, Weidenfeld and Nicolson, 1972) [in Hebrew]

Teveth, Shabtai. *Shearing Time/Calaban* (Israel, Yish-Dor, 1992) [in Hebrew]

Touval, Saadia. *The Peace Brokers: Mediators in the Arab-Israeli Conflict, 1948–1979* (Princeton, Princeton University Press, 1982)

Tzur, Tzvi. *Settlements and the Borders of Israel* (Tel Aviv, Yad Tabenkin, 1980) [in Hebrew]

Tzur, Zeev. *The Hakibbutz Hameuchad in the Settlement of Eretz-Israel*, vol. 4 *1960–1980* (Tel Aviv, Yad Tabenkin, 1986) [in Hebrew]

Van Arkadie, Brian. *Benefits and Burdens: A Report on the West Bank and Gaza Strip Economies since 1967* (New York, Carnegie Endowment for International Peace, 1977)

Warhaftig, Zorach. *Fifty Years, from Year to Year* (Jerusalem, Yad Shapira, 1998)

Weitz, Raanan. *An Overview of the History of the Settlement of Israel* (Jerusalem, Bialik Institute, 2003) Jerusalem, Yad Shapira

Yaacobi, Gad. *On the Razor's Edge* (Tel Aviv, Edanim Publishers, 1989) [in Hebrew]

Yahav, Dan. *The Settlement Project in the Yamit Region: The Lost Dream, 20 Years after the Establishment, 10 Years after the Evacuation 1971–1992* (Tel Aviv, Yaron Golan Books, 1992) [in Hebrew]

Yania, Natan. *Political Crises in Israel* (Jerusalem, Keter, 1982)

Yaniv, Avner. *Politics and Strategy in Israel* (Tel Aviv, Sifriat Poalim, 1994) [in Hebrew]

Yishai, Yael. *Land or Peace, Whither Israel?* (Hoover Institution Press, Stanford, 1987)

Zak, Moshe. *Hussein makes Peace* (Jerusalem, Bar-Ilan University, 1996) [in Hebrew]

Index

Abbas, Mahmoud 182, 188
Admoni, Yehiel 5, 151–2, 161, 164
Agranat, Shimon 132, 138
agricultural work camps 49–50,
    52–3, 152
Ahdut-Ha'avoda 9, 21, 27, 32, 43,
    48, 62–3, 84–5, 88–90, 133, 139,
    169, 176
al-Ja'bari, Ali 71, 76–7
al-Shaka'a, Walid 74
Allon Plan 5–6, 41–3, 54, 65, 70,
    79–80, 84, 87, 92–3, 97, 103,
    106, 108, 115, 117, 121, 126,
    136–8, 163, 165, 169, 171, 173–4,
    185, 187
Allon Road 66
Allon, Yigal 12, 18, 21, 28, 30, 33–4,
    41–2, 49, 51–2, 56, 66, 84, 88–9,
    91, 101, 103, 117, 123–4, 130,
    133, 139, 144–5, 170, 181
Aloni, Shulamit 140, 145–6
AMAN 17, 24–5, 40, 56, 58, 61, 72,
    129, 138, 166
Amit, Meir 17, 104
Arab League 51, 145–6
'Arab question' 4, 8–9
Arafat, Yasser 75, 109, 188
Aran, Zalman 19, 21, 27, 32, 79
Assad, Hafez 141
At-Tur settlement 106–7
Ayarot Pituah (development
    towns) 122

Ba'al-Hatzor settlement 154
Bar-Lev, Haim 57, 130–1, 170
Bar-On, Hanan 26, 30
Barbour, Walworth 20–1
Barkatt, Reuven 92
Barzilai, Yisrael 31–2, 53, 67
Bedouin tribes 111–12, 114
    see also Rafah plains
Begin, Menahem 11, 18, 21, 32, 34,
    93–4, 96, 101

Beilin, Yossi 8
Beit Jala 77
Ben-Aharon, Yitzhak 121–2,
    125, 169
Ben-Gurion, David 4, 9, 22, 29, 42,
    62, 70, 84, 176
'Benevolent Occupation' 47,
    114, 166
Bethlehem 77, 89
Black September 102–4
British Mandate 8, 10
Brown, George 35
Brownstein, Lewis 13

Can'an, Hamdi 75
Carmel, Moshe 32
Citizens' Rights Movement 140, 146
Committee of the Four 40–1, 67
'Concept' 129–31
constructive ambiguity 4, 6–7
Cook, Tzvi Yehuda 148–9

Dayan, Moshe 10, 12, 16–23,
    26–9, 32, 34, 44–7, 51–2, 56,
    66, 74, 80–2, 84, 88–90, 96,
    103–5, 109, 114, 118–19,
    124–5, 127, 130, 133, 157,
    163, 179, 181
    Functional Solution *see* Functional
        Solution
    meeting with King Hussein 135–9
    reluctance to talk to
        Palestinians 74–6
Dayan Plan *see* Functional Solution
'decision not to decide' 2, 5–8, 14,
    60, 72, 85, 89–90, 92, 126
decision-making process 12–13
development towns (*Ayarot
    Pituah*) 122
disjointed incrementalism 7–8,
    138, 175
Drobles, Matityahu 185
Druze Arabs 66–7, 143

East Jerusalem 2, 18, 22, 25, 30–1, 34, 42, 69, 73, 95
  annexation 36–7, 81
Eban, Abba 13, 19, 27–8, 34, 36–7, 66, 71–2, 79–80, 89, 95, 108, 111, 124, 130, 139, 169
economic integration 30, 46–7, 66, 76, 79, 81–3, 88–90, 92–3, 174–5
Egypt 85–6, 95, 97, 157
  acceptance of Rogers B 98
  interim agreements with 156–9
  relations with 24
  'War of Attrition' 85–7
  Yom Kippur War 5, 11, 103, 129–32
Eilat 58, 91, 93, 101, 106, 112, 156, 168
El-Arish 50, 69, 106–7
El'azar, David 19, 21, 49, 111
elections
  1973 134–5
  1977 167
Eliav, Arie 121, 125
Eliqa settlement 48–51
Elkana settlement 164, 174
enlightened occupation 24, 126
Eshkol, Levi 2, 7–8, 10, 12, 16–17, 19–20, 24, 26–8, 30, 36, 50–4, 59, 66, 68, 72, 76, 81–2, 105, 140, 178–9
  illness 84
  Washington visit 59–60

'facts on the ground' 3–4, 33, 49, 66–7, 89, 92, 97, 114, 117, 138, 143, 151, 153, 160, 176, 178, 181
Fatah movement 74–5, 102
Federal Plan 115–20
Five Principles 33–5, 177
Foreign Affairs and Defence Committee 45
Fourteen-Point Document 132–4
Functional Solution 84, 93, 97, 114–16, 118, 123, 125–6, 137, 166, 169–70, 174, 185

Gahal Party 11–12, 16, 43, 71, 88, 93–4, 99, 103
Galili Document 6, 127–9, 133–4, 176

Galili, Yisrael 1–7, 28, 32–4, 51, 55, 90, 96, 103, 105–7, 109, 125–6, 130, 140, 150–1, 153–4, 156, 159, 161, 163–4, 170, 179
Gavish, Yeshayahu 18, 57
Gaza Strip 2, 18, 20, 22–3, 25, 30–1, 42, 46, 72, 91, 93, 96, 103, 122, 156, 158, 165, 182, 184–5
  annexation 67–9, 185
  economic integration 81
  emigration from 68–9
  settlements *see* settlements
  unrest in 166
Gazit, Mordechai 95
Gazit, Shlomo 7, 25, 72, 125, 165
Geneva Convention 53
Gibli, Binyamin 9
Gidi Pass 105
Golan Heights 2, 20–1, 26, 28, 30–1, 52–3, 56, 91, 93, 97, 102, 111, 122, 128, 141–3, 158, 163, 168–9
  annexation 66
  development 142–3
  Eliqa settlement 48–51
  Nahal outposts 50, 53, 55, 66
'Golda's kitchenette' 104, 108–10, 130, 179
Goldberg, Arthur 28, 37, 58
Goran, Moshe 23
Grand Debate 121–6
Gromyko, Andrei 37, 58
Gush Emunim movement 11, 148–50, 154, 159, 164, 180
  Ma'ale Adumim settlement 65, 150–3, 164, 183
  Ofra settlement 153–5
  Sebastia/Kadom settlement 159–63
Gush Etzion settlement 52–5, 70, 128, 163
Gvati, Haim 50–2, 66

Haganah 46
Hakibbutz Hameuhad 48, 71
Hamas 182, 184–5, 187–8
Hammer, Zevulon 147, 164
Hammouda, Yahya 74
Hamtana (Waiting Period) 12, 23, 27
Harkabi, Yehoshafat 166

Hashomer Hatz'air
    movement   111–12
Hazan, Ya'akov   62, 67
Heads of Services Committee   40–1, 67
Hebron   19, 22, 33, 42, 69–72, 76,
    149, 163
    settlement of   70–2
Herman, Avraham   55
Hertzog, Haim   23, 26
Hertzog, Ya'akov   38, 57–8, 72
Hillel, Shlomo   103, 145, 151, 153,
    163, 169
Hussein, King of Jordan   17–20, 25,
    32, 38, 41, 56–8, 76, 78, 80, 102–3,
    110, 144–5, 175, 178, 184, 187
    Federal Plan   115–20
    meeting with Golda Meir   135–8

Independent Liberal Party   140, 146
Inter-Ministerial Committee for the
    Development of the Shlomo
    Region   106
international condemnation   20
'Invisible Occupation'   46
Israel Land Authority   124, 150
Israeli Defence Force (IDF)   7, 11,
    17–18, 25, 46, 71, 105, 125

Jarring Document   94, 105
Jarring, Gunnar   59–61, 94, 105,
    107, 142
Jericho   65, 77, 136–7
Jericho First plan   143–6
Jerusalem   28–9, 36–8, 89, 111
    Israeli control   101
    liberation of   27
    see also East Jerusalem; Old City
Johnson, Lyndon   17, 177
    Five Principles   33–5, 177
Jordan   78–81, 95, 101, 110, 144, 158
    acceptance of Rogers B   98
    see also Hussein, King of Jordan
Jordan River   30–2, 42, 44, 91,
    136, 163
19 June decision   2, 30–3, 35
June War see Six-Day War

Kadom/Sebastia settlement   159–63
Katzerin   143

Kerry, John   182
Kfar Darom outpost   113
Khartoum resolution   51
Kiryat Arba settlement   71–2, 149, 163
Kissinger, Henry   86, 97–8, 135, 141,
    144, 146, 157, 159, 180
Knesset   31, 36, 45, 70, 91, 94, 117,
    130, 142, 152, 157, 188
Kol, Moshe   51, 106, 140, 162
Kollek, Theodor (Teddy)   29

Labour Party   2, 7–10, 61–4, 88–9,
    94–7, 109, 134, 167, 171, 176
    Convention (1969)   91–4
    Grand Debate   121–6
Lahat, Shlomo   29
Land of Israel Movement   53, 70
land for peace   5, 14, 99
Lapid, Yair   183
Latrun Pass   25–6, 42
Lavon affair   9–10
Lavon, Pinhas   9
Lerner, Dan   49
Levinger, Moshe   70–1, 150
Liberman, Avigdor   183
Likud Party   134–5, 147, 184–6
Lincoln, Abraham   6

Ma'ale Adumim settlement   65,
    150–3, 164, 183
Ma'arach Political Committee
    (MPC)   27, 43, 78, 80
Mapai Party   9–11, 16, 21, 27,
    43, 48, 61–3, 84, 88–90, 135,
    139, 176
Mapam Party   31, 43, 45, 53, 61, 63,
    67, 88–9, 93, 111, 124, 129, 145,
    147, 153, 160, 165, 176
Meir, Golda   8, 27, 63–4, 79, 84–5,
    87, 90–1, 93–5, 97–9, 101, 103,
    107–8, 117, 126–7, 134, 144,
    168–9, 178–9
    'Golda's kitchenette'   104, 108–10,
    130, 179
    meeting with King Hussein   135–8
    resignation   138
Merkaz Harav *yeshiva*   149
Merom Golan see Eliqa settlement
Meron, Theodor   52–3, 66–8

Mescha outpost 161, 164
military administration 22–4
Ministerial Committee for the Held
    Territories 89
Ministerial Defence Committee 27,
    29–30, 44
Ministerial Settlement
    Committee 54, 106, 151, 163–4
Mitle Pass 105
Mossad 17, 40

Nablus 74–5, 159
Nahal outposts 50, 53, 55, 65–6,
    113, 164
    see also individual outposts
Nahal Sinai 106–7
Nahal Yam 106
Naksa see Six Day War
Narkiss, Uzi 20, 23, 25, 29, 46–7
Nasser, Gamal 'Abdel 16, 18, 61,
    85–6, 96–7
    death of 104
National Religious Party 16, 71,
    135, 140, 145–8, 157, 160,
    164, 178
national unity government 1, 12,
    16–17, 21, 27, 54–5, 61, 65, 85,
    93–4, 99, 174, 178
Netzarim outpost 113
Netzer, Moshe 66, 106–7, 154, 163
New Zionism 11
Nitzan, Yehuda 24
Nixon, Richard 86–7, 94, 97–9,
    101, 177
non-decision *see* 'decision not to
    decide'
nuclear capability 4

Occupied Territories 1, 11, 13,
    156, 173
    economic integration 81–3
    enlightened occupation 24
    lack of strategic policy 2–3
    military administration 22–4
    settlements *see* settlements
    unemployment 81, 83
    see also specific territories
30 October decision 55–7
Ofer, Avraham 143, 152

Ofra settlement 153–5
Old City 19–20, 25
    Temple Mount 29, 183
    Wailing Wall 22, 29
Open Bridges Policy 46–7, 92, 125
Oral Law 88–92, 101, 107–8, 124, 176
Oslo Accords 186–7

Palestine Liberation Organisation
    (PLO) 73, 102, 109, 136, 144,
    146, 157, 159, 165–6, 186–7
Palestinian Authority 182, 186
Palestinian people 4–5, 14, 25–6, 123
    emigration from Gaza Strip 68–9
    limited administrative
        self-rule 76–8
    meetings with 72–6
Palestinian self-rule 40, 46, 76–8,
    88–9, 93, 116, 120, 138, 165–6,
    171, 174–5
Palestinian state 33, 39, 41
partition plan 9–10, 21, 48, 176
Pedatzur, Reuven 6
Peres, Shimon 62, 139–40, 144, 153,
    160, 162, 164, 178–81, 186
policy of indecision *see* 'decision not
    to decide'
Political Committee 27
Popular Front for the Liberation of
    Palestine (PFLP) 102, 109
'price of unity' 8, 176
Primakov, Yevgeny 110–11

Rabat Summit 159, 165
Rabin, Yitzhak 18–20, 31, 56, 87,
    94–8, 107, 139–41, 144, 147, 149,
    153–4, 156, 158, 160–2, 166, 171,
    178–80, 186
    settlement policy 163–5
Rabinowitz, Yehushu'a 152, 167
Rafah plains 96, 101, 106, 108,
    110–15, 158, 163, 168
Rafi Party 10, 12, 16, 62–3, 84–5,
    88–9, 127, 139–40, 157, 176
Ramallah 89
Ramat Gan 90
religious revivalism 147
Religious Zionism 11, 22, 148
Resolution 242 58–9

Rifai, Zaid   117–18, 136–8, 144–5, 188
Rogers B   97–100
   acceptance of   99, 101
Rogers Plan   94–7, 99, 109, 118, 177
Rogers, William   86–7, 94
Rosolio, Danny   167
Rostow, Walt   20
Rusk, Dean   34, 60

Sadat, Anwar   104–8, 111, 129, 131,
   157, 168
Sapir, Pinhas   27, 32, 71, 79,
   81–2, 84, 89–90, 92, 122–3,
   134, 139, 171
Sarid, Yossi   152, 154, 169
Sarinu   27
Sasson, Eliyahu   28
Sasson, Moshe   5, 72–5, 77, 79
satisficing   7
Saunders, Harold   165
Sebastia/Kadom settlement   159–63
secret peace plan   101–2
self-rule *see* Palestinian self-rule
Settlement Department   43, 49–50,
   53–4, 66, 112
settlements   48–52, 65–7, 163–5, 175
   At-Tur   106–7
   Ba'al-Hatzor   154
   Eliqa   48–51
   Elkana   164
   Gush Etzion   52–5, 70, 128, 163
   Hebron   70
   Kiryat Arba   71–2, 149, 163
   Ma'ale Adumim   65, 150–3,
      164, 183
   Mescha outpost   161, 164
   Nahal outposts   50, 53, 55,
      65–6, 164
   Ofra   153–5
   Sebastia/Kadom   159–63
Shalev, Aryeh   26, 30
Shamgar, Meir   22–3
Shapira, Haim-Moshe   19, 28, 32, 52,
   83, 103, 130, 132–3
Shapira, Ya'akov-Shimshon   27, 32
Sharm el-Sheikh   91, 93–4, 96, 101,
   105–7, 110–12, 128, 156, 158,
   163, 168

Sharon, Ariel   113–15, 160, 185
Shehadeh, 'Aziz   75
Shem-Tov, Victor   104, 112, 161
Sherf, Zeev   33–4, 81
Shlaim, Avi   6
Shuqairi, Ahmad   74
Sinai Peninsula   2, 11, 16, 22,
   26, 30–1, 56, 86, 94, 106–7,
   110–11, 168
Sisco, Joseph   87, 94–7, 99, 107, 110
Six Day War   1–2, 8, 10–12, 16–22,
   48, 51, 72, 85–6, 102, 122, 147–8,
   167, 177, 180, 184
Siya Bet faction   9
Suez Canal   31, 86, 104, 157
Suez crisis   35, 42
Syria   141–3, 158–9
   separation-of-forces agreement   141
   Yom Kippur War   5, 11, 103,
      129–32

Tabenkin, Yitzhak   9, 43, 48, 62, 85
Tel Aviv   18, 90
'three no's'   51
Tiran Straits   16, 18, 22, 30–1,
   57, 158
Tomb of the Patriarchs   22, 70
transition   10–12
Tuchman, Barbara   188
two-state solution   9, 51, 121,
   182–3, 188
Tzadok, Haim   133, 170
Tzur, Tzvi   5, 57

United Nations   3, 37
   partition plan   9–10, 21, 48, 176
   Resolution 242   58–9
Upper Galilee   49, 102
US position   177–8
US-Israeli relations   59–60
USSR   97–8, 110

Van Arkadie, Brian   7

Waiting Period (*Hamtana*)   12, 23, 27
'wall-to-wall' coalition   48–64
'War of Attrition'   85–7, 93, 96
'War of Independence'   141, 176

Warhaftig, Zerach 19
Weitz Plan 43–4
Weitz, Ra'anan 43, 49, 106
West Bank 2, 18–21, 23, 25, 38–41,
 45–6, 94, 103, 148, 159, 165,
 169–72, 174
 Allon Plan *see* Allon Plan
 annexation 32, 56, 188
 economic integration 81
 settlements *see* settlements
 unrest in 166

Ya'akobi, Gad 145
Yadin, Yigal 28

Yadlin, Aharon 121–2, 128, 145,
 159, 168
Yamit 114, 122, 128, 158
Yariv, Aharon 25, 56, 58, 108, 145,
 167, 169
Yom Kippur War 5, 11, 103, 129–32,
 138, 148, 181
Yost, Charles 95
Yost Document 95, 97

Zionism 4, 48, 69–70, 159, 169, 175–6
 New 11
 Religious 11, 22, 148
Zore'a, Meir 151

CPSIA information can be obtained at www.ICGtesting.com
Printed in the USA
LVOW04*0912120615

442242LV00002B/13/P